The P(
D1549368

The Politics of Public Sector Reform

From Thatcher to the Coalition

Michael Burton

First published 2013 by
PALGRAVE MACMILLAN

Palgrave Macmillan in the UK is an imprint of Macmillan Publishers Limited, registered in England, company number 785998, of Houndmills, Basingstoke, Hampshire RG21 6XS.

Palgrave Macmillan in the US is a division of St Martin's Press LLC, 175 Fifth Avenue, New York, NY 10010.

Palgrave Macmillan is the global academic imprint of the above companies and has companies and representatives throughout the world.

Palgrave® and Macmillan® are registered trademarks in the United States, the United Kingdom, Europe and other countries.

ISBN 978–0–230–36364–9 hardback
ISBN 978–0–230–36365–6 paperback

This book is printed on paper suitable for recycling and made from fully managed and sustained forest sources. Logging, pulping and manufacturing processes are expected to conform to the environmental regulations of the country of origin.

A catalogue record for this book is available from the British Library.

A catalog record for this book is available from the Library of Congress.

Contents

The Politics of Public Sector Reform: From Thatcher to the Coalition

Introduction

The UK public sector faces an unprecedented long-term challenge. A decade of plenty in the public finances has been followed by a decade and more of austerity. Public services are undergoing long-term annual spending cuts even as demand rises from demographic change in health, education and adult care. Unless taxes rise substantially, which no political party advocates for fear of electoral oblivion, public sector managers and politicians, faced with a combination of major budget reductions and increasing demand, have a stark choice; either 'decommission' and remove services altogether or through increased productivity, reduction in overheads and new technology succeed in retaining them by lowering the cost of delivery.

But providing the same services with less income to fund them means public service managers must continually explore new ways of slimming down their own organisational costs and increasing productivity. In the short-term, it means 'salami-slicing' costs through efficiency savings. In the long-term, however, many public sector practitioners and politicians believe these will not be sufficient and that only substantial, 'transformational' change can deliver the sustainable savings necessary to meet the next decades of lower budgets, a process likely to be far more challenging than previous change programmes as demand outstrips the financial capacity of the public sector to meet it. As one prominent ex-union leader commented in 2011 in an inquiry he chaired: 'The scale of the challenges ahead is such that a comprehensive public service reform process must now be initiated'.[1] And in evidence to the Public Administration Select Committee in early 2010 on the level of efficiency savings required to meet reduced budgets, National Audit Office (NAO)

1

head Amyas Morse told MPs: 'I think that if you are not prepared to go to something more radical... you will only achieve a marginal improvement, worth having but not likely to meet the strategic needs we are talking about today'.[2] Supporters of more ambitious reform believe that millions of pounds remain trapped within public sector organisations that could be released to frontline services if only the process-driven hierarchies and bureaucratic barriers that make up so much of the public sector can be broken up.

But firstly, how should we define public services? These are not only services provided directly by the public sector as private and voluntary sector organisations are also providers of public services. More accurately they are services in which the public sector, as commissioner and purchaser, is the main decision-maker on the outcomes it aims to achieve. So for the purposes of this book, the public sector includes health, local government, police, Whitehall, education and welfare services, all of which commission goods and services from other providers and also decide the outcomes, but does not include the privatised utilities such as energy, telecommunications and water and national transport operators which answer to shareholders.

Secondly, what is the annual UK public sector budget? Whitehall departments like education, works and pensions and communities and local government as well as the devolved administrations of Scotland, Wales and Northern Ireland have their own allocated departmental budgets, but the Treasury also divides total spending into sectors such as social protection and public order which straddle various Whitehall departments and gives a better idea of costs. Total public spending for 2011–2012 in the United Kingdom (total managed expenditure or TME as the Treasury accountants call it) amounted to £695 billion. Of this the largest spending was on 'social protection' at £242 billion, namely welfare benefits, old-age pensions and personal social services, followed by health at £121 billion, then education at £91.6 billion and public order and safety at £32 billion including police at £16.5 billion. Local government in Britain spent £142.7 billion, which included some of the above such as personal services, housing benefit, education and welfare. The bulk of local government spending was on social services and education. TME of £695 billion on public spending for 2011–2012 was £5 billion more than that of the year before but after taking into account inflation, it represents a fall of 1.6% in real terms, only the seventh year since 1971–1972 that TME has fallen (in real terms). Most of the fall was due to a sharp drop in capital spending with current spending almost unchanged. TME has more than doubled since 2000–2001 and is three times the size it was in 1990–1991, not taking into account inflation.[3]

Thirdly, what is 'transformational change?' In the public sector, it means the radical reconfiguring of an organisation rather than piece-meal reform with the aim of delivering substantial savings alongside reduced costs and an improved, or at least no worse, service. Such change is difficult and complex, often lasts beyond the tenure of a minis-ter or even the lifespan of a Parliament and requires direction, leadership and a clear set of goals. It also invariably means job losses.

One inspectorate report comments:

> There are three different types of efficiency reform. The transactional approach includes unconnected initiatives that incorporate limited cost reduction or efficiency drives and deliver short-term easy wins that cannot be sustained in the long term. Transitional approaches deal with back office and frontline savings separately. This brings larger long-term savings but does not provide the challenge that delivers big savings. The transformational approach requires substan-tial organisational change and takes time and effort.[4]

But transformation is also about service as well as organisational recon-figuration, breaking down public sector silos by sharing departmental budgets, delivering early intervention in family care and criminal justice to save on long-term costs and focusing services on the needs of users not the producers. The public sector is good at dealing with symptoms but poor at tackling the root causes. Most welfare costs are on paying out benefits rather than on helping people get into employment or in health dealing with sickness rather than preventing it.

Transformation also involves the participation of the public in under-standing that they will in future access services differently, with greater use of online transactions at lower cost to the provider, that their expectations of what the state can provide will need to be managed downwards, and that they must take greater responsibility for their own well-being. The question is how this transformational change can be achieved when previous public service change since the 1980s has such a chequered record of success. The post-2010 recession in public finances is not the first opportunity for a government to address productivity in public services even though it is the most pressing. Since the cre-ation of the welfare state in the late 1940s, politicians from left and right have endeavoured to manage the way such services are delivered, both to improve outcomes to users and to control costs. Since the early

1980s, when greater attention was paid to public sector management and productivity, the policy has become known as 'public sector reform' involving an end to what ministers and others regard as inefficient managerial and workforce practices in the delivery of public services, aligning them with ever-growing customer expectations and opening them up to market forces.

The words 'public sector reform' have become in some circles politicised, inferring that the existing structure is imperfect, and they have been seen as a threat to the status quo, in particular by workforce unions and professional associations. The pattern of reform has therefore involved intermittent conflict between ministers wishing to impose changes against the resistance of producer interests such as unions and professional bodies, the latter sometimes with public support. But it has also involved ideological differences even between the supporters of reform, with those who believe privatisation of public services is the most successful way of improving their productivity and performance at odds with those who believe public services can be reformed from within without privatisation. In practice there is consensus between the main political parties about the need for reform which has continued unabated since the early 1980s under successively two Conservative governments, two Labour and a Coalition of Conservatives and Liberal Democrats.

But why do governments feel the need to reform public services at all? One answer is they believe that the public sector by itself is slow to react to the changing external environment and that governments intervene to ensure that it responds accordingly. One Downing Street strategy unit summed up the need for reform in the following words: 'The world doesn't stand still, and hasn't stood still. Public services need to adapt to social change, economic change, technological change and changing attitudes and expectations. Public services face users who have vastly higher expectations and need to modernise and adapt accordingly. In particular, public services need to be more responsive to and better able to meet the needs of all users'.[5]

A second reason is that politicians and governments like to leave their imprint on domestic policy, to have a beneficial impact on the lives of their citizens. While political, economic and foreign crises can blow governments off course from their manifesto aims, the desire of ministers to improve the lot of the public persists, even if it becomes diluted. While governments can influence behaviour through legislation and regulation, it is through the public sector that they can most directly effect the improvement of services used by all citizens.

Furthermore since the late 1970s, by which time the post-war welfare state was three decades old, politicians had begun to question the role and quality of public services. While some, predominantly on the right of politics, argued the case for reducing the role of the state altogether, others on the centre and left of politics called for managerial reform, an injection of private sector practices to make public services more responsive to the needs of its users. The process of reform carried out under the Thatcher Government continued through its successors and became absorbed into the lexicon of leadership, evidence of a prime minister's genuine commitment to improving people's quality of life. Tony Blair regarded public sector reform as his highest domestic priority. Yet when David Cameron became Prime Minister in 2010, he too announced reform as *his* biggest priority.

Governments in the past 30 years have used the public service reform agenda as a way of proving their abilities to voters. Evidence that key services like health, education or law and order have improved is invariably helpful for re-election because voters see public services as a government's responsibility. Politicians on the centre to right see public sector reform as evidence that they are being prudent about taxpayers' money. Those on the centre to left see reform as an issue about social justice and reducing inequalities as described by one Labour No 10 strategy unit: 'Public service reform is central to the achievement of the Government's objectives of greater social justice and a higher quality of life for everyone. This Government is determined that everyone has access to public services that are efficient, effective, excellent, equitable and empowering – and that continually strive to cater to the needs of all citizens'.[6]

But consumers too have driven the reform agenda. As a major government-commissioned study of the private sector role in public service delivery noted:

> In poorer countries, populations are more satisfied with standardised public services since 'one size fits all' is a significant step up from limited access to public services and a private market that many could not afford. This was clearly the case in the early post-war period in Britain and other European countries when the foundations of the public welfare state were laid. Today however, citizens want more varied, more immediately available, more modern (i.e. efficient and continually evolving) and, more customised and caring services. They are used to these qualities in the private services they consume.[7]

Critics of reform who argue that it is merely another word for public spending cuts ignore the fact that in the decade from 2000, reform was also accompanied by major above-inflation investment in public services, which to some observers masked stagnant productivity levels, a period which ended with the financial crash of 2007–2009 and the consequent ballooning deficit in UK public finances. The Institute for Fiscal Studies estimated that had public sector productivity levels in 2007 been the same as 1997, an extra £42.5 billion could have been released.[8] In December 2012, a report on decentralisation and reform by Treasury Minister Greg Clark commented: 'Record levels of spending channelled through top-down management systems have not delivered the excellence that the people of this country deserve and which they have paid for in their taxes. If the public sector had kept pace with average private sector productivity between 1997–2007, then it would be nearly a quarter more productive'.[9]

The downward pressure on public spending since 2010 has made the challenge of improving performance while cutting costs even more acute by providing a long-term backdrop of diminishing resources caused by budget cuts. Even aside from this, rising demand such as an ageing population means that for the next decades public services will continue to operate in an environment of fiscal constraint. It is for many middle management and senior public sector executives, whose careers progressed during the years of annual spending increases, a new experience. They will be managing declining, not expanding, resources, probably for most of the rest of their careers.

Reform is no longer a party political issue. Governments of all political persuasions agree that efficient, productive public services are a priority and that sound management is vital. The NAO says that while public services are different in the ways they are delivered, 'their quality and cost-effectiveness depends on a number of common minimum requirements. For example, service delivery requires a well thought-out delivery model, sound programme and project management, strong commercial skills, mature process management and a real understanding of customer needs'.[10]

But the task of reform is complex and difficult to pursue to its conclusion. Every prime minister since 1979 has demanded change and initiated it with mixed results. Efficiency programmes have proved to waste money rather than save it, huge investment has been made in IT projects that end in expensive failure, while many parts of the public sector continue to be riddled with poor procurement skills, inflexible workforces, lack of managerial expertise and ambition, and a focus on process and input rather than output. Numerous Commons select committees and auditing bodies have repeatedly criticised waste, incompetence and inefficiency in public sector reform programmes although their reports often appear too late to influence their direction. Statistics boasting of savings turn out, on closer and later scrutiny, to be 'smoke and mirrors'. Public services continue to be risk averse. The public sector is also hostile to sharing resources and staff, so that users frequently have to contact several agencies for help with issues such as births, death, divorce or house-moving which cross different departments. Health and social services still act as if joint working and integration of the two sectors is innovative rather than common sense, as it is to users. Ministers have been, and are, frequently the problem rather than the solution, demanding short-term changes that in the long term prove costly and wasteful by which time they have left office and take no further responsibility. The attention span of prime ministers on public service reform ebbs and flows along with their preoccupation with other more immediate events especially in foreign policy. As two seasoned public sector practitioners and commentators conclude in a recent study of the public spending challenge: 'The traditional pattern of UK public administration has been remarkably consistent. There has seemingly been an unwillingness to alter radically existing administrative and public service delivery units to match the needs of a rapidly changing economy'.[11]

For reform is difficult as big bureaucracies move slowly. Former Chancellor Alistair Darling says that 'every government, in every part of the world, knows it can do things more efficiently ... Of course improved technology can make government more efficient and less costly, though this is not entirely straightforward and neither can it be done quickly'.[12] A Commons select committee puts it even more bluntly:

> We have commented frequently in our past reports on the poor quality of management information on performance and delivery available within government, and this has contributed to the unconvincing claims made for previous efficiency initiatives. In our previous examinations of central efficiency initiatives, we found that only 38% of departments' claimed savings met the specific criteria set by the Treasury.[13]

There are also powerful vested interests blocking change from professional associations and union workforces to Whitehall departments reluctant to relinquish control over their fiefdoms. The prime minister might call for strategic reform across sectors, but ministers rapidly adopt the silo mentalities of their Whitehall departments. The public expect improving services, but driven by the media are critical if experimentation leads to errors and are intolerant of failure. Risk-aversion leads to fear by public sector leaders of innovation and an emphasis on process and box-ticking.

The private sector role is two-edged. On the one hand, it provides expertise, managerial leadership, investment, technology. On the other, it can outwit amateurish public sector procurement managers and lock them into costly inflexible contracts. The much-vaunted Private Finance Initiative has turned out to be a long-term millstone of debt. Private companies can also go out of business, leaving the public sector client, that is the taxpayer, to pick up the pieces. Some public sector markets are undeveloped and there is insufficient private sector capacity to meet need leading to domination by a few powerful suppliers.

But one stark fact is certain: lack of money means reform of the public sector is more urgent than ever before if increased productivity and more efficient management of resources is to fill the gap caused by stagnant tax revenues and rising demand on public services. A succession of alarming projections, outlined later in this book, about the state of public finances in the next decade disagree not over whether they will be constantly lagging behind demand but over the size of the deficit. The National Health Service (NHS) alone, even if health spending remains flat in real terms beyond 2015, is projected to incur a funding gap of as much as £54 billion by 2021–2022 unless offsetting productivity gains can be delivered.[14]

But the public cannot wait for the errors of previous reforms to be repeated again and again under successive governments, for ministerial short-termism to hinder long-term strategic change programmes or for Commons select committees to discover too late that reforms have been expensive failures.

This book is about how reform has been attempted across public services, where and how it failed and what lessons there are to be learned for the unprecedented changes the public sector faces in the next decades. It is about what taxpayers and consumers can and should expect from the political and managerial leaders of their public services despite spending reductions that will continue for a generation and more. It is how we all tackle this fundamental challenge, namely how services paid through taxes and frequently provided by monopoly suppliers respond to public expectations and how governments endeavour to make them respond, not always successfully.

It does not start from the premise that the public sector is by nature inefficient. Many private sector corporations have failed to adapt or become slow to respond to a changing external environment, the difference being that they then go out of business. But the public sector, lacking the impact of market forces to stimulate improvement and innovation, is more prone to inertia. The public sector also has a unique challenge in constantly rising demand over which it has little control. Faced with a financial crisis, the private sector cuts costs, increases productivity and solves its problem by selling more products – for more sales means more income and more profit. In contrast the public sector, faced with a crisis, cuts costs, increases productivity but then has to reduce demand for its services in order to balance its books.

As with all organisations, employees make up the largest cost of the public sector and it is on them that efficiency savings inevitably fall. The Coalition government from 2010 targeted staff costs, freezing salaries and reducing the cost of guaranteed pensions. Most public sector staff are dedicated to their valuable work, but 'the public service ethos', the idea that uniquely employees put service to the public first rather than the pursuit of profit, has in the past paradoxically often masked inefficiency and poor customer service. Even a Labour government report from the Prime Minister's Strategy Unit in 2006 dismissed the idea that opening up public services would undermine this ethos, commenting that 'the evidence is thin' and adding: 'While many public servants feel uncomfortable with the notion of "profit", most would agree that many of the characteristics of successful businesses and organisations in the voluntary sector should apply to public services – primarily focusing on and listening to customers'.[15]

The focus of this book is on how governments encourage the public sector to innovate, respond to consumer needs, increase performance through targets and inspection, exploit new technology and drive down back office costs, introduce competition for the delivery of services, streamline management and decision-making, improve procurement skills and ensure the workforce is productive and pro-actively managed. It is also about where and why these reforms succeeded or failed. I aim as well to provide some answers for while there are many studies on the fiscal and managerial challenges faced by the public sector they are light on practical solutions. As one former mandarin and Whitehall expert noted with some frustration at the launch of yet another report on the fiscal cliff ahead: 'Everyone has gone AWOL when it comes to solving the future of our public services. The problem is, everyone is obsessed with rearranging the Whitehall deckchairs, while gaping flaws aren't being addressed'.[16]

I have divided the book into four parts. Firstly, I deliver an overview of public sector reform under five prime ministers beginning with Margaret Thatcher (1979–1990) who was the first post-war politician to regard public sector reform as a priority after the huge expansion of the public sector from the late 1940s to the 1970s. I have not, however, devoted attention to the privatisation of the public utilities during this period as once in the private sector they are outside the remit of this book which examines public services. Mrs Thatcher's successor John Major (1990–1997) also regarded reform as a key part of his domestic policy, refining the more ideological aspects of Thatcherism and laying the grounds for his successor Tony Blair (1997–2007). Blair was a fervent believer in public sector reform and his term in office coincided, for the first time since the 1960s, with a major increase in public spending. He also had the advantage of a decade at No 10, in theory enabling a greater longer-term strategy for change to be implemented. In practice, as his memoirs testify, he was to be first frustrated by the institutional obstacles to change, then distracted by foreign policy. Under Gordon Brown (2007–2010) reform was less of a priority while the fiscal crash dominated his attention from 2008 onwards. The Coalition government of David Cameron in 2010 placed public sector reform at the top of its agenda, including a radical downsizing of Whitehall, transfer of powers to local government and structural changes in health, education and welfare. A Commons select committee called the programme 'the most ambitious reform of Whitehall since the Second World War'.[17]

I then look at the various drivers of public sector reform beginning with the Cabinet Office and No 10 and how through these departments prime ministers keep track, or more usually *not* keep track, of the reform programme while balancing their other priorities. I also look at the powerful influence of the Treasury on reform through its constant drive to keep down costs through improved efficiencies.

I then examine the role of Parliament through its select committees, which frequently and with much frustration account the catalogue of failings in so many reform programmes and which must be regarded as perhaps the most effective part of Parliament's watchdog role. I have found the select committee reports, particularly those of the Public Administration Select Committee (PASC) and the Public Accounts Committee (PAC) – along with the reports from the NAO which accompany those from the PAC – an invaluable source for this book. Accusations by politicians that these committees and the NAO represent the 'forces of conservatism' for constantly exposing the shortcomings of Whitehall efforts to innovate are wide of the mark. Sadly it is not innovation which is being criticised but the repeated waste of money and lack of understanding about what the innovation is supposed to achieve which are under fire.

I also mention the position of ministers who are often criticised for adopting the 'silo mentality' view of their Whitehall departments even against the cross-departmental approach of their own governments' reform programmes.

Reform is also not always driven just by governments. In the past three decades, consumerism, increasingly prevalent in the private sector, has also pervaded the public sector with people regarding themselves as customers rather than passive recipients of services. Increased choice and personalised budgets provided by a range of suppliers from the private and voluntary sectors are the trend for the future. Governments have had to respond to such demands for better and more customer-focused services. The application of technology is crucial in improving customer contact while also reducing costs. I thus conclude this section with the impact of consumers' increasing demands for better public services in driving reform, the trend towards more choice and personal budgets and the role of other providers in delivering these.

Next I look at the pattern of reform in the key parts of the public sector, namely Whitehall, the NHS, local government, the police, education and welfare (while generally funded centrally, there are some differences between the way these services are managed in England, Scotland, Wales and Northern Ireland but in the main I provide an overview across the United Kingdom). Fourthly, I examine how public sector performance management and productivity can be measured and monitored and whether it achieves its aims. Considering that the complex performance monitoring regime developed under Labour 1997–2010 coincided with a decline in public sector productivity then questions must be asked about whether such a top-down process is useful. Judging productivity in the public sector is far more complex than that in the private sector, and the challenge is to determine outcomes against input while recognising public services cannot always be measured like factory production lines.

My last chapter looks at the international context. I have not endeavoured to benchmark UK public services with those abroad in detail largely because the subject is so huge that it would take another book to cover it and because it is not easy to compare like with like, especially with different funding regimes. In the main, the United Kingdom is comparable to the United States, Canada, Australia, the larger EU countries and Scandinavia in the size, quality and spending level of its public sector. The World Health Organisation produces a hugely detailed comparable study of each nation's health statistics in its World Health Statistics. The Organisation for Economic Co-operation and Development (OECD) Programme for International Student Assessment produces comparative performance data for students on key academic subjects. There have been international studies looking at the quality of central government and at the proportion of public services provided by the private and voluntary sectors. Where relevant I touch on some of these international comparisons.

I then conclude with the lessons learned from reform programmes to date and suggest the way ahead. Throughout these chapters, I use case studies as examples of specific reforms, some of which were successful, some not.

It is important also to state that the UK public sector has a wider economic role which is easily overlooked in the private versus public debate. It is a major employer and in many areas is the single largest employer of local labour. While the role of the public sector is not fore-most that of a job-creation scheme, cutting costs through reducing staff can lead to similar costs ending up back on the public purse further down the line in welfare benefits. Public sector services are also deliv-ered by private and third sector organisations. The government through the public sector is a major supplier of contracts for private firms, large and small, many of which depend on them, and the United Kingdom's public sector economy is one of the world's largest.

The public sector also has a key role in the knowledge economy such as providing education for overseas students, developing health technologies with private sector partners and using arts and leisure to support regeneration projects. A study by the Work Foundation con-cluded that driving innovation should also be a key aim of public sector reform, concluding: 'The public sector will continue to play a major role in the wider UK economy particularly in the knowledge economy through the position of the public sector within the wider innovation system. Success in this challenging environment will depend on the public sector rapidly finding ways to better deliver public services, and to better leverage its support for the wider economy'.[18]

The challenge for the United Kingdom now is to meet public expec-tations that their services will continue to be maintained and improved against a long-term backdrop of spending reductions and rising demand. The mantra is 'more for less'. As Latham and Prowle note: 'The increas-ing size of public services in the economy and the current crisis in public finances can either be an opportunity to make a radical change... or provide the excuse for further partial, imposed and ineffective changes which seek to consolidate the existing structural weaknesses'.[19]

Public service reform will continue to be high on the agenda of politicians and the general public for years to come. The challenge is to ensure it is implemented fairly and efficiently without repeating the errors of the past decades. This book I hope will point the way.

Part I
The Background to Reform

1
Reform Under the Conservatives 1979–1997

The election of Margaret Thatcher in 1979 was to prove to be a watershed in the history of public services. Since the creation of the welfare state after the Second World War there had been a consensus through successive Conservative and Labour governments about the central role of government as a benevolent provider of public services from local government to water, telephones, rail and energy. Commentators, referring to the converging views of Labour's leader of the 1950s Hugh Gaitskell and Conservative politician Rab Butler, called this consensus 'Butskellism'.

But following the defeat of the 1970–1974 Heath Government, leading Tory politicians such as Sir Keith Joseph and Margaret Thatcher began to rethink their approach to the state. Mrs Thatcher in particular dismissed the post-war consensus as 'socialist, social democrat, statist or merely Butskellite' and in particular called it 'a centralising, managerial, bureaucratic, interventionist style of government'. In her eyes, the public sector had become synonymous with Labour and socialism and the post-war consensus was a sign of Conservative weakness. 'The result of this style of accommodationist politics was that post-war politics became a "socialist ratchet" – Labour moved Britain towards more statism, the Tories stood pat and the next Labour Government moved the country a little further left', she recalled in her memoirs. 'The Tories loosened the corset of socialism; they never removed it'.[1]

In her view the public sector, driven by its producer interests, the employees, had grown to the extent that it was now stifling private sector entrepreneurship. 'Already large and unwieldy after its expansion in two world wars, the British Government very soon jammed a finger in every pie', she later wrote in her memoirs. 'It levied high rates of tax on work, enterprise, consumption and wealth transfer.... It made

17

available various forms of welfare for a wide range of contingencies – poverty, unemployment, large families, old age, misfortune, ill-health, family quarrels – generally on a universal basis'.[2]

Her views had been reinforced by her experiences as a minister under Edward Heath whose initial attempts to expand the free-market sector in the early years of his 1970–1974 government ended in a U-turn, and his subsequent defeat at the hands of striking miners in the nationalised coal industry. She later accused him of trying to implement 'the most radical form of socialism ever contemplated by an elected British Government' through his proposals for state-run incomes and prices policy, adding: 'The Heath Government changed course radically and adopted a programme of corporatism, intervention and reflation'.[3]

In 1974 when asked to choose between supporting Edward Heath or the miners during an industrial dispute the public chose the latter, re-electing a Labour government. But the so-called 'winter of discontent' in 1978/79 when public sector unions took strike action against the Labour government over pay restraints leading to domestic rubbish piling up in the streets undermined public support for unions in general and public sector unions in particular. Not only did this pave the way for Mrs Thatcher's election in spring 1979 but it also provided some public sympathy for what was to become known as Thatcherism, a smaller role for the state with those services still in public control imbued with private sector management expertise and opened to competition.

Mrs Thatcher wanted the public sector reduced in size with the remainder galvanised through an injection of private sector management practices. Her government was the first since 1945 to challenge the fundamental role of the public sector and require it to reform. She was determined from day one in office to address what she regarded as the overmighty state and in her first Cabinet meeting 'began the painful but necessary process of shrinking down the public sector after years in which it was assumed that it should grow at the expense of the private sector'.[4]

Mrs Thatcher's immediate decision was to impose an immediate freeze on civil service recruitment and review the controls by central on local government, an initiative repeated 31 years later by the Coalition under David Cameron. Subsequently under Mrs Thatcher's governments of 1979–1990, key utilities including gas, electricity, telephones and water were privatised along with Britain's state-owned airline and council houses offered for sale to their tenants. Compulsory competitive tendering was introduced into local government manual services, firstly in highways, then from 1988 in refuse, street cleaning, cleaning and ground maintenance with private suppliers taking over services previously operated by council employees An efficiency review was undertaken throughout Whitehall to bring in private sector management practices. Some three quarters of Whitehall staff were transferred to over 130 external or 'Next Steps' agencies with a remit to manage themselves more efficiently outside traditional Whitehall working practices. In 1983 the Audit Commission was created to combine the auditing of health and local government spending with a focus on increasing performance.

On health she was more circumspect, recognising the popularity of the NHS. She recalled: 'Housing like education had been at the top of the list for reform in 1987. But I had reserved health for detailed consideration later'.[5] But she still believed that its 'monolithic, state-provided system' made it both unresponsive to patients and inefficient. She recalled: 'Dedicated its staff generally were; cost conscious they were not'.[6] And she added: 'The NHS was a huge organisation which inspired at least as much affection as exasperation, whose emergency services reassured even those who hoped they would not have to use them and whose basic structure was felt by most people to be sound. Any reforms must not undermine public confidence'.[7]

But she also admitted that change was more complex to achieve, the White Paper proposing more private sector involvement in delivery and self-governing hospital trusts, appearing only in 1989. Nonetheless, the momentum for reform was underway. As one commentator on her government, David Marsland, later noted 15 years after she had ceased to be prime minister: 'In [the Education Reform Act 1988 and NHS and Community Care Act 1990] the thrust of reform was similar – enhanced attention to the consumer's role, introduction of competition, devolution of management to local operating levels and tough central frameworking'.[8]

But while it maintained a clear ideological antipathy to the idea of the state as a primary provider of services, Thatcherism also conceived the concept of public services being more responsive to users' needs. Politicians on the right argued that the public sector was dominated by employees, through their trade unions and professional bodies, which created rigid, inflexible working practices. They saw public bodies like local authorities and health services as monopolies unwilling and unable to adapt to changing customer needs and burdened by expensive hierarchical structures. They saw them as unfairly protected from wider economic pressures affecting the private sector. They believed that competition would expose this inherent inefficiency and that where competition was not possible, public services must be monitored through inspection and regulation. These views, while initially articulated by politicians and theorists on the right, were soon to be shared by those on the left.

In addition public services were under financial pressure as Thatcher made lowering taxes a priority. As Latham and Prowle point out:

> The size of the UK post-Second World War public sector as a percentage of GDP rose to the point where it significantly exceeded the US but was significantly less than that of some European counterparts. In part this created a sense of dissatisfaction on behalf of the public who would like to see European level public services but are only prepared to pay North American tax rates. The pressure has therefore been on the delivery of more efficient solutions for public service delivery and administration.[9]

Reforms to the public sector initiated under the Thatcher government were to run like a thread through successive administrations, Conservative and Labour. As one observer commented in 2005:

> These two great reforms [of health and education] have provided, despite cosmetic changes under Labour since 1997, an essential basis for Tony Blair's attempts at modernisation since 2001.[10]

The principle that public services must be managed as efficiently as possible, with minimum bureaucracy, learning lessons from the private sector in being customer-centric and adapting working practices around the needs of users, not employees, was to acquire cross-party consensus in the following decades. The differences were over the scale and responsibilities of the public sector and over the degree of privatisation.

Many on the left of politics argued that public services were public precisely because they could not be adequately or equitably provided by private companies. Critics of reform believed that the 'public sector ethos' ran counter to the ethos of the private sector with its outcome focus on profit, that introducing the profit motive to public services would mean the poor losing access to universal services in favour of those who could pay. Opposition also came from public sector trade unions and professional bodies, the former using their leverage within the Labour Party as providers of funds, to attempt to discourage policies promoting public sector reform. Indeed unions continue to see the term 'public sector reform' as a cover for privatisation and cuts in services.

Reform under John Major 1990–1997

Under Thatcher's successor John Major, who became prime minister in 1990, the momentum for change in the public sector was maintained, but with key differences. In his autobiography (1999) Major recalled how improving public services was as much a priority as his predecessor when he wrote: 'I wished to improve the performance of public services. Where this could best be done in the private sector I would privatise. Where not, I wished to devolve decision-making so as to cut bureaucracy and improve the image of the service and the morale of public servants. There should be no excuse for poor performance'.[11] He added: 'The future of public services was high on my agenda in November 1990 when I entered Downing Street'.[12]

But there was a fundamental difference in approach. If Thatcher introduced the concept that public services needed to be challenged and preferably privatised or opened up to competition, Major believed they could be changed while still in state ownership. He argued that public services had value and that relying just on privatisation was 'too ideological, too lacking in vision or ambition'.[13] Unlike many in his own party, Major believed in the core value of state-owned services, his views coloured by his upbringing. As he later described, his own life history was 'different from that of most of my predecessors at Number 10' and 'when I was young my family had depended on public services'. He added:

> These personal experiences left me with little tolerance of the lofty views of well-cosseted politicians, the metropolitan media or Whitehall bureaucrats who made little use of the public services in their own lives and had no concept of their importance to others. They may have looked down on the public sector and despised it as second-rate but many of them knew nothing of the people who worked there or the manifold problems they faced.[14]

His approach, less ideological, more focused on change from within rather than wholesale privatisation, was to set the tone for reform during the following quarter century.

Major adapted the Thatcherite assault on the public sector by arguing that it did not require abolition but reform and admitting that his own party had been too quick to condemn it. 'Privatisation had brought huge improvements in the quality of service in the 1980s as well as lower price', he wrote. 'Yet the public face of the Conservative Party carelessly, sometimes tactlessly, still allowed itself to be seen as not caring about improving the public sector...The impression too often conveyed was that our support was grudging; and our policy of privatising some parts of the public sector led people to believe we were hostile to all of it'.[15]

Major did not only continue Thatcher's drive to change public services, he also as new prime minister made it his personal agenda and by inference suggested she had only half-completed the task. His view however was not that the state had become over-mighty but that the services it delivered were inept. He wrote in his memoirs that on becoming prime minister the state of the public sector 'dismayed and angered' him adding:

> Despite many excellent public servants the service offered was often patronising and arrogant...There was a mentality in parts of the public sector that no one had responsibility to give better service to the public...Services were run carelessly, wastefully, arrogantly and, so it seemed to me, more for the convenience of the providers than the users...I wanted to bring the discipline and effectiveness of the private sector into the public services.[16]

Major took the view that both the public sector and his own party's attitude towards it needed a step change and as he later remarked: 'The culture of the public sector needed changing and I believed I knew how to do it'.[17] This new managerially based approach to public service delivery was to become known as New Public Management.

Major and his ministers believed privatisation was right for certain services like British Airways, the railways, coal industry and British Telecom and he backed the contracting out of certain central and local government services, but he was lukewarm about it in schools or health. Nonetheless he faced opposition not just from public sector unions and from the right of his own party which believed only privatisation and competition were the solutions to poor performance but also the Treasury which believed services could be kept in-house with the proper funding. Major wrote later:

> In order to achieve improvement I knew I would have to confront old attitudes both towards public services and inside them. The Tory right were not the only ones with an attitude problem. They believed the only good public service was a privatised one; but the vast majority of civil servants, even in the Treasury, seemed to believe the only way a service could be improved was to throw money at it.[18]

Major began outlining his philosophy even before he became prime minister. In 1989 in a speech to the Audit Commission when he was chief secretary to the Treasury he warned against denigration of the public sector, calling instead for a focus on improving its performance and making its services more responsive to users. On becoming prime minister in November 1990 he told his Number 10 policy unit to make public sector reform 'a priority for action'. His Number 10 advisers, Sarah Hogg and Jonathan Hill, later recalled that in his first Cabinet meeting Major had noted in a notepad four issues 'on which he was determined to maker an impact: inflation and unemployment, Northern Ireland and public services'.[19] Major himself later wrote: 'We had to find new ways of raising sharply the general quality of public services and of empowering the consumer, patients, parents and passengers alike'.[20]

Major saw information as the way to improve performance, believing that 'publishing the performances of different schools, hospitals, local authorities or transport services would act as a kind of surrogate competition to raise standards. These bodies which were seen to be underperforming would come under pressure to explain why and to improve. An information revolution would be just as effective a way of doing this as the left-wing device of regulation by state, quango or local education authority'.[21]

He believed that standards for every service should be published, performance reports made available to the public and redress available for errors. This was underwritten in a pledge called the Citizen's Charter, an initiative which he personally drove despite initial scepticism within his own party, to the extent of initially ordering all 19 ministers with public service responsibilities to submit to him ideas on how to implement it. Officially unveiled in a speech in March 1991 and launched in July 1991, the Charter aimed to widen competition in public services, increase contracting-out, bring in more performance-related pay and introduce published performance targets locally and nationally. By 1997 there were 42 national charters and over 10,000 local charters and years later in 2008 a key Commons committee would describe it as 'a landmark shift in how public services are delivered' adding:

> The Citizen's Charter has had a lasting impact on how public services are viewed in this country. The initiative's underlying principles retain their validity nearly two decades on – not least the importance of putting the interests of public service users at the heart of public service provision. We believe this cardinal principle should continue to influence public service reform, and encourage the Government

to maintain the aims of the Citizen's Charter programme given their continuing relevance to public service delivery today.[22]

Number 10 advisers Sarah Hogg and Jonathan Hill saw it as an update of Thatcher's agenda for reform. 'The Charter was a statement of hard policy principle, about the application of market disciplines – information, competition, direct accountability to consumers, reward for performance – to public services. It was, in that sense, the lineal descendant of privatisation'.[23] They added:

> Departments and the Treasury tended to shy away from talk about standards or quality [the departments would want more money and the Treasury feared it would mean them getting more money]. The Citizen's Charter was an explicit effort to break out of this trap; to stimulate public services to use public money better.[24]

Like his successor Tony Blair, Major soon complained of Whitehall institutional inertia and set up a committee – later a unit – based in the Cabinet Office to oversee progress on the Charter. One of the ministers involved was Francis Maude, who two decades later as Cabinet Office minister was to oversee public sector reform. After the 1992 election Major created an Office of Public Service Standards to 'ensure that the drive for higher standards was not sidelined' and later introduced an awards programme for good services, the Charter Mark.

However, while Major envisaged the Citizen's Charter as a ten-year programme and its principles carried over into successive governments the name itself quietly disappeared under Tony Blair. As Major later commented ruefully: 'The Citizen's Charter failed to catch the public imagination as it should have done with the sheer scale and breadth of its attack on old-fashioned working methods and poor public service'.[25] But he also believed that while it was 'not a magic wand' and instead 'the launch of a long, slow process of change' in the 40 years of public service before it 'too little progress had been made.[26]

His advisers, Hogg and Hill, believed the Citizen's Charter had a lasting impact. 'A huge programme it scored over time many unsung successes in improving the quality and efficiency of public services', they later wrote and added:

> Departments are large, heavyweight institutions with a very big turning circle and infinite capacity for obstruction and delay. It is a rare policy that succeeds without the momentum of one of these

institutional tankers behind it. Yet the essence of the [Citizen's] Charter was that it was non-departmental. The miracle is that it managed to turn the public sector feet as far as it did.[27]

In 2008 a Commons Public Administration Committee report said the Citizen's Charter had a lasting impact on 'how public services are viewed' and continued to influence public service reform. It concluded: 'Despite being somewhat unkindly judged by history, the Citizen's Charter was nonetheless a significant milestone in public service reform'.[28]

Major's focus on information and inspection as a means of driving up performance across education, police, railways, health and utilities was to survive his own departure from Number 10. Another lasting innovation of his government was the creation of schools inspectorate Ofsted in 1992 which replaced a less vigorous monitoring regime. Two decades later with its remit wider than ever, Ofsted chief and former Headteacher Sir Michael Wilshaw would write:

> Over the last 20 years, Ofsted has been instrumental in changing the educational landscape by challenging an establishment that is sometimes too cosy and complacent, and occasionally attempts to defend the indefensible. Like many other headteachers, I would not have been able to achieve so much without the confidence of being backed by Ofsted's criteria and judgements when setting expectations of both staff and students.[29]

Another, more controversial, legacy was the private finance initiative (PFI) set up in the United Kingdom in 1992 and copied across the world. PFI used private sector management expertise and funds to develop major infrastructure projects such as roads, hospitals, schools and waste plants with the added advantage that it was off-balance sheet and therefore excluded from public spending figures. PFI was to be widely used under the next governments of Blair and Brown, though became less popular under Cameron as the full impact of the long-term liability to the taxpayer of PFI-funded projects became apparent.

Many of the Major reforms and certainly the philosophy that public services must be customer-centric and adapt to changing demands were to survive into consequent governments. Indeed Major later commented ruefully: 'We peeled back the layers of complacency in the system that had left the public expecting the worst from the services their taxes paid for. New Labour was to take office in time to win some of the plaudits'.[30]

Conclusion

The first major attempts to reform public services with a view to making them more efficient, more responsive to consumers and less costly began under Margaret Thatcher. The reforms encountered hostility and were seen by critics as ideologically driven particularly as Thatcher regarded public services as part of an over-mighty state. For the first time however she engendered a debate about the level of services the public should expect. However, even Thatcher avoided reform of the health service leaving its implementation to her successor John Major.

Major took a less ideological view about public service reform although was no less keen. His government developed the concept of customer-focused services through the Citizen's Charter, launched the education inspectorate Ofsted and introduced PFI for the first time. Many of Major's reforms were to be refined and developed under his successors.

2
Reform Under Labour 1997–2010

The key test of whether public sector reform would survive the end of 18 years of Conservative governments came in 1997 when Labour was swept into power on a landslide. Would Labour now turn the clock back to 1979, scrapping the legislation that had led to privatisation and opened up public services to competition?

In fact far from rejecting wholesale the reforms of Thatcher and Major, the new Prime Minister Tony Blair took the view that their changes had been only the beginning. His Chief of Staff Jonathan Powell was later to recall: 'Our main strategic focus in government was reform of the public services'.[1] Blair's Press Chief Alastair Campbell also later wrote: 'Once in power [Blair] was clear about the initial priorities...in establishing Labour's competence on the economy; in showing that modernising public services did not just mean pouring in money but forcing them too to face up to difficult reform'.[2]

In his memoir *A Journey* Tony Blair wrote: 'Whatever the enormous impact of the Thatcher reforms had been on the private sector of the 1980s we had inherited a public sector largely unreformed; and we weren't instinctively inclined to reform it. The state was still as it had been since 1945'.[3] His autobiography devotes many pages to his frustration with the pace of public sector reform in which he refers to 'the vested interests of the state' and how 'left to its own devices, it grows'[4]. He believed that public services did not need to be provided on a monopoly basis within the public sector 'controlled in a rigid way by national and local bureaucracies often deeply resistant to innovation'.[5]

Blair backed some of the reforms initiated by Thatcher and Major but he felt that the Tories had 'not properly thought through' crime and welfare policy and had only begun to be radical 'at the end of their time'. But on education and health he felt their reforms needed to be examined and if necessary developed by New Labour rather than dismissed. Later he wrote:

> On health and education … while the Tory reforms may have been badly implemented and badly explained their essential direction was one that was in fact nothing to do with being 'Tory' but to do with the modern world. These reforms were all about trying to introduce systems where the money spent was linked to performance and where the service user was in the driving seat.[6]

Blair and his supporters believed that changes in the way local government, health and Whitehall delivered services were essential and that the principle of opening up public services to other providers was conducive to improving quality. He and his New Labour ministers maintained that monopolies were inefficient, private or public, and that inefficient monopolistic public services hit the people they were supposed to help. It followed therefore that Labour as champion of the poor should be on the side of increasing efficiency. As he later wrote: 'Driving value through public services is not a question of being efficient rather than just – it is just. Spend less on bureaucracy and you spend more on front-line care'.[7]

The shorthand for public service reform was 'modernisation'. Blair initially called his political philosophy the Third Way, neither statism nor capitalism. In theory his approach appeared both practical and ideologically sound. In practice, it aroused hostility from unions and the party's left which saw it as a cover for privatisation and reduced terms and conditions for the manual workforce as competition and the drive for efficiency drove down labour costs.

In the case of local government for example, Blair's New Labour government refused to abandon the market testing of in-house manual services. Instead it scrapped the compulsory stipulation replacing it with a voluntary regime with value for money at its core. As the historian of the Audit Commission later noted, 'No slouching at local level by councils of any political allegiance could be allowed to impede Labour's drive for radical improvement in Britain's public services'.[8] Indeed the commission itself, once earmarked by Labour in opposition for the axe, instead took on a greater inspection and performance monitoring role.

In the health sector the government moved towards breaking down the monopolistic NHS provision of hospital care by creating more autonomous foundation hospitals. The same applied to education where Blair used new academies, injected with private sector management and funding, to break what he saw as the rigid management of schools by local education authorities and teaching unions.

But Blair was to confess in his memoirs that he felt his programme for public sector reform was too unambitious despite the immense battles he had within his own party and with other ministers to implement it. He later wrote that in public services he and his supporters had 'all the right language and all the right intentions' but change had to be driven from the centre. He added: 'The origins of later, far more radical change were discernible in those starting months yet the policy prescriptions were too tame'.[9]

He later recalled that during the winter break in 1997 he re-read the party manifesto on public services and 'laughed at their modesty' although recognising the difficulties of being more radical added: 'To go deeper, to start changing systems was a whole different order of political as well as practical task. Adjust a system and people hardly notice. Change it and out of every channel come the interests the system maintains'.[10]

His Chief of Staff, Jonathan Powell, later wrote: 'Government is a "precious egg" carried by the prime minister in a thousand mile egg and spoon race.... and we didn't want to drop it ... This fear led us to be too timid on public service reform as well'. He saw reform as shifting from 'producer-driven public services to health and education services driven by the patient, the parent and the pupil but still free at the point of use'. Powell argued the government should have moved 'directly to radical reform to bring this about' but was limited by a commitment to upholding John Major's spending plans for the first two years 'to demonstrate that the Labour government was financially competent'.[11]

Referring to what he perceived as producer interests blocking reform Tony Blair wrote of 'major small "c" conservative interests within the services that were hostile to change, essentially vast vested interests that were pretty unscrupulous about defending themselves on the spurious grounds of defending the public interest'.[12] In 1999 he complained in a speech to the British Venture Capital Association: 'You try getting change in the public sector and public services. I bear the scars on my back after two years of government'.[13] To the Labour conference in September 1999 he referred to 'the forces of conservatism' and he did not necessarily just mean the big 'C' Conservatives.

Frustration at his perceived inability to effect change in the public sector later stalked the pages of his memoirs. He recalled: 'Across the piece – in schools, universities, the NHS, law and order and criminal justice – we were still only tinkering, not transforming... As 1999 wore on and the year 2000 turned I began to look at how we could propel the whole question of reform further and faster'.[14] Mindful of his own lack of experience of managing organisations he even considered working on the front line to better understand how the system worked. 'At points I wanted to give up everything else and just spend days on the front line learning what it was like to manage a service, what its real pressures were, what could be done within the conventional parameters and how the parameters might be changed'.[15]

Blair felt he only truly worked out his agenda on public service reform – choice and diversity – after the start of his second term. Later he commented: 'I had worked out the crucial failure of the first term [1997–2001]; the mistaken view that raising standards and performance could be separated from structural reform.... Above all we had to divest power away from the dominant interest groups, unions and associations, and put it into the hands of people, the consumer, the parent, the patient, the user'.[16] He added: 'As one of my longer year 2000 notes put it, we needed to become more searching, more radical, more groundbreaking in our approach to the whole post-war settlement around public services and the welfare state'.[17]

Blair's view was that changing the poor performers was no longer sufficient. It was now about addressing the performance of what he regarded as the mediocre. He wrote later: 'We had a much greater ambition for change. The trouble was for many people, including ironically the public we were wanting to serve, a coasting or average service seemed fair enough'.[18]

But many in his own Labour party were lukewarm about his proposals for more radical change. Blair wrote: 'Though much of the party could accept radical reform in the event of chronic failure, most would not accept that radicalism in the case of passive mediocrity'.[19]

He later regarded the period in working up the 10-year NHS Plan in 2000 as when he had 'a clear break' with the idea that the private and public sectors were different entities adding: 'The truth was that the whole distinction between public and private sector was bogus at all points other than one: a service you paid for and one you get free'.[20] He also dismissed the concept of a 'public sector ethos' as a cover for poor performance saying that 'if the status quo resulted in a poor service, then that was the true betrayal of that ethos; and so if the poor service arose from the wrong structure the structure had to change'.[21]

Part of the problem was that reforming public services, as his predecessors had found and his successors were to find, was like turning round an oil tanker. In his memoirs Blair complained that by 2000 he was learning how 'complex the institutions of public service were' and added: 'The intricacy of the issues involved was really hard to unravel and reconstruct'.[22]

In 2001, after his second general election win, Blair was determined to step up the pace of public service reform. A new delivery unit was created in Number 10 with a brief to oversee the performance monitoring programme of the key public services, education, health, crime and transport. A strategy unit was set up to plan strategy and develop ideas for tackling longer-term issues. He believed that by the beginning of his second term, in 2001, he had created a 'template of reform'. He later described this as 'changing the monolithic nature of the service, introducing competition, blurring distinctions between public and private sector, taking on traditional professional and union demarcation of work and vested interests and in general trying to free the system up, letting it innovate, differentiate, breathe and stretch its limbs'.[23]

Despite his preoccupation in his second term after his 2001 election victory with international affairs, 9/11 and Iraq, he was convinced in his own mind about what change needed to occur in public services. In autumn 2002 he still continued to regard public sector reform as 'at the heart of what he wanted to achieve in his remaining time as Prime Minister' despite having already been in power for five years.[24] By this he meant more foundation hospitals, academies freed from council control, more patient choice in the NHS.

At the same time, after adhering in its first term to the Conservative government's public spending targets, the Labour government after 2000 began to increase spending, especially in health sector. It also hired a private sector director Sir Peter Gershon to run the Office of Government Commerce overseeing Whitehall procurement. In 2004, Sir Peter presented a report on how to achieve greater efficiencies across public services which was included into the next comprehensive spending review and underpinned efficiency reform for the next four years. He estimated savings of £20 billion could be made of which £8 billion was through productivity improvements.

Blair later maintained that many of his reform aims in health, education, law and order had been achieved. 'By the time I left choice and competition were embedded in the NHS; academies were powering ahead; the crime bills had passed; tuition fees were in place, and welfare and pension reforms were formulated, if not introduced. These weren't small items. They were major changes'.[25]

His agenda was summed up in a paper from his Number 10 Strategy Unit in 2006 which wrote: 'The UK Government's current approach to public service reform combines pressure from government (top down performance management); pressure from citizens (choice and voice), competitive provision; and measures to build the capability and capacity of civil and public servants and central and local government'.[26]

Towards the end of his premiership, 'Blair's mantra of choice and diversity had come to define his approach to public services. By freeing up schools and hospitals and giving more choice to their users, the theory went, services would become more responsive and standards would improve'.[27] But he also expressed regret after his departure that he had not gone further and faster on public sector reform, a sentiment that was noted by his Conservative opponent and later Prime Minister, David Cameron.

Looking back on his term in office Blair said his government brought in competition, blurred distinctions between the public and private sectors and took on 'vested interests' adding: 'Each reform was painfully iterated and reiterated ... Together they added up to a substantial corpus of change and set the system in a new direction. They will form the essential basis of any future reform and where departed from, will, over time, be returned to'.[28]

But one of his ministers, Alistair Darling, was more critical about what he regarded as a missed opportunity to pursue the reform agenda in his second term, blaming Blair's preoccupation on foreign affairs, especially Iraq:

[Blair] became distracted from domestic affairs at just the time when we still had a mandate to carry through the reforms needed to improve public services. By the time he returned to address domestic issues, following a historic third election victory in 2005, it was too late. Everyone in government knew that he was going and the political centre of gravity swung towards Gordon [Brown]. In the two years between the election and Tony standing down in June 2007 the business of government was paralysed.[29]

Blair also presided over a huge increase in public spending which led to improved public services. However, this was not matched by proportionate increases in public sector productivity and recent studies since attempted to separate improvements which were down to higher investment and those which can be attributed to reforms.

Reform under Brown 2007–2010

His successor, Gordon Brown, had as chancellor been a critic of Blair's more radical proposals for public sector reform particularly in health, over foundation hospitals, and in education, over academies. Even in 2000 Blair had noticed that 'the direction of reform was not shared, not agreed and not much liked' by Brown and his Treasury team. 'I noticed that the term "marketisation" of public services started to be used in discussion between us... and the term was not meant as a compliment'.[30] And he added: 'The nearest I got to giving up my job voluntarily was during 2004 when I thought I had had enough and would yield to Gordon, since I felt he might continue the reform agenda. And the clearest I became that I should stay despite it all was when I realised he wouldn't'.[31]

In his own memoirs of his years at Number 10 as Blair's Chief of Staff, Jonathan Powell suggested that the Conservatives were able to 'pivot their entire election campaign around Gordon [Brown] as a block on reform' and that had any other Labour politician taken over as prime minister from him, 'the Tories would have been left without a campaign in 2010 and perhaps the Labour Party would have won the election'.[32] But Blair was not without critics of his reform programme. Brown's biographer noted that while early pledges on academies and foundation hospitals were absent this was a 'conscious decision' as 'Blair's insistence on constantly altering the way in which public services were delivered had drawn increasing irritation from practitioners during his final years as Prime Minister'.[33]

Gordon Brown's own short reign as prime minister from 2007 to 2010 was dominated by the financial crash to which he responded with vigour and leadership but he was less enamoured with radical public service reform. The biographers of his government wrote in 2010:

[Brown] deserves little credit for his health policy... overall tough decisions in health were sidelined and no clear lead was given... in education... innovation and the drive in school improvement stalled. On law and order he began by reversing the Blairite agenda and only late in the day as the election approached did he seek to make it a priority... Overall Labour lost significant ground under Brown on public service reform.[34]

Another commentator wrote: 'Only halfway through his second term and especially after his third election victory in 2005 did Blair settle on a bold agenda for reform and by then Gordon Brown was doing his best to obstruct it'.[35] By nature more of a statist than his predecessor, Brown remained committed to choice in health and to improving standards in schools through the Children's Plan but was less convinced of the need for structural change. His attempt to put his views on reform on paper led to the document *Excellence and fairness* in June 2008 but it 'lacked popular resonance' and appeared, said one aide, 'civil-service inspired'.[36] Unlike Blair public service reform did not define Brown's approach to domestic policy. In a 2009 Cabinet Office document Brown revealed his view that the state was back in fashion when he wrote: 'The state has an inescapable responsibility to promote fair chance and fair rules for all. This is the moral compass that guides the new agenda of public service reform'.[37]

Brown 'cared deeply about education' but took a different stance to Blair. His biographers wrote: 'The Prime Minister was never [an] ideological opponent of academies and diversity ... but his heart beat faster to educational tunes different from Blair's'.[38] Through the Children's Plan and the 'National Challenge' education policy focused on improving exam standards and tackling failing schools rather than rolling out the academies programme. 'Choice, diversity, academies and empowering parents were all downplayed or mothballed'.[39] Brown's biographers wrote that his 'relatively bare cupboard of achievement on schools and universities is striking.' Their book quotes a Number 10 aide saying in 2009 they were ' "heading for polling day and no one knew what our education policy was." '[40]

Blair's vision for choice and diversity defined his approach to public services, proving in the view of his biographers 'a substantial asset, not just driving work in Whitehall but also acting as an anchor to steady his premiership against the storm of events'. In contrast, Brown 'had no such anchor'.[41] From anti-social behaviour (ASB) to schools policy Brown kept asking whether a policy constituted change or continuity with Blair 'rather than the more fundamental question: "What am I myself trying to achieve?" '[42]

Two years into his premiership in summer 2009 and with an election just a year away, Brown defined his own domestic policy agenda through a document drawn up with the Policy Unit *Building Britain's Future*, which included his approach to public services 'even though in truth Brown had yet to seriously engage in public service reform'.[43]

In his preface Brown wrote: 'We embrace radical modernisation in the welfare state and public services'. Anticipating the impact of deficit reduction on public spending, he warned that 'over the coming years there will need to be even sharper reforms with tough choices about where to target investment and a determination to get value for money'.[44]

In its pledge to move away from a system based primarily on targets and central direction to one where individuals 'have enforceable entitlements over the service they receive', the paper signalled the direction of travel of reform which was to crystallise in the next government's own promises of decentralisation. It pledged hospital treatment within 18 weeks, access to a cancer specialist within a fortnight and free health checks for the middle-aged. It stated that while it did not envisage users taking public service providers to court, giving them powers 'through clear redress mechanisms will not only drive up standards and the quality of public services... it will lock in and guarantee fairness'. It added: 'The public services of the future will continue to play a crucial role in ensuring fair chances for all and promoting social mobility'. It also noted that the public sector had delivered efficiency savings of £26.5 billion between 2004 and 2008, 'way beyond' the £21.5 billion target identified by Sir Peter Gershon in his review commissioned when Brown was at the Treasury.

In education every secondary school pupil would have access to a personal tutor with one-to-one tuition for those falling behind and successful headteachers would work across more than one school 'as we radically expand federations of schools, trusts and academies'. An education White Paper *Twenty-first century schools* published in June proposed ways of allowing high-performing schools to take over poor-performers. The problem was Brown's government had little time to see the fruits of more long-term changes with a general election due in May 2010.

In the government's last year a new concept emerged which was to be overtaken by the election. The idea, driven by the communities and local government department and the Treasury through the Operational Efficiencies Programme, was that of pooling public sector budgets locally and allocating according to need. Dubbed Total Place it led to over a dozen pilot schemes covering services from family intervention and adult care to youth justice and re-offending and the 2010 Budget envisaged a dramatic expansion of the programme. Momentum was lost with a change of government though the concept re-emerged a year later, and with yet more pilots, as 'community budgets'.

Conclusion

Tony Blair regarded public service reform as the defining feature of his government and developed some of the existing Conservative initiatives in health and education while dropping others like the Citizen's Charter. He introduced major changes in the NHS, Whitehall, local government and education backed up by a complex system of top-down performance management. In his support of opening up public services to new providers, to introducing academies operating outside local government and to more independent foundation hospitals Blair was often at odds with his own party as well as with what he saw as the 'forces of conservatism' within the public sector. But he was also criticised for creating a bureaucratic system of inspection and targets.

His successor Gordon Brown was less enamoured with public sector reform and was soon preoccupied with the fiscal collapse from 2007. Under both Brown and Blair public spending saw its biggest increase since the 1940s but this was not accompanied by proportional increases in productivity.

3
Reform Under the Coalition 2010–2015

The sidelining of Blair's ambitious public sector reform programme under Brown was to provide a policy opportunity for the Conservatives and their Liberal Democrat allies when they formed the Coalition government in May 2010.

The lack of clear direction under Brown enabled the Coalition to maintain that standards in public services were declining as reform had lost its way and that it needed to be relaunched. In a speech in January 2011 Conservative leader David Cameron said: 'I want one of the great achievements of this Government to be the complete modernisation of our public services. Like every other western industrialised nation we won't sustainably live within our means with unreformed public services'. The idea that despite ten years of Blair's changes the Conservatives and their partners could still use the state of public services as an election issue and claim they were 'unreformed' reflected the uneven pattern of the Blair 'modernisation' programmes.

Many commentators believed that having Liberal Democrats as Coalition allies would temper Conservative plans for public service reform and certainly there were rows about the level of private sector involvement in services like the NHS. But the Coalition, perhaps mindful of Blair's regrets that he was not much more ambitious about introducing public sector reform early in his first term, and despite its sometimes uneasy alliance of anti-big state Conservatives and pro-state Liberal Democrats, proved surprisingly ambitious in its reform programme outlined in the first few months of taking power. Indeed its plans for welfare, health and education reform both borrowed and developed initiatives launched by Blair which in turn borrowed from Major. One historian of the Conservatives commented:

> Measures to extend choice in the public services and to reform the cumbersome welfare system chimed with Team Cameron's approach – not least because they believed they amounted to a continuation (or more accurately an adaption) of policies that the Conservatives introduced during the 1990s.[1]

In the way that Blair had supported aspects of Thatcher's radicalism, so the new Prime Minister David Cameron too was an admirer of Blair's determination to press ahead with public sector reform despite opposition from professional interests and his own party and to focus on the needs of the public as consumer. He also believed that Blair had been too timid in tackling public service reform. One of his colleagues noted:

> Blair came into power with many good intentions but for several years wandered around in the mists trying to work out how on earth to deal with things like schools and crime and hospitals and so on and not really having very much idea.[2]

Cameron's government aimed to expand Blair's choice and diversity agenda in education, law and order, welfare, health and local government. In particular its philosophy was that the public must be allowed more involvement in their public services, even to the extent of running them, and that services must be opened up to a wider variety of outside providers to deliver, not simply from the private sector but from the third sector such as social enterprises and mutuals. The inspection regime must also be scaled back, relying less on government-appointed officials to monitor services and more on the public themselves as consumers. The mantra of the Coalition government's first year was 'Big Society', the concept that the public should take on more responsibility for local services and helping neighbours on a voluntary basis, rather than assuming that the role must always be fulfilled by government agencies. In practice the idea proved difficult to develop, particularly as the voluntary sector was hit by local authority spending cuts. Critics also maintained that Big Society was simply a way of persuading the public to run services like libraries without pay in order to save money.

For whereas Blair's reform agenda from 2000 had taken place against a backdrop of rising public spending, reform under the Coalition operated in an environment of sharply reducing expenditure. The Treasury maintained that public spending in the 20 years to 2007/08 averaged

40% of GDP, then rose to 'a historically high level' of 48% of GDP by 2009/10 leaving Britain with the 'largest deficit in its peacetime history' at 11% of GDP.[3]

The fiscal collapse in 2007/8 had led to recession in the private sector at a time when the lag in budget planning meant the public sector remained insulated from cuts. From 2010/11 this changed. In the June 2010 budget the Treasury announced that welfare reform, including benefit cuts and the introduction of a new Universal Credits system to replace benefits and tax credits, would deliver savings of £11 billion by 2014/15 and government efficiency savings a further £6 billion. As part of its four-year deficit reduction plans confirmed in the Spending Review in October 2010, an average of 19% cuts in spending from 2011/12 to 2014/15 across all government departments other than health and overseas aid were announced. Across Whitehall, including agencies, the target was a 34% cut in administration costs by 2015, driven by a new Efficiency and Reform Group based in the Cabinet Office. Central government funding to police would fall by 20% in real terms by 2015, part funded by efficiency savings.

The Coalition exploited public resentment at generous senior salaries and guaranteed pensions in the public sector at a time when private sector pensions were disappearing to initiate workforce changes. They included pay freezes, redundancies and reductions in pension entitlement, provoking opposition from unions and professional associations with even GPs taking strike action in spring 2012, although with little public sympathy. But even with these cuts the 2010 Spending Review claimed that 'public spending as a percentage of GDP will return to the level seen in 2006–2007 (41%), and in real terms it will return to around the level seen in 2008–2009'.[4]

The review also maintained that the NHS, with its £102 billion budget in 2010/11 – up 70% from 2000/01 – would continue to be 'free at the point of use and available to everyone based on need not the ability to pay'. Furthermore it claimed that NHS spending would be increased 'in real terms in each year of the Parliament' though the NHS was tasked with delivering £20 billion of efficiency savings by 2015 (the Coalition's claim it was increasing real terms NHS spending was later disputed by the UK Statistics Authority which said that spending on the NHS in real terms was lower in 2011/12 than in 2009/10).[5]

The Spending Review described reform as:

localising power and funding; extending the use of personal budgets for service users, cutting burdens and regulations on frontline staff, including policing, education and procurement; increasing diversity of provision in public services through further use of payment by results; removing barriers to greater independent provision, and supporting communities, citizens and volunteers to play a bigger role in shaping and providing services; and improving the transparency, efficiency and accountability of public services.[6]

The Treasury review also laid out the Coalition government's new plans for public service reform. It went on:

> The Government will pay and tender for more services by results rather than be the default provider; look to set proportions of specific services that should be delivered by non-state providers including voluntary groups; and introduce new rights for communities to run services, own assets and for public service workers to form cooperatives.

It envisaged more 'innovative payment mechanisms' based on payment by results in areas like community health services, prisons, probation and children's services as well as welfare to work and offender rehabilitation. Overall, it saw a greater role for volunteers, community groups, social enterprises and mutuals in providing localised services.

The review added that these priorities were to be 'underpinned by radical reform of public services to build the Big Society' with greater involvement by the voluntary, or third, sector. This is defined as 'non governmental organisations that are value driven and which principally invest their surpluses to further social, environmental and cultural objectives'. It includes charities, local community groups, social enterprises and mutuals but one select committee report noted that 'the breadth of the sector presents a real challenge for policymakers looking to design the relationship between the sector, citizens and the state'.[7]

While the third sector has delivered services for centuries, its involvement in delivering public services, that is those funded by the taxpayer with a remit to ensure they are delivered to every person who needs them, is more recent but has grown steadily since the 1980s. By 2006 public funding for the third sector was some £11 billion, a third of the sector's total. In 1996/97 the value of government contracts to the third sector was around £2 billion. By 2005/6 it was almost £6.9 billion.[8] Ironically, this was a case of 'back to the future' as many of the voluntary sector's philanthropic works in the nineteenth century such as in the provision of social housing, hospitals and schools had been later taken on by the state.

The Labour government 1997–2010 saw the voluntary sector as having a key role in its public sector reform programme and in 2002 even set a target of having 5% of public services delivered by this sector by 2005/6, later abandoned. In 2008 the PASC noted:

> While in the past the development of a market has been justified on the grounds of driving down costs, which is a legitimate goal in itself, the aim of involving the third sector is also about improving the quality of services for their users. Government hopes – ambitiously – that the distinctiveness of third sector organisations will have a 'transformative' effect on public service delivery.[9]

Conservative leader David Cameron also saw a transformational role for the third sector in public service delivery, along with greater involvement by local voluntary groups, mutuals and social enterprises in running local services such as libraries and care facilities as the cash-strapped state retreated from its previous levels of provision. Cameron termed his philosophy of greater third sector and public involvement The Big Society, a phrase he first used in November 2009.

But inevitably the term took on political connotations because of spending cuts and was seen by critics as a smokescreen for closing down or transferring services previously run by the public sector. In Cameron's *Opening up Public Services White Paper in 2011* Big Society was hardly mentioned and by 2013 the phrase was out of fashion. MPs on the Commons Public Administration Select Committee were also unimpressed, warning 18 months into the Coalition government that the concept was little understood in Whitehall and was difficult to implement in practice. Even if were understood it would still take a generation to succeed.[10] Furthermore third sector groups were having as much as £3 billion in contracts and grant funding cut by local and central government due to the public spending squeeze. Big Society involvement in the NHS and welfare reform also proved challenging.

There is a paradox at the heart of Big Society. In the case of the Work Programme where the voluntary sector hoped to win a sizeable share of contracts, the requirement for high levels of capital funding and turnover tipped the scales in favour of private sector firms which won some 90% of the prime contracts leaving the third sector as subcontractors. The emphasis on payment by results makes it difficult for smaller voluntary groups with poor cash flow to compete. The government's emphasis on economies of scale to drive down supplier costs further militates against smaller enterprises. In its audit of Big Society, think-tank Civil Exchange concluded:

> The Big Society, despite its increased emphasis on a greater role for civil society, seems to be no exception to the general thrust toward greater competition and larger contracts, making it especially hard for small local voluntary and community organisations to compete.[11]

Academic David Lewis in a study of Big Society noted its basic contradictions as threefold which contributed to its being a 'flawed idea'. These were firstly that Big Society tried to build a legitimacy with 'a largely unconvincing appeal to an idealised and essentially unreal past'. Secondly it became enmeshed in public spending cuts, 'the result of either design or bad timing' which associated it with a particular politics. Thirdly, there was enough evidence from similar attempts to build civil society in the former Soviet block after the collapse of centralised state control to show that 'such approaches were flawed'.[12]

In education the Coalition announced an expansion of the academies programme – first unveiled by Blair – to all schools, not just those regarded as under-performing, along with invitations to create 'free' schools, set up by parents and others independent of the local authority. By September 2012 there were 2,309 academies, a 1,000% increase since May 2010 while the Department for Education spent £8.3 billion on the academies programme between April 2010 and March 2012.[13] When the deadline for the first wave of free schools closed in February 2011, the DfE had received 323 proposals of which 24 opened in September that year and a further 55 by September 2012.

In welfare, the coalition determined to address not only the cost of providing benefits and to end what it regarded as the perverse disincentive for welfare recipients to seek employment but also to reform the system itself. With the working age welfare budget having risen by 40% in the previous decade despite a strong economy, the Coalition determined to address the root cause of the increase. In the opinion of the minister in charge of the Department for Work and Pensions, former Conservative leader Iain Duncan Smith, the system trapped people into benefit dependency. Duncan Smith, who had in opposition set up a Centre for Social Justice, saw reform as a means of tackling Britain's persistent deprivation, much of it involving generations of the same families living on welfare. In November 2010 he said: 'I concluded that tackling poverty had to be about much more than handing out money. It was bigger than that. I could see we were dealing with a part of society that had become detached from the rest of us'.[14] A Welfare Reform Bill introduced in February 2011 proposed a new universal credits system, an integrated working age credit that merged out of work benefits with in-work support. It aimed to replace working tax credit, child tax credit, housing benefit, income support, income-based jobseeker's allowance, and income-related employment and support allowance. The aim was to ensure that 'all amounts of work will be more financially rewarding than inactivity' and ambitiously forecast that 500,000 adults would be taken out of poverty because of the changes.[15] It also aimed to cut the £3.5 billion a year cost of administering the system by reducing the number of overlapping agencies involved, including the DWP, HM Revenues and Customs and local authorities. The government also announced cuts to welfare, with a cap on housing benefit, the withdrawal of child benefit to higher rate taxpayers and a cut in housing benefit costs.

Alongside its drive to reform the welfare system and make it worthwhile for benefit recipients to return to work, the Coalition turned to the private and voluntary sectors to help the out-of-work find the jobs and stay in them. In June 2011 it launched a new Work Programme delivered by private and voluntary organisations as well as the public sector to replace existing job programmes like New Deals, Employment Zones and Flexible New Deals. In the new programme, which launched with 18 'prime' providers involving 1,000 organisations – half from the voluntary sector – delivering 40 contracts across 18 areas of England, for the first time providers were to be paid by results rather than through fixed fees.

In health, despite the fact that no structural changes to the NHS were heralded in the Conservative manifesto, one of the biggest pieces of health legislation ever published was unveiled in the Health and Social Care Bill in January 2011, later to become an Act in 2012. The Department of Health described it as 'a crucial part of the government's vision to modernise the NHS so that it is built around patients, led by health professionals and focused on delivering world-class healthcare outcomes'. It proposed giving consortiums of GPs powers to commission healthcare for their patients along with the budgets, abolishing the 152 Primary Care Trusts and ten Strategic Health Authorities by 2013, reducing management costs, making all hospitals foundation hospitals, creating a health scrutiny watchdog Healthwatch for patients to monitor services and setting up Public Health England to reduce health inequalities and improve public health working alongside local authorities.

In local government the mantra was 'localism' – the devolution of power down to local level, not merely down to local government but also beyond to local groups. The Localism Act in autumn 2011 heralded new powers for community groups to take over public assets and to block development. Regional development agencies were abolished, their planning powers transferred to councils. The Audit Commission, set up under Thatcher's government in 1983 to monitor local government and health spending, was also scrapped along with its performance monitoring regime and its audit functions transferred to private suppliers, along with a variety of quangos from the Standards Board for England to the General Social Care Council. With echoes of Major's drive for making more public services data available, the coalition stipulated that all items of spending of £500 by local authorities and central government departments and above had to be publicised online. The idea was that this would help the public in their new role as 'armchair auditors' monitoring wasteful spending.

One of the more dramatic reforms concerned the police. While Thatcher had been reluctant to include the police in her reform programme, Major set them performance targets under the Citizen's Charter and advocated more managerial professionalism within police forces. Blair appreciated that low-level crime, vandalism and ASB were key concerns for the public; the problem was that the police themselves in practice often did not partly because ASB issues involved several public sector agencies such as schools, social services and housing so Blair up an ASB Unit based in the Home Office to work across these Whitehall departments and coordinate their activity in tackling ASB.

Many advocates of reform became disenchanted with the way police interacted with the public. Underlying the inevitable calls for more 'bobbies on the beat' was a growing sense among the public, especially the elderly, that the police had little interest in tackling low-level crime and ASB, precisely the issues which most concerned people. High-profile cases of street crime and ASB in which the police failed to respond added to public unease about the priorities of the forces of law and order. Advocates of reform – on the left and right – came to view the police as affected by the same inherent weaknesses as other parts of the public sector such as institutional inertia, cultural conservatism, powerful unions and over-generous pay and conditions. Under Blair the police had been drawn into the performance-monitoring regime while a National Police Improvement Agency was created to support and drive through managerial change.

However, Blair had stopped short of restructuring and an earlier attempt to reduce the number of forces was abandoned. The 2008

Flanagan report into the police performance rejected a US model of directly elected commissioners, proposing instead a reform of the existing system of indirectly elected police authorities. But once in power the Coalition took the dramatic step of announcing its intention to restructure the police service, pledging to introduce directly elected police commissioners in what it called 'the most radical change in policing in 50 years' arguing that this would make the police more responsive to public concerns and bring a renewed focus on frontline policing. The Coalition introduced the Police Reform and Social Responsibility Bill – subsequently passed in November 2011 – to set up directly elected police and crime commissioners outside London from November 2012 and scrapping police authorities. In a consultative paper in July 2010 *Policing in the 21st century: reconnecting the police and the people*, Home Secretary Theresa May said the police 'have become disconnected from the public they serve'.

The centre-right free-market think-tank Reform noted in its online 'scorecard' in February 2011:

> The Government has set out the principles for successful reform: accountability to the user; diversity of provision; and value for money. These are exactly the same as those espoused by figures in the last Government including Tony Blair, [former health secretary] Alan Milburn and [former Foreign Secretary] David Miliband. They will deliver the pressure on managers to innovate, change services and save money along with the freedom to enable that to happen.

Supporters of reform argued that the public sector deficit provided the so-called 'burning platform', the urgency to drive transformational change in service delivery to meet the new reduced spending targets. Opponents maintained public sector reform was now a codeword for cuts.

Running a Coalition government with Liberal Democrats also tempered pressure from the Conservative right to push for more privatisation of public services. In February 2011, Deputy Prime Minister Nick Clegg expounded the view of the Coalition Liberal Democrat partners when he told a conference in St Albans:

> I categorically do not believe that private providers are inherently better than public-sector providers, and I would not support an approach to reform that implied that they were ... Moving from a monopoly to diverse providers doesn't mean closing you down and bringing in

someone new to do your job at half the salary with half the training as it did in the past.[16]

The health reform Bill had to be put out for further consultation in spring 2011. A White Paper from Cameron on opening up public services – trailed as his vision for public service reform – due in early 2011 was delayed until July. This was due to behind-the-scenes rows with Liberal Democrat allies about a greater private sector involvement in the NHS, not helped by leaks in February 2011 to the *Daily Telegraph* suggesting the Cameron paper would include 'an assumption' of more privatisation across the public sector which duly rang alarm bells among opponents.

Cameron's delayed Open Public Services White Paper published in July 2011 laid out for the first time his and the Coalition's reform strategy for what it termed 'the next few years' even though by then the Coalition had been in office 14 months and several of the key initiatives in health, police, welfare and local government had already been announced. Cameron told the Commons that while much of Britain's public services were 'amongst the best in the world, we can still do even better'. He summed up its aims as more choice, more decentralisation 'to the lowest possible level', a more diverse range of providers, fair access and accountability, themes that had run through reform since the early 1980s. He told MPs this would include personal budgets for adult care and children with special needs, funding that followed the pupil, student and patient, and premium payments for children from poor backgrounds and to councils which achieved improvements in public health. In their joint introduction to the paper he and Nick Clegg said that 'reform of public services is a key progressive cause'.[17]

The White Paper said that total public spending went up by 57% in real terms from 1997/8 to 2010/11, from 28% to 48% of GDP but on key international comparisons 'the UK has been treading water' particularly in education and health inequalities. The paper said 'a new approach to delivering public services is urgently needed' because 'giving people more control over the public services they receive, and opening up the delivery of those services to new providers, will lead to better public services for all'. Alluding to spending cuts it added that opening up services was necessary if the government were to deliver better services for less money [and] improve public service productivity. It said the state's role would be in 'overseeing core standards and entitlements (such as school floor standards and NHS waiting times), fair funding (such as the Pupil Premium or tiered payments for different client groups within the Work Programme) and equality of access (such as setting the School Admissions Code)'. It concluded:

> Our reforms are the best way to deliver better services; indeed, they are the only way we can deliver improved, modern public services in a time of fiscal consolidation and growing demand.[18]

In a speech on July 11 in London at think-tank Reform announcing the White Paper, Cameron alluded to media speculation about its delay saying:

> I know there are those who thought we might be pulling back or losing heart for the task ahead. So let me assure you of this: we are as committed to modernising our public services as we have ever been...This is a job that urgently needs to be done, and we are determined to see it through.

He argued that despite improvements, public services were still lagging behind those of other countries and he claimed that investment had not been matched by a similar increase in productivity. He told his audience:

> Total public spending increased in real terms by 57% between 1997 and 2010 but on no measure can we claim that things have improved by more than 50%. Even if we weren't deeply in debt we would have a responsibility to do something about this.

A later update on progress in March 2012, following a period of turbulence in the euro and a deteriorating economic scenario, emphasised that far from 'going slower' on public service reform 'it has become increasingly clear that the medium and long-term prospects for the UK's competitiveness, growth and jobs depend heavily on public service reform'. The update added that the case for reform had 'become even stronger' because of a lack of finance and that 'the only feasible way of making the gains in quality of service that our economy and society so urgently need is to make a step change in the productivity of the public services'.[19]

But reform was not simply about money. Like Thatcher and Blair, Cameron too was concerned about the minority of households who existed outside the system on welfare, often causing huge costs for the taxpayer through their demands on the benefits and criminal justice system. Under Blair they were the 'socially excluded' and a Social

Exclusion Unit was created to tackle the problem. To Cameron – while in opposition – they were the 'broken society' and he launched his 'broken Britain' campaign in August 2007. In government they were 'troubled families'. To the media they were the 'the underclass'.

But they were also evidence of the failings of public services, with various different public agencies including police, probation, housing, social services, GPs and schools all focused on the same families through multiple interventions at great cost, with little coordination and often with little tangible result. In the last months of Brown's government the 'Total Place' pilot programme had attempted to ascertain how the system, where it involved overlapping public sector agencies, could be streamlined both to be more efficient and to improve its outcomes. The pilots looked at a variety of problem areas such as drugs and alcohol, crime, offender rehabilitation and troubled families where more than one agency was involved. One of its most energetic advocates was a prominent ex-permanent secretary and former council chief executive Lord Bichard who led the programme at cross-departmental Whitehall level. The programme was sidelined when the Coalition took power in May 2010 and resurrected as a more modest pilot study focused on troubled families called community budgets.

This cross-party recognition that public services often operated in silos and resulted in overlapping and ineffective multiple interventions was emphasised in a study by the Christie Commission into the future of public services in devolved Scotland, led by the Scottish National Party. The June 2011 report concluded that the purpose of reform was socio-economic, namely to reduce inequality, arguing that current structures were failing to deliver this end and that reform was now essential in the light of budget cuts and rising demand. It argued that the combination of spending cuts and rising demand caused by demographic and social changes meant Scottish public services had to 'embrace a radical, new collaborative culture' or else 'both budgets and provision will buckle under the strain'.

Commission Chair Dr Campbell Christie, a former union leader, noted: 'Experience tells us that all institutions and structures resist change, especially radical change. However the scale of the challenges ahead is such that a comprehensive public service reform process must now be initiated'.[20]

The report, whose conclusions resonated south of the border, maintained that some 40% of spending could be prevented by adopting a more preventative approach and it said the structure of public services was often 'fragmented, complex and opaque', resulting in persistent inequality and deprivation. It added: 'Tackling these fundamental inequalities has to be a key objective of public service reform'.[21]

The surprise riots in August 2011 renewed the Coalition's focus on the troubled families agenda, especially when research into those convicted of looting found a large minority came from deprived backgrounds with poor parenting, had criminal records and low educational attainment. A Troubled Families Unit was set up in the Department of Communities and Local Government led by Louise Casey, ironically the former head of Blair's ASB Unit, to work across Whitehall while the community budgets programme with its focus on pooling public sector budgets locally was also rolled out and expanded. In November 2012 early results from four pilot areas, Cheshire West and Chester, Greater Manchester, Hammersmith and Fulham/Westminster City/Kensington and Chelsea, and Essex, claimed that savings of hundreds of millions of pounds could be made through greater integration of services and earlier intervention.[22]

Conclusion

Despite a decade of public sector reform, the Coalition in 2010 also regarded reform as its own key priority in particular to open up public services to private and voluntary sector providers. In education the academies programme was expanded to include all schools while 'free' schools were introduced, in health Primary Care Trusts were abolished as part of a controversial restructuring of the NHS, local government was given more 'localist' powers along with less funding, and an ambitious reform of the welfare system was launched. The changes occurred against a backdrop of sharply reduced spending which put pressure on public sector management to opt for 'transformational' rather than incremental change. The long-term squeeze on their budgets means public service providers must reconsider how they deliver services in order to maximise efficiencies and early pooled budget pilot studies show evidence of major savings.

Part II
The Drivers of Reform

4
Number 10 and the Cabinet Office

The office of the Prime Minister, Number 10 Downing Street, is the powerhouse of government. It makes decisions, sets policy, directs strategy and meets the daily crises that afflict the government machine. But when it comes to dealing with complex, difficult and long-term challenges, the type that public sector reform invariably involves, the influence of Number 10 is much less certain. One of its longstanding and most powerful officials observed that 'in truth political power does not reside in Number 10'.[1]

How can that be? The United Kingdom's official government archives, the National Archives, after all describes the role of Number 10 thus: 'The Prime Minister is at the very centre of British government, as principal advisor to the Sovereign, head of government, leader of the majority party in Parliament, principal minister for the civil service, having overall responsibility for defence, national security and diplomacy, and wide powers of patronage on official appointments. The Prime Minister has a wider public role in interpreting Britain's strategic aspirations and interests both nationally and internationally'.

Yet all is not as it seems. One of the greatest challenges for prime ministers is ensuring government departments work jointly to deliver policy decided at corporate, or Cabinet, level. But departments and their ministers are protective of their powers, reluctant to cede authority and both fearful and resentful of intervention from Number 10, in theory the powerhouse of the government, the driving force of policy.

It is Number 10 through the Cabinet Office that sets and determines the direction of the government and in particular its domestic agenda, notably its public sector reform programme. One Whitehall expert commenting on Coalition civil service reform plans noted: 'It is an unusual minister who takes a deep personal interest in civil service reform... Past reforms that succeeded required clear direction from the prime minister and senior ministers – and visible prime ministerial support to the officials who must shape the ideas and actions for civil service reform'.[2] But the style of Number 10 depends heavily on the character of the Prime Minister. Tony Blair for example was determined to drive forward public sector reform himself, expanding Number 10's remit across government, often ahead of his own ministers. David Cameron, in contrast, took fourteen months to produce his much-vaunted vision for public sector reform, in the White Paper *Open Public Services*. By then many of his Cabinet ministers were already forging ahead with their own reform plans, especially in schools, local government, health and welfare and the Cameron vision looked unoriginal.

But in practice the power from Number 10 is a good deal more ephemeral and its disconnection from Whitehall departments and the frontline of public services has often frustrated prime ministers wanting to drive through public sector reforms. Unlike their Cabinet ministers, prime ministers do not have a huge Whitehall machine behind them and Number 10 does not have direct responsibility for a government department other than the Cabinet Office indirectly. The staffing complement at Number 10 is modest in comparison to that of the rest of Whitehall despite its growth under Blair. Even the Cabinet has no legal powers, which reside with the secretaries of state. Tony Blair's Chief of Staff Jonathan Powell, who spent a decade at Number 10, later wrote:

> The only formal powers the prime minister has is the power of patronage. He can appoint and dismiss ministers and certain other office holders but he has no budget and no army of civil servants behind him, unlike every other cabinet minister.[3]

Describing Number 10 as more 'senior common room than buzzing office', Powell recalled his entry into Downing Street after the 1997 general election win:

> The main thing a prime minister himself notices on entering Downing Street for the first time is how illusory power really is. When you are in Opposition you are convinced that, if only you can get through the door, you can start making things happen. But power like the crock of gold at the end of the rainbow is never there

when you arrive. Prime ministers...become convinced that power lies somewhere else.[4]

Powell's memoirs, *The New Machiavelli*, are peppered with disparaging comments about the lack of real power at Number 10. Regarding it as only one of many centres of influence in politics, he wrote: 'In truth political power does not reside in No 10 but is instead widely diffused in the British elite, not just in government but outside it as well. The only way a prime minister can govern is by persuading that elite, by building coalitions of support and by carrying his colleagues with him'.[5] During the tanker strike crisis of 2000, Number 10 'pulled every lever available and none of them seemed to be connected to anything' while during the 2001 foot-and-mouth crisis 'again we pulled on every lever and none of them was working'.[6] And he added: 'The little secret of the British constitution is that the centre of government is not too powerful but too weak'.[7]

Mrs Thatcher described her own challenges at taking on the Whitehall machine when in her autobiography she recalled asking Derek Rayner to set up an Efficiency Unit 'that would tackle the waste and ineffectiveness of government. We were both convinced of the need to bring some of the attitudes of business into government. We neither of us conceived just how difficult this would prove'.[8]

Number 10's lack of real power was a particular frustration for Blair when trying to push through his public sector reform programme. Blair's immediate team, which included Powell, press chief Alastair Campbell, Sally Morgan and a succession of bright policy and strategy unit heads, was regarded as a high-powered operation and became the size of a small department. Yet even with these talented advisers around him, Blair was constantly irritated by what he perceived as the inability of Whitehall officials, their ministers, the health service, police, local government to respond at sufficient speed to his demands for reform.

There were plenty of ideas emanating from Number 10 but they disappeared into the system. Powell recalled:

> Tony used to complain that all the new ideas came from Number 10 rather than the departments. This was to some extent our fault for dominating the system in the way we did but it was also extraordinary how little capacity for original thought the [Whitehall] departments seemed to have. Departments were almost as weak in policy making as they were in terms of delivery.[9]

In his memoirs Blair described how the prime minister was akin to that of a chief executive, with a need to get into the detail of driving through change rather than relying on others to do it for him. He wrote that changing public services inevitably meant 'getting into the details of delivery and performance management in a radically more granular way. Increasingly prime ministers are like CEOs or chairmen of major companies. They have to set a policy direction; they have to see it is followed; they have to get data on whether it is; they have to measure outcomes'.[10]

The role of Number 10 units in reform

To stiffen the Number 10 machine, prime ministers create their own units. In 1971 Conservative Prime Minister Edward Heath created the Central Policy Review Staff (CPRS) to deliver strategic advice. The new think-tank followed a 1970 White Paper, *The Reorganisation of Central Government,* which looked at how the expanded state and governments could cope with longer-term challenges by planning and preparing and evaluating different strategies to meet them. But as a later Commons committee report noted: 'The 1970s arrangement was not wholly satisfactory. The economic downturn that began in 1973 and continued for the remainder of the decade meant that the CPRS became enmeshed in short-term crisis management'. David Howell, a Conservative minister during the 1970s, explained that by 1979 '[The CPRS] had become a sort of trouble shooting body...any role it was originally supposed to have, as a systematic, regular bringing together of reports of programme analysis throughout Whitehall to present an overall strategic picture to the Prime Minister and the Cabinet had long disappeared'.[11]

The CPRS was supposed to 'think the unthinkable' but when its report on what might occur if the NHS were replaced with a private insurance scheme was leaked in 1982 even Margaret Thatcher as prime minister decided this was too controversial a concept. After her second election win in 1983 she dispensed with the CPRS which in her view 'had become a freelance "Ministry of Bright Ideas" some of which were sound, some not...' adding that 'the CPRS could become a positive embarrassment' and used instead the Number 10 Policy Unit.[12]

The Number 10 Policy Unit had been created in 1974 under Labour Prime Minister Harold Wilson and carried on under Thatcher and her successor John Major who recalled in his autobiography: 'The future of public services was high on my agenda in November 1990 when

I entered Downing St. I set out my priorities at my first two full meetings with my new policy unit in January 1991'.[13]

Like both his predecessor and successor, Major found government departments moving at a glacial pace. He decided to strengthen the Policy Unit by drafting in the support of the Cabinet Office to drive through his new Citizen's Charter programme for public service reform. He wrote that the Policy Unit 'was pushing as hard as they could but it was soon clear that I needed to reinforce the unit with strengthened official machinery'. An ad hoc committee was set up in the Cabinet Office to work with the unit and Treasury in overseeing progress.[14]

One of the Policy Unit's members from 1992 to 1994, Jill Rutter, later recalled her own frustration with its lack of progress recalling:

> What became clear then was that it was too small to do anything other than get drawn into day-to-day fire fighting on behalf of the Prime Minister. Eight of us – a mix of civil servants and advisers – shadowed the whole domestic policy agenda. The Cabinet Office played its traditional coordinating and brokering role – but did nothing to move departments from their entrenched positions and look for positive solutions that cut across departmental boundaries. A meeting on policy on lone parents chaired by the Cabinet Office, full of Grade 7s briefed not to concede an inch of departmental turf, was one of the most dispiriting two hours I ever spent in government. The Prime Minister – and the government – lacked a capacity to develop forward looking policies and to do the hardest of all things – renew itself in office.[15]

Tony Blair, suspicious of the civil service, was determined to ensure Number 10 could command Whitehall's machinery when he became prime minister in 1997. During his premiership Number 10 grew to a size akin to that of a small department of state. The number of staff serving him grew to a peak of 782 in 2005/6 'which exceeded the figure from any previous era by more than 500, that is over 300%. It dropped later but in 2007/8 still stood at 399, higher than any time before 1997'.[16]

As well as the existing Policy Unit – which he merged with his private office in 2001 to form a small policy directorate of less than a dozen staff – he set up the Delivery Unit under an ex-adviser from the Department of Education, Michael Barber. Blair later recalled that the unit was 'much resisted but utterly invaluable and proved its worth time and time again'. Although small and staffed by civil servants, it also included outsiders from leading private sector companies whose task was to track the delivery of key government priorities. Blair said it would 'focus like a laser on an issue, draw up a plan to resolve it working with the department concerned, and then performance-manage it to solution'. This included data for Blair to discuss with his ministers every month and a progress report.[17]

He described how the Delivery Unit, among its achievements, helped to reduce the number of unfounded asylum cases, drove up literacy and numeracy in schools and worked on reducing NHS waiting lists and street crime. Blair said it was like 'an independent private or social enterprise at the heart of government' in which whole areas needing reform would be 'illuminated' since often the challenge required 'wholesale change to the way a public service worked, rather than a centrally or bureaucratically driven edict'.[18]

Long-term planning was addressed by a Performance and Innovation Unit set up in 1998 to work on 'time limited projects, with teams given the time and space to develop forward looking policies rather than reacting to short-term pressures'.[19] The Prime Minister's Forward Strategy Unit (PMFSU) was also created to 'provide a complementary capacity for doing more private work, generally working bilaterally with departments rather than on cross-cutting issues, and reporting directly to the Prime Minister and secretaries of states'.[20] An Office of Public Services Reform was set up in 2001 to drive through Blair's agenda on change but it was quietly disbanded in 2006.

In 2002 Blair merged both the Performance Innovation Unit (PIU) and PMFSU into a new combined Strategy Unit based in the Cabinet Office but reporting to him to oversee the wider programme of public service reform across departments and to look at emerging public service challenges that were likely to require action in the near future.

The Commons Public Administration Committee later described the remit of the Strategy Unit:

> The decision to establish the PMSU was influenced by the work of the [Central Policy Review Staff] in the 1970s. Like the CPRS, the PMSU was designed to be close enough to the issues, politics and personalities in government to understand the contexts and challenges, but distant enough from everyday matters and from those closely associated with existing policy to provide new thinking. It can be seen as a kind of internal consultancy or think-tank.[21]

The Strategy Unit had three key roles, namely reviews and policy advice on domestic policy priorities, helping departments develop strategies and policies and identifying emerging issues. Working in project teams of between two and four based around public service reform, home affairs, economy and infrastructure, welfare reform, social justice and communities, its staff ranged between 45 and 90 and drew on high fliers from the civil service, think tanks and academia who developed strategy for public service reform especially the choice agenda in health and schools. Between 1999 and 2007 it published some 90 reports.

Blair said its brief was 'to look ahead at the way policy would develop, the fresh challenges and new ideas to meet them. That also was highly successful'.[22] He saw its role as clearly distinct from the more granular Delivery Unit which focused on specific public service targets such as reducing waiting lists or increasing school results and the Policy Unit which provided advice on implementation. Blair later wrote that while the Policy Unit handled the day-to-day, the Strategy Unit looked into the future to develop policy in challenging areas like pensions, welfare to work, public health and further education.[23]

In a discussion paper about the Blair government's approach to public service reform, the Strategy Unit wrote: 'The UK Government's current approach to public service reform combines pressure from government (top down performance management); pressure from citizens (choice and voice), competitive provision; and measures to build the capability and capacity of civil and public servants and central and local government'.[24]

The paper, carefully trailed as 'not a statement of government policy' to avoid the unit going the way of the CPRS under Thatcher, was produced just before the onset of the credit crunch in 2007 and slide into recession but in its anticipation of future challenges facing public services it was advanced in its thinking. It described these challenges as 'fundamental drivers behind the need to reform Britain's public services'. Chief among these were an ageing population, a shift in the composition of households leading to smaller units and a need for more and diverse forms of housing and greater expectations of choice by users in their public services to match their experience in the private sector.

The government intended meeting these with public services that were 'citizen-centred and responsive, universal, accessible to all and in the case of health and schools free at the point of use and efficient and effective'.

The report described the government's response as having four main elements: 'top down performance management (pressure from government); the introduction of greater competition and contestability in the provision of public services; the introduction of greater pressure from citizens including through choice and voice; and measures to strengthen the capability and capacity of civil and public servants and of central and local government to deliver improved public services'.[25]

Four months before Blair stood down as prime minister the Commons Public Administration Committee issued a report on government strategic thinking in which it called the unit 'highly regarded' and agreed that a 'strong central strategy unit is essential' but needed greater involvement of ministers whose departments 'have practical experience and in-depth knowledge'.[26] The Strategy Unit survived Gordon Brown's premiership but was absorbed into other Cabinet Office units by David Cameron in 2010. The Delivery Unit was also abolished and its functions were transferred to the Treasury.

Two commentators on the power of the prime minister's office rejected the idea that big was necessarily better when they wrote in June 2010:

> Simply possessing a large staff with interventionist functions cannot necessarily overcome the prevailing political circumstances, such as those faced by David Cameron, who must accommodate a second party within government. We do not suggest that the Cameron premiership will necessarily be weak, but that it cannot achieve its goals simply by endowing itself with an enlarged support structure.[27]

Jonathan Powell, despite his criticisms about the weakness of the Number 10 machine, also praised the idea of a small-scale Downing Street when he wrote in 2011: 'No 10 has the advantage of small size, personal contact and nimbleness. It would be a terrible thing to sacrifice this...A prudent prime minister should always realise that Number 10 is in the end a court and not the HQ of a multinational corporation'.[28]

The Cabinet Office role in reform

The Cabinet Office is at the centre of government with the remit of making government work smoothly, supporting the prime minister, the deputy prime minister and the cabinet, and ensuring the civil service is providing the necessary means to help government implement its policy. It was once described as the 'junction box' of government with power coming from its centrality for 'as a secretariat it operates and services all the complex machinery of cabinet government'.[29]

But Alistair Darling, a former chancellor, was dismissive of its power, stating: 'The Cabinet Office, despite its name, is there to service

Whitehall rather than the Prime Minister. In my experience it is a mixed bag, an amalgam of various functions that can't be fitted into other government departments'.[30]

After the Coalition took power in May 2010 the Cabinet Office was tasked with supporting the new government in the implementation of its key aims outlined in the *Programme for Government*, the joint document between the new ruling Conservatives and Liberal Democrats. It stated:

> In the crucial area of public service reform, we have found that Liberal Democrat and Conservative ideas are stronger combined. For example, in the NHS, take Conservative thinking on markets, choice and competition and add to it the Liberal Democrat belief in advancing democracy at a much more local level, and you have a united vision for the NHS that is truly radical: GPs with authority over commissioning; patients with much more control; elections for your local NHS health board. Together, our ideas will bring an emphatic end to the bureaucracy, top-down control and centralisation that has so diminished our NHS.[31]

In June 2010 the new Coalition created the Efficiency and Reform Group jointly with the Treasury based in the Cabinet Office out of the Office of Government Commerce and the public sector procurement body, the Buying Agency, and later the Government Property Unit, responsible for the government estate, to drive efficiency reform across Whitehall. Its brief was to cut back Whitehall spending and use technology to drive down back office costs. A report by Sir Philip Green for the Cabinet Office in October 2010 highlighted savings that could be made by Whitehall departments centralising their procurement functions and using their bulk buying power to drive down prices. These proposals for centralised bulk buying were at odds with another Cabinet Office task to open up public services to new providers, especially third sector, small firms and social enterprises, or what Cameron had termed the 'Big Society'. A Mutuals Taskforce was also created to champion staff-led mutuals across the public sector.

In its business plan for 2011–2015, published in November 2010, the Cabinet Office said its brief was to return to its traditional role after the Labour years of an expanded Number 10: 'By reforming and coordinating, driving efficiency and transparency, and helping to build the Big Society, we want the Cabinet Office, which includes the Prime Minister's Office, to return to its historical role at the centre of government'.

In its redefined role under the Coalition, the Cabinet Office outlined its public sector reform duties as driving efficiency and effectiveness in government; increasing transparency in the public sector by publishing information that would 'give taxpayers the ability to hold public servants to account and enable users of public services to choose between providers'; reforming the political and constitutional system 'by supporting efforts to give power to people and communities by redistributing control away from Britain's over-centralised state'; building the Big Society and promoting social mobility.[32]

The regularly updated Structural Reform Plans aimed to replace 'the old top-down systems of targets and central micromanagement' for Whitehall and were 'key tools for holding departments to account for the implementation of Programme for Government commitments'. In spring 2011 the Cabinet Office and Treasury jointly announced the creation of the Major Projects Authority to improve the success rate of the high-risk central government projects.

But the Cabinet Office was criticised by the Commons Public Administration Select Committee for not providing leadership for the civil service in delivering the change programme across Whitehall. The PASC concluded:

> Ministers seem to believe that change will just happen. It is essential that the Cabinet Office take leadership of the reforms and coordinate the efforts in individual departments and across Whitehall as a whole. The scale of the challenges faced by the Civil Service calls for the establishment of a world class centre of Government, headed by someone with the authority to insist on delivery across Whitehall.[33]

The respected Institute for Government was also critical noting in 2012:

> The Cabinet Office must provide excellent support and make further resources available to those leading the work. It is unclear that this capacity exists in the present Cabinet Office structure. The creation of a Director General for Reform would be a good point at which to clarify the capacity and lines of management needed in the Cabinet Office to best support the reform programme.[34]

The Cabinet Office duly took note. In September 2012, after some delays, it appointed a director general of civil service reform. As outlined in the Civil Service Reform Plan in June 2012, the Cabinet Office minister also took personal responsibility for the change programme chairing a monthly Reform Board.

Conclusion

The prime minister's office, Number 10 Downing Street, is the focus of power in any government. In reality its ability to initiate difficult, complex change involving the public sector and follow this through is far less certain. Even a powerful Number 10 such as Tony Blair's could not ensure that its reform agenda was fully implemented.

But Number 10 is a court, not the headquarters of a multi-national company and lacks the weight of a Whitehall department of state. Its power often depends on the personality of the prime minister. In theory Number 10 has the Cabinet Office to enact corporate policy. In practice the Cabinet Office serves Whitehall.

The Cabinet, as the corporate executive of the government, often lacks the ability to implement its policies on a cross-departmental basis. The result has been a weakness at the heart of government when it comes to driving through complex and challenging policies such as public sector reform. The Coalition attempted to redress this through the creation of a director general of civil service reform reporting to the head of the civil service.

5
The Treasury

In its role as custodian of government fiscal and economic policy the Treasury has faced flak for the lamentable state of the United Kingdom's public finances. It failed to put the brakes on public spending in 2005 which might have avoided the huge deficit five years later, presided over a decline in public sector productivity during the boom years in spending, failed to predict the fiscal collapse in 2007/8, has consistently over-estimated GDP growth rates since 2010 and must now manage a long-term decline in the public finances. Even its much-vaunted efficiency programmes have been criticised by auditors and Commons select committees for over-egging their results.

Yet the Treasury is the most powerful government department in Whitehall, one of the three great offices of state along with the Foreign Office and Home Office, and traditionally led by a chancellor who is a close political associate of the prime minister. It is responsible for formulating the government's financial and economic policy and for ensuring that Whitehall departments meet their public spending targets, including making ongoing efficiency savings. It is also responsible for improving the quality of financial management and reporting across central government.

To go back to the origins of the current crisis in public finances we need to return to the mid- and late 2000s. The Treasury was run by the same powerful chancellor, Gordon Brown, for ten years (1997–2007) during a huge increase in investment in the public sector funded by a boom in financial services which came to an end with the fiscal crisis of 2007/09, precipitating a recession and a sharp reversal in public spending from 2010/11. Even as the fiscal crisis was breaking, the 2008 Budget boasted that since 1997 spending on the NHS had almost doubled in real terms and that when it celebrated its 60th birthday in 2008/09 the NHS would have a budget of £96 billion, 'representing the largest sustained funding increase in NHS history'. Total spend on education was 60% higher, that on transport 90% higher, and on public order and safety up by 50% since 1997. This investment, it added, had helped reduce NHS inpatient waiting times from 284,000 in 1997 to 'virtually zero' in 2007/08, push up the percentage of children receiving A-C GCSE passes to 60% from 45% in 1997 and cut crime in England and Wales by 32%.[1]

This was at a time when the Treasury, under its powerful Chancellor Gordon Brown, had enhanced its traditional role to become almost a department of domestic affairs, determining and developing social and economic policy alongside and often contrary to Number 10's strategic aims. The rivalry between the two architects of New Labour, Tony Blair and Gordon Brown, was reflected in the rivalry between the Treasury and Number 10, especially over the pace and scale of public service reform. Two commentators later wrote that under Brown the Treasury expanded its remit outside its traditional Ministry of Finance role, adding:

> The role of the Public Services and Growth Directorate grew. It still comprised the spending teams shadowing departments but it now combined that role with tracking performance against [Public Service Agreements] and efficiency targets... In short the [PM's Strategy Unit] and the Treasury reforms ran concurrently. They co-existed. They were not co-ordinated nor could they be because one agenda was driven by Blair and the other by Brown... the Treasury sponsored much strategic work that would normally have been produced by a central strategic unit in the Cabinet Office. The Chancellor or the Chief Secretary to the Treasury, rather than the Prime Minister or the Cabinet, were directly associated with these reviews. The Treasury and not the Cabinet Office provided the secretariat support for them... the consequence was that the Treasury became a policy department.[2]

Despite this unprecedented role the Treasury failed to plan for a scenario in which the taxes from the booming financial services sector that funded the public spending boom suddenly declined, though it was by no means alone as an institution in this lack of foresight. Because public spending is planned in advance there is inevitably a time lag before reductions or increases can take effect. The taxes which funded public services were dangerously dependent on the United Kingdom's financial services sector and if these dipped then public spending levels would be potentially under-funded. An indication of the huge long-term damage wrought by the fiscal downturn on the public finances is that, had the trend in GDP growth continued from March 2008 until 2016/17, eight years later, it would, according to the Institute for Fiscal Studies, be 13% higher than the GDP actually forecast for that year in 2012. That extra economic activity would have met the growing demand for public services. According to a separate survey the total tax contribution of the United Kingdom's financial services sector fell by 9.4% between 2007 and 2009 mainly down to lower corporation tax payments. Despite this even in 2009/10, well into the fiscal recession, the United Kingdom's financial services sector still contributed 11.2% of all tax revenues or £53.4 billion and was the largest payer of corporation tax. In 2011/12 the figures were 11.6% and £63 billion.[3]

The arguments over whether Labour should have cut spending earlier and was therefore profligate or whether any political party or its leading politicians, including those which were to form the Coalition in 2010, had any inkling of the severity of the recession have raged ever since. In his memoirs as chief of staff at Number 10 until 2007, Jonathan Powell maintained he had been concerned about increased public spending. 'I was worried about the spend, spend, spend nature of some of our Budgets and noted in my diary that without reforms to save money in the public sector we would have no cushion if the economy turned south'.[4]

The same chancellor who had presided over 'spend, spend, spend' moved to Number 10 in 2007 leaving his successor to face the imminent fiscal tornado. In his memoirs Brown's successor as chancellor, Alistair Darling, recalled arriving in his new post in June 2007 to find the Treasury generally relaxed about the government's dependency on City tax revenues:

> Reading through the briefing papers prepared for the new Chancellor I remarked to Nick Macpherson [the permanent secretary since 2005, later to continue in office under George Osborne] almost in passing that we seemed very dependent on taxes coming in from the financial services industry. About 25% of our corporate taxes came from that sector...Treasury officials voiced no concerns about the banking system in the course of the early briefings I was given as a new minister.[5]

Darling was clear that the Labour policy of pouring money into public services was the right one and that it merely corrected previous decades of under-investment. He said that in 1997 there was a 'near-consensus' that the government had to increase investment in 'neglected public services'. Such under-funding, he argued, came from low economic performance in the 1970s which had deprived the Treasury of tax revenues coupled with spending cuts and privatisation under Thatcher. The 2008 Budget predicted a continuing rise in public spending which by 2011 'will have delivered the longest sustained real increase in public spending since 1945'.[6]

In his defence as to why the Treasury had been so unprepared for the fiscal crisis he maintained that it was clear by 2008 that 'the assumption that the economy would continue to grow uninterrupted could no longer hold'. Had he realised what was to follow, 'I would almost certainly have fixed public spending for the following year, making plans for a further review the year after'. As it was in the autumn of 2007 he had decided it was 'time to apply the brakes on the amount we were spending' and had decided to cut the rate of growth in public spending by half. He added: 'After ten years of almost uninterrupted increase in public spending we could afford to do so'.[7] By spring 2008 as the financial scenario worsened he realised that 'the problem was that it had been assumed that taxes coming in from the financial sector would go on and on'.[8] Darling's argument, which underpinned the government's approach to the recession, was that maintaining public spending, albeit with the rate of increase reduced, would alleviate the effects of the fiscal crisis and the recession that followed.

He also recognised that a post-Thatcherite political consensus over recognising the value of increased public spending to fund public services was breaking down under the impact of the first recession in the United Kingdom since the early 1990s. 'For most of the New Labour years the story of Labour investing in public services and the belief that the private sector and public sector should complement each other dominated the political scene. The banking crisis changed all that'.[9] He said that the 'Tories changed their minds at the end of 2008' and began calling for spending cuts.[10]

The breakdown was not only with other political parties but with his own boss, Darling insisting the government should be honest and admit some cuts were necessary, although health and education were protected with inflation-only increases in 2009, Brown preferring to stick to the line it was continuing to 'invest' in public services and avoid any mention of cuts. Within the Treasury 'hard-line orthodox economists' whom Darling called 'the Taliban wing' argued for a more traditional deflationary response to the budgetary crisis. He, in turn, maintained he had no intention of 'doing a Snowden', a reference to Labour's deflationary chancellor in the 1929 slump, though he found himself in the unpalatable position of having to rein back spending departments, arguing with ministers late into the night before his December 2009 Pre-Budget Report.[11]

In his last Pre-Budget Report in 2009, by now having to both defend previous high rates of public spending while also explaining why spending had to be curbed due to the deficit, Darling boasted that 'since 1997 a combination of investment and reform has radically improved the quality of Britain's public services, delivering real and lasting improvements'. He added that total public spending had increased by 57% in real terms over this period compared to 15% in the preceding 12 years, that NHS spending in England had more than doubled, that spending on education in the United Kingdom had increased in real terms by £31.2 billion since 1997 and that spending on the police had grown by 19% in real terms since 1997. Public sector net investment was now at its highest in 30 years. In the PBR he pledged to stick to planned levels of public spending in 2010/11 'to help the economy through the downturn' but envisaged a reduction in spending growth from 2011/12 to halve the deficit within four years although health and education had inflation-linked rises.[12]

Darling's plans were overtaken by the 2010 election. The new Chancellor, George Osborne, tore up many of his predecessor's more cautious deficit-reduction targets and announced the aim of balancing the budget within a rolling five-year period, later extended to 2016/17. Osborne delivered an emergency Budget in June 2010 which maintained that the spending assumptions behind the Comprehensive Spending Review 2007/11 were based on 'unsustainable revenue streams' namely the property boom and taxes from the financial sector. Public spending increased from 41% of GDP in 2006/07 to 48% in 2009/10. The Budget envisaged this would fall to 40% by 2015/16 under its measures to reduce the deficit, or a reduction in spending of £83 billion. Ambitiously the Budget envisaged a 'fiscal consolidation', that is a combination of tax rises and spending cuts, of £128 billion a year by 2015/16 of which £99 billion would come from spending cuts and £29 billion from tax increases. Over the previous 45 years the average figure for total public spending as a proportion of GDP had been 42.7%. The Budget plans aimed to reduce cyclically adjusted public sector net borrowing by 8.4% of GDP between 2009/10 and 2015/16, similar to that achieved in the United Kingdom between 1993/4 and 1999/2000 (6.5%), in

Sweden between 1993 and 1998 (9.4%) and Canada between 1992 and 1999 (7.5%).

The Budget also envisaged public sector net debt peaking in 2013/14 at 70.3% of GDP and declining to 67.4% of GDP in 2015/16 (in 2008/09 public sector net debt was 44% of GDP and in 2010/11, 60.4% according to Budget figures). The forecasts proved wildly optimistic. Two and a half years later in the Autumn Statement (previously known as the Pre-Budget Report under Gordon Brown) in December 2012 public sector net debt was forecast no longer to be falling in 2015/16 but to be peaking at 79.9% of GDP that year – 12.5% higher than the June 2010 Budget's prediction – and to only start declining in 2016/17 when it would still be 79.2% of GDP and 77.3% in 2017/18. In other words, the 2012 forecasts were that after seven years of austerity to 2017/18 public sector net debt would still be three quarters more than it had been in 2008/09 and almost 17% higher than the first year of the Coalition government.

Osborne also set up an Office for Budget Responsibility, a non-departmental public body, to provide independent analysis of the public finances and scrutiny of the Treasury's costings. The OBR's role is also to produce five-year forecasts alongside the Budget and Autumn Statement and assess whether the government is on course to meet its fiscal plans. It too has found predicting the economy difficult, announcing over-optimistically in March 2012 that the United Kingdom would avoid entering recession that year.

Reform case study (1): Efficiency programmes

The Emergency Budget in 2010 promised £6.2 billion of efficiency savings in 2010/11 and set up the Efficiency and Reform Group in the Cabinet Office to oversee Whitehall back office reductions. Yet this followed a decade of much-trumpeted efficiency savings under the previous government. Is it possible that there is still so much inefficiency in the public sector or were the previous figures merely accounting 'smoke and mirrors'?

The original drive to improve public sector efficiency had coincided with spending increases from 2000 onwards. That year the government set up the Office of Government Commerce to improve procurement expertise in Whitehall. Its first Chief Executive Sir Peter Gershon, a former private sector business director and ironically also later adviser in 2010 to the Conservatives on efficiency, claimed that the OGC saved £1.6 billion in its first three years by improved procurement processes.[13]

As part of the Treasury's Spending Review 2004 setting out policy for 2005/2008 and previewed in the 2003 Budget, the Treasury ordered a major efficiency drive across Whitehall which included plans to reduce civil service headcount, relocate offices out of London and the South East to cheaper regions and cut overheads. A review into relocation was undertaken by former local authority Chief Executive Sir Michael Lyons while Sir Peter Gershon, then head of the Office of Government Commerce, headed a review into efficiency across the public sector. In its consultation document the Gershon Review said the aim of the efficiency review was to cut back on back office costs and release them into the frontline.

But what is efficiency? In his groundbreaking 2004 review for the Treasury Sir Peter Gershon described efficiency as 'making best use of the resources available for the provision of public services'. He added:

This review has defined as 'efficiencies' those reforms to delivery processes and resource (including workforce) utilisation that achieve:

- reduced numbers of inputs (e.g. people or assets), whilst maintaining the same level of service provision; or
- lower prices for the resources needed to provide public services; or
- additional outputs, such as enhanced quality or quantity of service, for the same level of inputs; or
- improved ratios of output per unit cost of input; or
- changing the balance between different outputs aimed at delivering a similar overall objective in a way which achieves a greater overall output for the same inputs.[14]

The Gershon Review, published in 2004, identified £20 billion in annual efficiency gains that could be made from across the public sector's budget, 60% of them cash releasing, including £6.45 billion from local government, or 2.5% a year, and £6.5 billion from health, plus a cut of 84,000 Whitehall posts of which 13,500 would be reallocated to frontline services, all this spread over three years of the Spending Review from 2005/06 to 2007/08. Most of the savings were in procurement, back office and transactional services. Projected efficiency savings were itemised by government department such as £4.2 billion in education, £6.5 billion on health, £785 million in transport and

£960 million in work and pensions and the report called the efficiency targets 'stretchable but achievable'.

Not surprisingly the review said accountability for delivery of this efficiency programme would be 'critical'. It added, in hindsight with some optimism, that: 'Ministers and officials need to be held to account on the basis of good information on performance. The Government has therefore agreed that there will be effective and continuing parliamentary and public accountability systems for the delivery of agreed efficiency targets...this will be a highly transparent system'. The report noted: 'The challenge now is to sustain the process of making these proposals a reality'. One method was to ask government departments to produce Efficiency Technical Notes which would 'be a key mechanism for ensuring accountability of progress towards the Government's headline target of £20 billion in annual efficiencies by 2007–2008'. Some upfront funding would come from the £300 million Efficiency Challenge Fund. The efficiency proposals were backed by a detailed implementation timetable and framework. Responsibility for delivering the Efficiency Review was given to the OGC and a new Efficiency Team working closely with the Treasury and reporting directly to the prime minister and the chancellor. A Public Value Programme was set up to continue the momentum for value-for-money savings.[15]

Four years later the March 2008 Budget announced that Whitehall and local government had by then delivered over £23 billion of efficiency savings, including £8 billion from better procurement and £1 billion from the back office, and a reduction of 77,600 in the civil service workforce. By the Pre-Budget Report in November 2008 the efficiency savings reported so far stood at £26.5 billion with 86,700 posts removed.

A further £30 billion was earmarked in the March 2008 Budget to be saved by Whitehall and local government through 'value for money' (VFM) over the next three years, later increased to £35 billion. These VFM savings were to be sustainable, that is ongoing, rather than one-off cuts, with no impact on service quality.

The Treasury therefore had three ongoing efficiency programmes until 2011: VFM, the Operational Efficiency Programme (OEP) and the Public Value Programme (PVP), the latter two not due to report savings until 2010/11. The OEP focused on five areas of operational efficiency such as the ratio of HR staff to employees, the PVP on departmental spending areas with poor value for money. Total efficiency savings envisaged over the six years of the two spending review periods, 2005–2011, amounted on paper to £70.5 billion.

But the optimistic figures were met with scepticism. In July 2009 the Treasury Select Committee published its own analysis of the efficiency programme, including the Gershon Review, the OEP and the PVP announced in the 2008 Budget. The select committee noted that 'the efficiency programmes of the past have not always achieved their desired results and indeed some have questioned the extent to which these programmes actually achieved savings'. It added:

> We note that the [National Audit Office] interim report about Gershon efficiency savings highlights serious problems in measuring efficiency. We raise concerns that the NAO did not audit the final Gershon efficiency savings and that this has led to a lack of confidence on the part of some organisations in respect of the reported savings. We believe that, at a time when the public sector will be pressed to make further efficiencies, it is vital that any savings made are properly recognised and quantified. We call on the Government to continue to work with the NAO to ensure that future efficiencies are accurately measured.

The Commons Treasury committee also questioned the feasibility of the extra £5 billion of value for money savings earmarked in the 2009 Budget for 2010/11 which it said had been announced without consultation with departments and as a result 'does not inspire confidence'. It suggested that the government 'considers a more business-led approach to cost cutting in the public sector than setting an arbitrary target and requiring the civil service to meet it'.[16]

The £35 billion VFM savings target came under further attack from the central government finance watchdog, the NAO. In December 2009 the NAO published two reports looking at the value for money savings claimed by government departments, part of the £35 billion target by 2010/11. It found that of the Department of Transport's reported savings of £892m, only 43% could be described as cashable savings, 22% 'had some uncertainty', and 35% 'may be overstated'. Of the Home Office savings of £338m it examined, 24% were uncertain and 17% were of 'significant concern'.

The NAO later issued a further report into the £35 billion VFM programme by which time the Labour government had been superseded by the Coalition. It pointed out that the VFM savings did not necessarily mean a reduction in spending; indeed 11 of the 17 departments increased their budgets in real terms between 2007/08 and 2010/11.

The total increase in departmental budgets over the CSR07 period was £21.3 billion.

The NAO report reviewed five of the main departments which were due between them to deliver 40% of the savings across central government and found only 38% of the £2.8 billion VFM savings claimed by them so far actually 'represented sustainable savings'. It concluded that it was 'unlikely' that the £35 billion savings target would be met by 2011. The VFM programme, it said, 'was not well enough understood across government, there was 'insufficient quality control within departments before savings were reported publicly' and insufficient incentives for them to make savings. Ominously, it warned, that spending cuts now underway 'means that departments will have to think more radically about how to reduce costs and how to sustain this in the longer term'. Looking at the lessons for the future it concluded: 'The recommendations of this report remain relevant as it remains essential to understand the impact of cost reductions on the quality of public services, and to accurately measure the cost and impact of improvements to value for money'.[17]

The NAO report was followed by an equally robust critique of the VFM programme in 2010 by the House of Commons Public Accounts Committee with much harsher criticism of the Treasury. The PAC stated bluntly, and considering what was to lie ahead with spending cuts, alarmingly:

> The current financial environment is fundamentally different from the position when the programme was launched in 2007, with substantial cash reductions required over the next four years by most departments. The scale of savings needed will require much more radical action, but the results from this programme left us with grave concerns as to whether departments are ready to implement effectively a programme of value for money savings. There is a serious risk that departments will rely solely on cutting front-line services to reduce costs, without adequately exploring the potential to reduce costs through other value for money improvements.

The PAC's study found that by March 2010 total savings from the VFM programme amounted to just £15 billion, less than half the total, with just one year left to meet the £35 billion target. The PAC added:

> Despite the importance placed on the programme at the top of government, departments could not even measure adequately what

savings they had made, and the Treasury failed to create a framework for reliable reporting. Neither the Treasury nor departments had an incentive to report only soundly-based savings. The programme did not enable departments to find cost reductions by rethinking the way services are delivered.

The PAC concluded, 'In future appearances before the committee we will expect to see evidence of the Treasury's leadership: taking full responsibility for the delivery of efficiency savings across government as a whole; demonstrating a full grasp of the causes of under performance in any department; and intervening where performance does not meet expectations'. But it also added that the Treasury 'acknowledges that it alone does not have the internal capability or resources to direct value for money programmes across government' and needs to work with the new [Cabinet Office] Efficiency and Reform Group.

It added, 'We are concerned at the implication from Treasury that it will simply reduce departments' budgets and then walk away from responsibility for the delivery of the level of savings required across government. Bearing in mind the disappointing performance of this programme, we believe the Treasury will need to take a very different approach to value for money improvement in the next spending period'.[18]

Questions were also raised over Whitehall's ongoing efforts to improve its procurement expertise. The 2008 Budget had set up the OEP and the PVP to 'capitalise on best practice and leading thinking in the private and public sectors'. The OEP had suggested savings of a further £15 billion from back office cutbacks in IT, procurement and asset management in 2013/14 compared to 2007/08.

Some years later the Coalition was still arguing that there were substantial savings to be had from better procurement. A report by Sir Philip Green for the Cabinet Office in 2010 highlighted Whitehall's failure to maximise its buying power. It said departments procured in silos, lacked procurement and negotiating expertise, paid different rates for the same products and services and needed to centralise its purchasing. As an example it said the centralising of 75% of the buying of the government's gas and electricity needs had saved £500m over four years. Other examples were given of different prices paid for travel, accommodation, printing, office supplies, computers, vehicle hire, mobile phones, office catering and property.[19]

Furthermore the claimed efficiency savings were accompanied by a huge, expensive investment in a Whitehall shared services programme costing £1.4 billion in the seven years to 2012 with very little return (see chapter on Whitehall).

Even police efficiency savings also proved to be less than at first appeared. Between 2004 and 2008 police forces and authorities declared £1.4 billion of efficiency savings against a target of £1 billion, around half cashable. But as the inspectors later noted these savings added up to 2% of police budgets during that period while overall police spending rose by 7.7%.[20]

In his 2011 memoirs Darling admitted that despite the much-vaunted efficiency savings there were still areas of public services requiring reform, especially welfare and health. Of the latter he wrote: 'There are two areas in particular that remain to be resolved. We must get control of costs in a system where there is no incentive to do so and we must figure out how to drive up standards in a system that can never operate as a free market'.[21]

Despite the mixed record of previous similar programmes the Cabinet Office claimed further efficiency savings of £3.75 billion achieved in 2010/11 and £5.5 billion in 2011/12 by cutting back office costs across Whitehall 'driven by the Efficiency and Reform Group'.[22] Doubtless these too will be examined in future reports by the NAO and the PAC.

But if previous efficiency savings have proved to be suspect can the Coalition be any more successful in implementing them? There have been many claims by ministers of savings already made, notably in Whitehall back office costs, but real evidence through auditing and select committee studies will take time to surface.

There is little major difference between government approaches, whatever their politics, to savings, only in the method. All parties want public services to be run efficiently and productively exploiting IT to streamline back offices and to allow resources to be focused on the frontline. The 2008 Budget noted that 'where public services are delivered by a combination of public, private and voluntary sector providers, fair competition means that services are provided by whichever can offer best value for money', a sentiment which would not have been out of place as Coalition policy years later.

The difference is in the degree of urgency, Labour's efficiency programmes operating mainly in a climate of rising spending until 2010, with the Coalition's operating against one of spending cuts, and in their respective methods. The Coalition set its face against 'top down' targets which had been the feature of Labour's performance system, certainly in its early years, preferring to allow transparency to act as a spur for improvement.

Reform case study (2): The private finance initiative

The private finance initiative (PFI), the scheme to fund major public sector projects like hospitals, schools, roads and waste plants by using private sector management expertise and capital funding in return for regular payments, was first set up in 1992 under John Major's government but expanded rapidly under New Labour. Its advantage to Treasury ministers, in attracting funding that did not appear as capital government spending and transferring risk to the private sector, overcame its disadvantages, namely that the payments by the public sector to the private sector stretched far into the future with 30 year contracts. Indeed a House of Commons Library study into PFI as early as 2001 warned that PFI 'must be paid for by higher public expenditure in the future, as the stream of payments to the private sector grows. PFI projects signed to date have committed the Government to a stream of revenue payments to private sector contractors between 2000/01 and 2025/26 of almost £100 billion'.[23] By March 2011 Treasury figures showed PFI payments of over £9 billion a year stretching to 2027 and over £1.6 billion still payable for the year 2033/34.[24]

When the Coalition took over in 2010 it decided the chickens were coming home to roost: the costs of meeting PFI payments were saddling the public sector with long-term debts which it could ill-afford at a time of spending cuts. In July 2011 a Commons Public Accounts Committee report noted that private finance borrowing had always been more expensive than government borrowing but that since the financial crisis the gap had widened. The cost of capital for a typical PFI project was 8%, double the then government long-term gilt rate.[25] In November 2011 the Chancellor George Osborne announced a review of PFI with the aim of creating 'a new model for delivering public assets and services that takes advantage of private sector expertise, but at a lower cost to the taxpayer'.[26] The revised PFI2 was announced in the Autumn Statement in December 2012 and included the government becoming a minority public equity co-investor in projects and a more value-for-money approach to partnering.

While Infrastructure UK, a division of the Treasury, was created to help major projects, in May 2011 the Major Projects Authority (MPA) was set up to improve the delivery success rate of major projects across central government which required Treasury approval and entailed tougher monitoring and revised assurance procedures. The MPA, run jointly with the Cabinet Office, followed a 2010 NAO report which had warned of the major risks inherent in major government projects. The Treasury said that to meet spending cuts 'the Government will need to effect a step-change in spending control. On the one hand, this means strengthening arrangements for scrutiny and control of spending, both within departments and by the Treasury. On the other hand, it means focusing this enhanced scrutiny where it is most valuable. In line with these objectives, the Treasury has strengthened its project approval processes. Alongside this, the Coalition's *Programme for Government* makes a clear commitment to achieving better value for money for public spending. This includes a strong will to improve the success and delivery of Major Projects'. The new MPA, it expected, by bringing 'proportionate scrutiny and assurance that is deployed at the right times will significantly improve major project performance'.[27]

Conclusion

As the custodian of the country's finances the Treasury has faced criticism for its handling of macro-economic policy in the past few years although the United Kingdom is not alone in failing to predict the severity of the recession after 2008. But even aside from its failure to prepare for the eventuality of a recession, failure to predict the recession when it happened and its optimistic growth forecasts afterwards, the Treasury's public sector efficiency programmes have also been questioned.

Select committees and auditors have complained that there is insufficient independent current monitoring of efficiency programmes and that when they finally evaluate them their reports are too late to influence outcomes. They also complain that the Treasury cannot just cut departmental budgets and then abandon responsibility for helping departments to implement them.

The PFI has proved to be an expensive way of funding capital projects even though it was enthusiastically adopted by governments from 1992 to 2010 and has been revised.

6
The Role of Parliament

Through its select committees of MPs in the Commons, which shadow the government departments, and peers in the Lords, where they examine specialist subject areas, Parliament maintains a watchdog role on whether the government is performing efficiently in the best interests of the public. The management of public services and the way governments handle change programmes is a particular focus of parliamentary select committees. But in comparison to government departments select committees are not well resourced, are often investigating weaknesses in public sector management in hindsight when it is too late to influence improvements and depend on the individual abilities of committee members. Nonetheless the fact that both ministers and senior civil servants have criticised select committees suggests the latter's salvoes have found their mark (see below).

MPs also respond to their constituents' complaints about public services by referring them to ministers or raising the issue in the House. A regular complaint from local government is that ministers criticise local councils because so many MPs hear only negative feedback from their constituents through their regular surgeries which are then passed up to government departments. It in these meetings that constituents come to their MPs with problems they have encountered as users of public services, in particular housing, planning, health, police, benefits and social services even though in theory MPs can only deal with matters for which Parliament and central government is responsible, such as health or tax (the devolved governments in Scotland, Wales and Northern Ireland have different arrangements and powers).

MPs can contact ministers or if they feel an issue needs to be made public can raise it in oral questions, adjournment debates, early day motions or even a Private Member's Bill. Although MPs are not responsible for those services which fall under the remit of the local authority, they will still pass on complaints to councillors or officers. If the council happens to be run by an opposing political party then the MP is likely to be more vociferous in their criticism of the service. But MPs, in reflecting their constituents' interests, may be opposed to the aims of the government in driving through public sector efficiencies such as closing smaller hospitals in favour of larger, better-resourced ones.

The principal form of scrutiny of public services is through select committees. The Commons select committees, with at least 11 MPs each, shadow every government department, scrutinising its spending, policies and administration and also report on associated public bodies like regulators and non-departmental public bodies, gathering written and oral evidence and publishing their conclusions in print and online. Membership reflects the party balance in the Commons while the committee chairs are allocated to MPs from the three main parties in proportion to their strength in the Commons. Committees like Public Administration or Public Accounts look at issues that cross departments. The Liaison Committee looks at the work of all the select committees as well as hearing evidence from the prime minister on aspects of public policy. The Lords committees look at the specialist areas of the European Union, science and technology, communications, constitutional affairs and economic affairs. The PAC, the PASC and the departmental select committees are the watchdogs on spending in Whitehall departments and their reports receive wide media coverage, in print and online while their more newsworthy hearings are watched live on television. Their reports also feature prominently in this book.

Around 40% of select committee reports call only for a small policy change while the remainder call for larger changes. They are also highly productive, one study finding that during 1997–2010 the 20 Commons committees ran around 1,450 inquiries and produced almost 40,000 recommendations and conclusions of which 19,000 were aimed at central government.[1]

Do they have an impact and influence? The answer is clearly yes, especially the Public Accounts and Public Administration Committees (PAC and the PASC) which are highly effective watchdogs on public spending. The former attracted national and international media coverage when in November 2012 it grilled chiefs of major multinational companies over allegations of tax avoidance. The coverage reflected public anger that with public services under pressure from spending cuts, large corporations were not contributing their fair share of tax.

The first large-scale cross-committee analysis of the policy impact of select committees also concluded they are effective. The Constitution Unit at UCL, with the support of committee staff, traced back the recommendations of seven committees over the 13 years of the Labour government 1997–2010 and found that 'about a third' of substantive recommendations make it into policy and 40% receive a 'positive' government response. But the report stressed that the impact of the committees' work is more subtle, exercising behind the scenes influence. Some recommendations may be 'ahead of their time' and emerge as government policy years later, and 'sometimes the government changes policy before the committee reports because of the need to pay extra attention to the area that the committee is investigating'. It added: 'A committee can catalyse opinion and act as a tipping point in a debate'. It cited the example of the Public Administration Select Committee's success in 'getting the core values of the civil service on a statutory footing'. Committees hold government to account in a way which helps Whitehall departments think through their policy options and justify their decisions while committee reports are ignored at civil servants' peril.

It concluded:

> Committee reports are therefore simply one factor contributing to policy debates, but one which is taken seriously. When reports are timed correctly, or built on a particularly firm body of evidence, or come up with new and sensible policy ideas, they can be successful. When they are overly media-driven, superficial, or make overambitious recommendations, they may be more likely to fail...They are largely taken seriously in Whitehall, many of their recommendations go on to be implemented (though sometimes not until years later), and they have an important preventative effect in encouraging more careful consideration of policy within government departments.[2]

An example of how a select committee study can influence government policy was highlighted in the PAC's summer 2011 study into the PFI whose borrowing costs it said were double that of long-term government gilts. Furthermore, as PFI debt did not appear in government debt or deficit figures the PAC said these created artificial incentives 'unrelated to value for money' avoiding short-term capital spending but incurring higher long-term costs and should be removed. The Office for Budget Responsibility estimated that if PFI debt appeared as part of the national accounts it would add a further £35 billion to the national debt. The PAC said PFI should be used 'as sparingly as possible' and only where it displayed value for money rather than as a means of pushing capital spend off balance sheet. It added: 'Evidence we have seen suggests that the high cost of finance in PFI has not been offset by operational efficiencies. Much more robust criteria governing the use of PFI are needed'.[3] In November 2011 the chancellor launched a review of PFI with the aim of replacing it with a different model of capital borrowing.

Earlier in 2009 the Treasury select committee added its voice to concerns about whether the then Labour government's much vaunted efficiency savings programme was actually achieving the targets it claimed (see previous chapter on the Treasury).

The Commons liaison committee whose members chair each of the other select committees examined the work of the committees in 2012. Written evidence from Dr Ruth Fox of the Hansard Society, Peter Riddell of the Institute for Government and Dr Meg Russell and Professor Robert Hazell of the Constitution Unit (UCL) concluded: 'That permanent secretaries are now talking more about committees than in the past, and not always in warm terms, is itself a sign of impact'.[4]

The two select committees that comment on cross-departmental aspects of efficiency are the Public Administration and Public Accounts committees both of whose reports feature regularly as sources in this book.

Public Administration Select Committee

The Public Administration Select Committee (PASC) looks at the quality and standards of administration within the civil service, shadows the Cabinet Office and scrutinises the reports of the Parliamentary and Health Service Ombudsman. It also takes a cross-departmental interest in public service reform and examines the impact of public sector reform plans on Whitehall such as efficiency programmes and opening up public services to new providers. It has produced reports both criticising and praising aspects of government public service reform policy.

In evidence to an inquiry by the Commons liaison committee on the effectiveness of select committee the PASC described its remit as 'scrutiny of the quality and processes of our national government and to make recommendations which will lead to their improvement'. It added that its reports had a 'central theme of Civil Service reform, and the belief that change in Whitehall and better government will be defeated by inertia without a coordinated reform programme, led by a strong centre of government'.[5]

The PASC has continued to be an outspoken critic of government 'smoke and mirrors'. As an example in December 2011 the committee delivered a highly critical and prescient report on the Coalition's public services reform plans for encouraging more volunteers and charities to participate in delivering local public services, the Big Society agenda. The committee warned that there was 'little clear understanding of the Big Society project among the public' and 'confusion over the government's proposals to reform public services'. The report asked for 'clarity' over the role of private and third sector providers, over how accountability for public money would be maintained under Big Society and whether there was even sufficient interest or capacity from the voluntary sector to take on local service delivery. It proposed a step change in the way Whitehall and local government commissioned services if Big Society was to achieve the government's aims, adding: 'The redistribution of power from Whitehall to communities, central to the Big Society project, will by its very nature necessitate a substantial change to Whitehall itself, and to the nature of government'. The report also alleged there was a lack of understanding in Whitehall and local government about mutuals and the government should have already addressed this skills weakness 'if it had a coherent implementation plan' and the PASC recommended a single Big Society minister with a cross-cutting brief. It concluded that without such changes the Big Society project would not succeed.[6]

This was not the first time the PASC had commented critically on the role of the third sector in service delivery. In June 2008, when although Big Society as a name and concept was embryonic – it was first mentioned by Cameron in 2009 – the voluntary sector was taking on an expanding role in delivery, the committee looked at what this might mean for public services. Its report concluded: 'Whatever transformation of public services is about, it should not be about transferring responsibility for delivering large areas of public service out of the state and into the third sector. It appears that government accepts this. Despite the emphasis given in government publications to involving the third sector, only 2% of public service spending is on third sector delivery'.

The PASC said it could not confirm evidence that the third sector was necessarily always the best provider and that 'the Government's priority ought to be understanding the needs of the users of particular services, and then working out what organisations might be best placed to meet those needs'. Its report called for 'a vigorous mixed economy of provision, with all prospective service providers judged on their merits'. While it welcomed the government's 'general direction' the PASC said there needed to be greater evidence of the benefits of having more third sector delivery.[7]

The committee had also expressed previous concern about Whitehall's capacity to meet the post-2010 Coalition agenda of opening up services to new third sector providers and mutuals while also downsizing. In July 2011 the PASC criticised the lack of strategic leadership at the centre of government over how Whitehall was adapting to the change programme arising from the spending cuts and Coalition reform agenda. It pointed out that by the first anniversary of the coalition, only 6 of 16 Whitehall departments had not had a change of permanent secretary. Describing the Coalition's reform plans for Whitehall 'as the most ambitious since the Second World War' it said the new focus on third sector provision coupled with spending cuts and downsizing of Whitehall required a more flexible civil service with new commissioning skills but the government had failed to initiate a reform programme to help civil servants meet this. It added:

> Whitehall has traditionally performed three core roles: policy advice, the management of public services, and the supervision of public bodies. If the civil service is to connect with ministers' ambitions for public service reform a fourth capability will need to be added to this trio: the ability to engage with groups from the voluntary and private sectors through the contracting and commissioning process. Every government department must focus on developing this fourth capability, and the Cabinet Office must ensure that this is embedded in the civil service change programme across government.

The report welcomed the Coalition's transparency programme but warned that 'data dumping' on its own was not sufficient and asked how the public might be 'empowered' to use such information. It concluded: 'Unless there is a comprehensive change programme, there will be little of the real change which was the watchword of David Cameron's manifesto for government, which the Coalition was formed to implement and which is critical to the success of the Government's wider public sector reform programme'.[8]

Again, this was not the first time the committee had looked at Whitehall weaknesses, or pulled its punches. A 2007 PASC report said the then ongoing Capability Reviews into departmental performance 'paint a bleak picture of civil service performance' and added:

> There is a clear consensus that the Civil Service is weak in its perfor-
> mance management. We accept that this problem is not unique to
> the Civil Service. Nonetheless, it is clear that the way poor perfor-
> mance is currently managed is not acceptable. A radically different
> approach may be needed, and it should be a top priority for the
> Cabinet Office to find one.[9]

The committee has also commented on the wider reform agenda and its impact on users. In July 2008 the PASC produced a study of the long-term impact of the – by then defunct – Citizen's Charter which had been set up by John Major in 1991 and its role in implementing a consumerist approach to public services. The PACS's predecessor committee, the Public Service Committee, had in 1997 concluded that the Charter had 'to a great extent swept away the public's deference towards the providers of public services, and their readiness to accept poor services, and has taught providers to welcome the views of users as a positive assistance to good management'. The PASC in *its* 2008 report 11 years later said, the Charter 'has had a lasting impact on how public services are viewed in this country' and its principles 'retain their validity nearly two decades on' and should 'continue to influence public service reform'.[10]

A related earlier report into user-driven public services warned it was still unclear as to whether they

> offer better value for money or improved outcomes for all or most ser-
> vice users. What is clear is that stronger variants of user participation
> and control would have far-reaching effects on the shape of some of
> our public services. In particular, there would be fundamental impli-
> cations for the role of public service professionals, their relationship
> with service users, and the way that public services are organised and
> assessed.[11]

The suggestion that ministers, rather than simply criticise public servants, might set an example of efficiency savings by downsizing themselves was also raised by the PASC. In its study of government ministerial numbers it noted that while in 1900 there had been 60 ministers in the UK government, by January 2010 there were 119 despite devolution to Scotland, Wales and Northern Ireland. The growth periods were in the 1930s, 1960s and 2000s and were mainly in posts below

Cabinet rank. Furthermore there was also an increase in the number of parliamentary private secretaries, regarded as the first rung on the ladder, and often dubbed 'the payroll vote' because they are guaranteed not to rebel against the government. The proportion of MPs on the payroll vote doubled between the 1920s and 2010 to a fifth of the Commons and a third (39) of the then governing party, Labour.

The PASC added, 'there is a growing consensus that the ever increasing number of ministers harms the effectiveness of government' and that they were simply creating more work for civil servants. Former Cabinet Secretary Lord Turnbull told MPs that by the time a minister had been allocated three private secretaries, a press officer, a driver, a car, there was 'not much change from half a million pounds'. The committee concluded that cutting the number of ministers by a third would be 'consistent with smaller, smarter government' and suggested 75 in total.[12]

Public Accounts Committee

The PAC's task is to scrutinise public spending or according to Standing Order No 148 'to examine the accounts showing the appropriation of the sums granted to Parliament to meet the public expenditure, and of such other accounts laid before Parliament as the Committee may think fit'. Unlike the select committees it does not look at the formulation or merits of policy but at the value for money issues which underpin the efficiency and public sector reform agenda. The committee also draws on reports from the NAO, which itself answers directly to parliament. Together, in the words of one Cabinet minister, they are 'the most influential watchdogs in the country'.

In September 2011 the PAC looked at the role of the new Efficiency and Reform Group (ERG) set up within the Cabinet Office in May 2010. Its report described the challenge in the ERG having to help deliver half of the £81 billion through efficiencies when it had limited influence or none over big spending bodies such as the NHS or local government as 'huge'. It also expressed its scepticism over government's claims of efficiencies generally when it commented: 'Our past experience of reviewing efficiency savings shows that departments' reported savings are frequently unreliable and impacts on front line services are often unclear'.[13]

The PAC's relentless focus on Whitehall incurred the wrath of outgoing civil service head and Cabinet secretary Lord O'Donnell in 2012 when he complained at the treatment of civil servants by its MPs.

Committee Chair Margaret Hodge accused Lord O'Donnell of acting 'like a shop steward for aggrieved permanent secretaries' adding,

> It seems that the [PAC] has been rattling the cage too much for some. There are those who say that shows we're doing our job properly, but there is a real challenge from the Civil Service on how we are approaching our work on behalf of Parliament and the taxpayer...Some have upped the ante, even asserting that the PAC's activism affronts some constitutional principle (of which the civil servants consider themselves custodians). Anonymous briefings suggest that some would even like to dismantle the committee itself.

But the MPs' particular concern was that senior civil servants were hiding behind the doctrine of ministerial accountability to escape scrutiny and called for a new relationship between Parliament, government and the civil service.[14]

The PAC was also on the receiving end of criticism from a Cabinet minister, Education Secretary Michael Gove. In a speech to think-tank Politeia in October 2012, Gove accused the PAC and the NAO of being 'some of our fiercest forces of conservatism' for criticising Whitehall's efforts to innovate. He added:

> Time after time the NAO and PAC report in a way which treats any mistake in the implementation of any innovation as a scandalous waste of public money which prudent decision-making should have avoided. And yet at the same time it treats the faults of current provision as unalterable facts of nature – like the location of oceans and mountains – which should be accepted as the design of a benign Providence. What we need – across the Westminster village – is a decisive shift in the culture in favour of risk and open-ness and away from small c-conservatism.[15]

Needless to say the NAO rejected the accusations saying the taxpayer was entitled to expect both innovation and value for money.

Conclusion

MPs maintain a watchdog role over the quality of public services, particularly in local government, through feedback from their 'surgeries'. But often the concerns of their constituents do not match the wider goals of public service policy for example in running fewer but larger and better-resourced hospitals.

Parliamentary select committees, in particular the PAC and the PASC, perform an invaluable role in monitoring government policy as it is implemented in practice, especially in the administration of public services. Research shows governments listen to the conclusions of select committee reports and implement their findings.

But their reports are often after the event when whatever the select committees are hoping to improve has already come and gone and any identified wasteful spending and inefficiency has already occurred. The watchdog role of parliament over public spending and administration needs to be reviewed to give select committees more resources to do their vital role.

7
The Role of the Consumer and Competition

Public service reform is driven not only from the top but also on the frontline where the public interact directly with providers. People expect from the public sector the similar customer-focused service they receive from the private sector for as taxpayers who fund the public sector they regard themselves as customers. Even while not all recipients of public services are taxpayers they still expect to be treated in the same way. As Sir Ronnie Flanagan, a prominent commentator on police reform, noted: 'As private consumers we do not go out of our way to buy an average product. We aim to buy the best that we can afford and this principle should apply equally, if not more so, to the public sector'.[1]

This was in marked contrast to the first three decades of the post-war welfare state when there was a view from public service providers that recipients of their largesse should be grateful. The idea that services should fit round the needs of the consumer rather than the other way round is comparatively recent, occurring from the early 1980s. It followed a sea change in attitudes in the private sector to customer service, especially in areas of high customer contact such as the hospitality industry, inspired by US practices. The success of the UK TV comedy *Fawlty Towers* in the mid-1970s with its inept and arrogant hotel manager expecting his customers to be grateful for their poor service struck a chord with the public.

But from the 1980s onwards the concept of customer service began to take hold in the public sector, the idea that users of publicly funded services were also paying for them through their taxes and therefore deserved to be regarded as customers just as if they were purchasing goods in the private sector. As one study of consumerism in public services noted:

> In the UK, the Thatcher-led Conservative Party that came to power in 1979 inaugurated programmes of marketisation and privatisation of public services, including a central discursive role for ideas of 'choice'. Although there were other views of 'consuming' public services before then, the trajectory of the contemporary figure of the citizen-consumer took off from this political-cultural conjuncture.[2]

Similarly, the idea that there was a 'public service ethos' with public sector workers being motivated by altruistic reasons was increasingly accompanied by the view that they were just as 'producer-driven' as any other workers but without the restraint of market forces to spur them into focusing on the consumer. Governments from Thatcher's onwards therefore decided it was up to themselves to create the stimulus to improve customer-driven services by reforming public sector bureaucracies and their culture, thereby satisfying growing citizen expectations.

Citizens are no longer supine and grateful recipients of services but consumers with rights and demands. They expect to be treated as customers just as they are in the private sector with similar high levels of personal service including choice. As one Labour pro-reform minister, Alan Milburn, put it: 'We are in a consumer age whether people like it or not. What will destroy the public services is the idea that you can retain the ethos of the 1940s in the 21st century'.[3] Blair's Number 10 Strategy Unit noted in 2006:

> The majority of the population want public services that are responsive, flexible and match the level of customer service they find in the private sector. The challenge is for public services established originally on the assumption of uniform provision to a relatively compliant, homogenous population to adapt to meet the complex needs of an increasingly diverse and assertive population.[4]

But consumers of public services, as they expect from the private sector, also want value for money. Just as they do not expect prices to rise in the private sector so they do not want taxes to increase. For politicians trying to square the circle of providing higher quality, more responsive public services without noticeably increasing taxes means making them more productive, more efficient and better managed. The consumer demand for higher quality without higher taxes helps drive the reform agenda.

Governments are both leaders and followers of consumer trends. Being seen to offer better public services is good for votes. Politicians harness the power of voters through the media to put pressure on public sector deliverers and improve performance. But citizens also pressurise MPs and governments to force change on unresponsive public sector providers. Much of MPs' 'surgery' caseload concerns their constituents' complaints about their experiences with local service providers such as health, police or local government. The MPs feed these complaints back to ministers. The media highlight weaknesses in services such as adult care, health or schools to which they expect politicians to provide an answer. As the public demand more choice in public services so governments press service deliverers in health, local government and Whitehall agencies to respond accordingly, setting targets and expected levels of service.

But what do customers want from their public services? Research into measuring customer satisfaction describes its key drivers as prompt delivery, timeliness, information, professionalism and staff attitude. The first, *delivery*, is judged by the final outcome, the way the service keeps its promises, and the way the service handles any problems. The service delivers the outcomes it promises and successfully deals with any problems it faces. The second, *timeliness*, is determined by the initial wait, how long it takes overall and the number of times the user had to contact the service. The service responds quickly to the initial customer contact and does not pass the customer to other staff. The third, *information*, is measured by accuracy, comprehensive and being kept informed about progress. The fourth, *professionalism*, is judged by the competence of the staff and if the user is treated fairly and the final driver, *staff attitude*, is measured by whether staff are polite, friendly and sympathetic to users' needs.[5]

Ipsos MORI identifes three key needs for public service users. The first is the security net that public services provides. The second is fairness, the perception that services are being offered to the recipients who need and deserve them, though there is an inherent conflict between whether these should be of a uniform standard across the country or vary locally. Ipsos MORI says that 'it is clear that policy ideas that fail to meet some combination of security and fairness tend to be poorly received or rejected out of hand'. Thirdly, there is a 'common desire' for public services to respond to specific need in local areas or for specific groups and provide 'the best possible experience'.

In a survey of 16 discussion groups its market researchers tested three concepts of funding public services namely personal budgets, user charging and insurance schemes. The groups concluded that personal budgets might be construed as being unfair – fairness being a key value among users – while charging for services like health was seen as an extra tax and an insurance scheme as a further cost.[6]

The Public Administration Select Committee also looked at how customer satisfaction could be measured and concluded that 'satisfaction' was subjective and did not necessarily reflect the true quality of a service particularly where users had low expectations. It warned: 'Measures of user satisfaction can shed some light on the quality of public service provision. They should, however, be treated with care because they are subjective and are sometimes based on less important considerations than service quality'.[7]

Age Concern told the committee that older people often recorded higher satisfaction with their services even though evidence showed they received a worse service than younger people. The committee concluded that users' experience of services or outcomes would be a better way of enabling public sector organisations to improve.[8]

Reform case study (1): The Citizen's Charter

The notion of the parent, or patient as customer with a right to expect certain levels of service, formed the basis of the groundbreaking Citizen's Charter launched in 1991 under the Major government. The Commons Public Service Committee, predecessor body of the Public Administration Select Committee (PASC), said in 1997 that the Charter 'has to a great extent swept away the public's deference towards the providers of public services, and their readiness to accept poor services, and has taught providers to welcome the views of users as a positive assistance to good management'.[9]

Eleven years later the committee's successor the PASC said the Charter 'represented a landmark shift in thinking about how public services are delivered in this country – a shift that saw the interests and perspective of service users given much greater prominence'. In a report published in July 2008 the PASC said the Charter 'put people first in the delivery of public service … a policy goal that remains relevant to this day'. It added:

It is still the case that the Charter programme was one of the clearest articulations of the need to focus on the experience of public service users, and for services to be responsive to the people using them. It also popularised the ideas that performance should be measured and measurements made public, and that information about services should be readily available in plain language.

The MPs recognised that while the Charter itself eventually went out of fashion its impact on attitudes to how public services should deal with its customers has continued under successive governments. Its report concluded:

> The Citizen's Charter has had a lasting impact on how public services are viewed in this country. The initiative's underlying principles retain their validity nearly two decades on – not least the importance of putting the interests of public service users at the heart of public service provision. We believe this cardinal principle should continue to influence public service reform, and encourage the Government to maintain the aims of the Citizen's Charter programme given their continuing relevance to public service delivery today.[10]

The Charter Mark scheme, a validation of customer appreciation of public services, which survived the change of government from Conservative to Labour and lasted from 1991 to 2008, was a voluntary method of encouraging public service providers to think in terms of customer satisfaction. In 1991, 35 organisations received a Charter Mark for customer service. By 2002 there were 949 winners and that year it was rebranded 'as a tool of customer service excellence, promoting it as a benchmark that all should aspire to, rather than a badge to collect'. By 2005 there were 1,452 holders of Charter Marks. Of the winners 94% said the Charter Mark had helped them increase customer focus and user consultation and 82% claimed to be delivering more cost-effective services. Analysis showed that the service improvements attributed to the Marks were:

- Better customer focus based on more choice and greater consultation with users.
- Development of user-led strategies where user feedback was strategically embedded in the policy-making process.
- Improvements to handling complaints where complaints were logged, analysed and fed into policy.
- Better published information by organisations to ensure greater transparency and clearer guidance on services.[11]

The Citizen's Charter programme was one of the most pioneering initiatives in encouraging more customer-responsive public services. Although it later became derided for its simplicity of approach, its impact permeated public sector reform for over two decades.

Reform case study (2): Choice in public services

The Blair government developed the concept of choice in public services, the idea that the citizen should have a menu of options from which to choose whether it be schools, hospital treatment or adult care. Choice was defined in one report by the then Prime Minister's Strategy Unit in the following ways:

- choice over the quantity or quality of a service consumed such as type of social housing
- choice over the specific form or content of the service.
- choice over the channel through which the service is delivered such as the Internet, by phone or face-to-face
- choice between alternative providers
- choice through personalisation by tailoring services to fit the specific needs and preferences of individual users[12]

But for choice to work it also needs competition. As the Strategy Unit noted: 'In the absence of competition, providers have few incentives to introduce choice and may only do so if forced to through top-down pressures. Where choice is introduced alongside competition, and funding follows users' choices, providers face stronger incentives to make the best possible use of resources'.[13]

Critics of choice argue that it is a meaningless concept in that it will always be limited by budget constraints. One critic from the Royal College of Nursing, writing in 2005 during the Blair health reforms, commented:

It would seem the Government wants public services to be provided more like privately supplied goods. By overlaying a market-based mechanism – choice – they believe people will gain more control over their lives ... The current presentation of choice seems to suggest that choices are unlimited – but the RCN believes there should be more honesty in the public debate about the limitations of choice. We have repeatedly pointed out that unconstrained choice in a constrained health and social care budget is undeliverable.[14]

The drive to encourage customer-focused services moved in the 1990s and 2000s through centrally set performance targets to more localised levels of service. In September 2009 Liam Byrne, responding as Cabinet Office minister to a select committee report on public services, noted:

> The next stage of reform in public services will be characterised by moving from a system based primarily on targets and central direction to one where individuals have entitlements over the service they receive...a move to a range of entitlements in the core public services. The aim is to ensure high quality standards for all and, by increasing the power of people to demand services reach these standards, help drive up service performance and efficiency.[15]

Choice however continued to be the main theme of the Coalition government's approach to public services. The Open Public Services White Paper published in July 2011 described choice as 'giving patients the right to choose which hospital they get treated in; helping parents choose where their child goes to school; rolling out personal budgets across health and social care, giving people the choice between private or tenant housing'.[16]

Choice has also led to 'personalised services' with recipients of adult care receiving their own personal budgets which they can use to buy care services as they desire. The Open Public Services White Paper in July 2011 pledged to increase more choice in adult care, education, skills training, children's early years, family services, health and social housing. In this case, personalised services also have a budgetary implication, enabling recipients of expensive residential or hospital care to live more independently at home.

But choice in itself is not sufficient to empower the citizen. Users need to access information to make the right decisions, need to be aware they have a genuine alternative and may need a third-party organisation to help them. As the National Audit Office comments:

> Service users need to be aware that they have a choice and to be genuinely able to exercise that choice as far as is practicable. Providers must believe that users will switch to another provider if they are not satisfied with the service. Oversight bodies need to ensure that users have reliable and useable information about the choice and quality of services and the quality of outcomes (where available). This is a complex task in public services markets. The goods and services being purchased, such as hospital services, school places or social care, may

be relatively complex and outside users' normal domains of expertise. In addition, there may be relatively high proportions of vulnerable users who need support to access and understand the information and responsibilities underpinning their choices, for example personal budget users who choose to employ carers.[17]

Choice also requires a different set of commissioning skills by the public sector. As the NAO comments:

> In personalised services, individual service users make their own purchasing decisions (though usually without knowledge of the price of the service they are purchasing). This is different from the traditional ways that the government uses taxpayer funding to provide services, such as employing staff to deliver them directly or purchasing them, on behalf of the taxpayer, from the private or not-for-profit sectors. It therefore requires government departments and agencies to possess and deploy a very different skill set suitable for a commercial market environment, and brings a new set of risks to achieving value for money.[18]

Reform case study (3): Using technology

The focus on the customer has been facilitated by increasingly sophisticated technology, especially mobile, which has transformed the back office, the infrastructure which supports the frontline. It has enabled local authority staff to reduce the amount of laborious face-to-face time spent on handling routine inquiries from the public by providing information online thereby reducing queues and enabling staff to focus on more serious issues where a personal approach is necessary. It enables staff out in the field to access data from their smart phones without having to return to the office or for GPs to view records at their terminals.

Technology has both made the public sector more productive and increased the quality of service to the user. From 2000 the government began to move public information and transaction services online through its Government Gateway, later rationalising online services through Directgov and Business.gov. An NAO report found that in 2010/11 the Gateway cost £22m to run and the other two £59m together and user satisfaction levels were high. By November 2011 Directgov was receiving 30 million visits a month before later folding into the new site Gov.uk.[19]

The introduction of the Oyster card on London's transport system not only enabled passengers to avoid ticket office queues by topping up their own cards but also formed part of Transport for London's programme to reduce ticket office staff costs. The public can fill in entire income or car tax forms online at their convenience without needing any human contact with a call centre. The transformation agenda in public services has been as much about using IT to improve the customer experience as it has about re-engineering the organisation.

But transformation is also about fitting the service around the customer. A perennial complaint about the public sector is its aversion to cross-sector working. The public are expected to deal with a myriad of different bodies when undergoing a life-changing experience, whether moving house, divorce, birth or death. In his groundbreaking study of transformation in public services Sir David Varney said that while the public sector was wedded to the concept of customer-service it tended still to revolve this around a transactional process rather than the needs of the whole individual.

Sir David added:

> People rarely identify themselves as being customers of a particular government service. Often they are trying to deal with a task or an event that does not fall neatly and obviously on any one part of government, such as becoming unemployed, getting married, starting a business or dealing with a bereavement. As these events will often cut across departmental responsibilities, the focus has to be on understanding what the individual needs. If the government continues to interpret the term 'customer' as being limited to those who transact with government at single points then government will continue to serve citizens and businesses without fully addressing their needs.[20]

Belatedly the government has tried to address this weakness by focusing on one group of public service users, namely troubled families, who frequently find themselves dealing with multiple agency interventions including social services, police, housing, probation officers, youth justice boards and welfare. Not surprisingly research has shown these multiple interventions are not only expensive in staff and time but ineffective and could be far more productive if channelled through just one agency. The Troubled Families Unit set up in 2011 within the Department of Communities and Local Government was tasked with driving this particular reform via local authorities. Further pilot projects, the so-called community budgets, are also looking at sharing local funding with the aim of providing a more holistic public service to their residents, the customers.

Reform case study (4): Creating a public sector market

The state does not need to be the sole producer of public services. Other providers from the private and voluntary sectors can also supply not just goods but services on behalf of the state in order to meet rising customer expectations. The history of public sector reform, especially from 2010, is about the public sector moving increasingly towards a primarily commissioning role and away from that of a monopolist producer, opening up its markets to alternative private and third sector – voluntary – providers.

It was the Thatcher government which first compelled local authorities in the 1980s to test their services, initially manual but later white collar, against external providers. Compulsory competitive tendering was abolished by Labour but private sector involvement in municipal services was encouraged as a means of delivering efficiencies and choice to users while the private and voluntary sectors developed an increasing role in the NHS, social care, welfare and schools. One 2012 study found there were 22,000 different organisations, voluntary and private, involved in social care and some £30bn–£40bn of private money had been invested in the sector in the previous two decades.[21]

A 2008 study commissioned by the then Labour government, the DeAnne Julius Report, described the UK public sector market that had built up around delivering public services, anything from refuse collection and hospitals to welfare and adult care, as 'a world leader' second in size to that of the United States and worth 6% of GDP. In 2007/8 its turnover was £79 billion employing 2.9 million staff with the largest sectors being in health and social care. In the period from 1995/96 to 2007/8, virtually all of it during a Labour government, the public sector market grew by 130% aided by such initiatives as the PFI. One of the paradoxes of such an expanding market is that with so much of the private and voluntary sector economy dependent on public sector contracts, it is adversely hit by public spending cuts.[22]

The question is, how does the use of external providers improve public services? DeAnne Julius cited savings of 20% when services are market-tested, irrespective of whether the contract is won in-house or externalised, adding that 'the primary benefits come from competition and the contractual process itself rather than any innate efficiency advantages of the private sector'.[23]

Looking ahead from publication in 2008, as the fiscal crisis was engulfing the United Kingdom, her report concluded:

> Major challenges remain if Britain is to develop the personalised, easily accessible, world class public services that are being demanded by its increasingly diverse population. This will require a range of providers – from the public, private and third sectors – with more autonomy for front-line staff to take decisions in the interest of users. It will require more sophisticated ways of measuring and contracting to deliver outcomes that match users' expectations, and it will require experienced public sector commissioners who are as adept at long-term market development as they are at procurement and project monitoring.[24]

The NAO says that 'markets present opportunities for services to become more personalised, responsive, efficient, diverse and innovative. Evidence from international and national research suggests that, under certain conditions, competition can deliver higher quality services and improve efficiency'.[25] But markets can also be imperfect and the public sector commissioner needs to ensure a degree of regulation. A market does not mean the government withdraws. Providers can keep prices artificially high if users are uninformed about costs, or they may not provide universal services or they may go out of business leaving the public sector commissioner to pick up the pieces. As the NAO says: 'When markets are used to deliver public services, the government typically retains a reversionary interest if services fail, yet it has much less ability to intervene than when it delivers services directly'.[26] The government, through its regulators, needs to ensure a delicate balance between allowing poor performing providers to exit the market while ensuring there is a continuity of service. If the government errs too much on ensuring that providers do not fail then it can encourage poor performance.

The NAO sets out what it calls ten principles governments need to follow to obtain value for money when using the market to provide public services. Among them there needs to be rules and regulations governing the way the market operates; arrangements in place to protect users in case of market failure (when a provider goes out of business); users need to have reliable and accurate information to make decisions about choice or personal budgets; the market needs to be dynamic with new businesses coming on stream to replace those that leave and monitoring bodies need to ensure that policy outcomes are being met. The NAO concludes: 'The introduction of market mechanisms into public service delivery does not remove the role of government. In fact, it puts the onus on government at all levels to develop an effective understanding of markets, including the practical and commercial considerations of making their market work effectively'.[27]

Increasingly providers, especially in health, welfare and criminal justice, are being remunerated on a 'payment by results basis' placing the financial risk on the provider.

Reform case study (5): Big Society and mutuals

Voluntary bodies, commonly described as the third sector, are also a long-standing feature of external provision which politicians of all parties are keen to expand as a way of creating more pluralism in service delivery, greater local flexibility but without the profit motive of the private sector. The third sector is defined as 'non governmental organisations that are value driven and which principally invest their surpluses to further social, environmental and cultural objectives'.[28] It includes charities, local community groups, social enterprises and mutuals but one select committee report noted that 'the breadth of the sector presents a real challenge for policymakers looking to design the relationship between the sector, citizens and the state'.[29]

While the third sector has delivered services for centuries, its involvement in delivering public services, that is those funded by the taxpayer with a remit to ensure they are delivered to every person who needs them, is more recent but has grown steadily since the 1980s. By 2006 public funding for the third sector was some £11 billion, a third of the sector's total. In 1996/97 the value of government contracts to the third sector had been around £2 billion. By 2005/6 it was almost £6.9 billion.[30] Ironically, this was a case of 'back to the future' as many of the voluntary sector's philanthropic works in the nineteenth century such as in the provision of social housing, hospitals and schools had been later taken on by the state.

The Labour government 1997–2010 saw the voluntary sector as having a key role in its public sector reform programme and in 2002 even set a target of having 5% of public services delivered by this sector by 2005/6, later abandoned. In 2008 the PASC noted:

> While in the past the development of a market has been justified on the grounds of driving down costs, which is a legitimate goal in itself, the aim of involving the third sector is also about improving the

quality of services for their users. Government hopes – ambitiously – that the distinctiveness of third sector organisations will have a 'transformative' effect on public service delivery.[31]

Conservative leader David Cameron also saw a transformational role for the third sector in public service delivery, along with greater involvement by local voluntary groups, mutuals and social enterprises in running local services such as libraries and care facilities as the cash-strapped state retreated from its previous levels of provision. Cameron termed his philosophy of greater third sector and public involvement Big Society, a phrase he first used in November 2009. MPs on the Commons Public Administration Select Committee however warned 18 months into the Coalition government that the concept was little understood in Whitehall and was difficult to implement in practice. Even if were understood it would still take a generation to succeed.[32] Furthermore third sector groups were having as much as £3 billion in contracts and grant funding cut by local and central government due to the public spending squeeze. Big Society involvement in the NHS and welfare reform also proved challenging.

There is a paradox at the heart of Big Society. In the case of the Work Programme where the voluntary sector hoped to win a sizeable share of contracts, the requirement for high levels of capital funding and turnover tipped the scales in favour of private sector firms which won some 90% of the prime contracts leaving the third sector as sub-contractors. The emphasis on payment by results makes it difficult for smaller voluntary groups with poor cash flow to compete. The government's emphasis on economies of scale to drive down supplier costs further militates against smaller enterprises. In its audit of Big Society, think-tank Civil Exchange concluded: 'The Big Society, despite its increased emphasis on a greater role for civil society, seems to be no exception to the general thrust toward greater competition and larger contracts, making it especially hard for small local voluntary and community organisations to compete'.[33]

One study of Big Society noted its basic contradictions as threefold which contributed to its being a 'flawed idea'. These were firstly that Big Society tried to build a legitimacy with 'a largely unconvincing appeal to an idealised and essentially unreal past'. Secondly it became associated with public spending cuts, 'the result of either design or bad timing' which associated it with a particular politics. Thirdly, there was evidence from similar attempts to build civil society in the former Soviet block after the collapse of centralised state control to show that 'such approaches were flawed'.[34]

Nonetheless, in April 2012 the government announced its first ever public sector joint mutual when 475 staff were offered a stake in the organisation My Civil Service Pension, which administers the civil service pension scheme, with ownership split between the staff, the government and the private sector, despite union opposition. In July 2012 responsibility for historic canals and rivers in England and Wales was transferred from the NDPB British Waterways to a new charity, the Canal and River Trust.

A new voluntary sector funding initiative, social impact bonds, is also developing as a means of attracting investment into public services. Social impact bonds are upfront investment backed by institutional charitable investors whose returns, paid by the public sector, are based on achieving designated social outcomes such as reduced rates of re-offending. Their attraction is that if the outcomes are not met then the public sector does not pay out. One example is Essex County Council which awarded a contract in November 2012 to a provider to deliver a bond to support adolescents at risk of going into care (see more in Chapter 11 on local government).

Reform case study (6): Changing behaviour

Expectations, once raised, are difficult to dampen down again. The end in 2010 of the longest period of public expenditure growth since the Second World War posed long-term challenges for public sector providers having to produce services on diminishing budgets. The public have become used to being treated as consumers, expecting steadily improving standards and choice without concomitant increases in taxation to fund them. But trying to bridge the gap between their expectations and the reality of reduced public spending has placed strains on the concept of the citizen as empowered consumer.

Many public sector providers argued even during the years of investment in public services that with consumer rights must come responsibilities and that the latter was missing from the equation. In 2008 the PASC recognised this weakness in the system when it noted that

> rights or entitlements to public services do not exist in a vacuum … there are limits to the resources available for public service provision. This means that discussions about the nature of

entitlements to public services must explicitly take into account the resources available to fulfil those entitlements. It also suggests that people need to be made aware of the responsibilities arising out of their use of public services, as a concomitant of their rights to publicly provided services'.[35]

The British Medical Association in its response to the committee commented: 'With patients' rights should come patients' responsibilities. The patients' charter was a rights-only charter, with no mention of responsibilities'.[36]

The challenge posed by consumers to public sector managers is to run the same services with less money and to do so with little obvious impact on service quality, an increasingly unsustainable balancing act. As the Institute for Fiscal Studies noted in a 2012 analysis of public finances which predicted cuts to council services beyond 2017: 'What is clear is that individuals will need to either expect less from their local authority in terms of the services provided or the quality of those services, or be willing to pay more for them through higher council tax or user charges'.[37]

The problem is that the public took time to adjust to the new age of austerity. The 2020 Public Services Trust report identified rising citizen expectations, 'particularly service standards that meet the best that the private sector can offer' as one of the five key challenges for public services over the decade from 2010.[38]

The Coalition government attempted to solve this conundrum by being seen to 'slash red tape' in the back office and management while hoping to limit cuts to frontline, customer-facing services. But there is a limit to how much cutting 'red tape' can meet deficit reduction targets. While many public sector managers have seen the downturn in public finances as a 'burning platform' moment, an opportunity to initiate transformational change in their organisations, this too is a back-room, long-term process. Until such transformation can deliver significant savings, the public must become involved in the debate about prioritising services. But for the public to appreciate that budgets are finite they need to know the facts.

The 2020 Public Services Trust, writing on the eve of major spending cuts, warned that for the public to understand and accept the downsizing of public services they must be better informed.

Public service reform is the flip side of the deficit and rising demand pressures. There is a £40bn black hole in public finances that will

have to be filled over the next four years. Simply maintaining existing services and commitments, and caring for an aging society could
add 6% to the proportion of GDP which has to be spent on public services. Unless the public is willing to accept levels of taxation at
unprecedentedly high levels in the future, change must come. Yet the
public has been denied the debate it deserves on what change should
look like'.

Its survey found that the public were not prepared for major change and
'in general the current recession was not yet seen as being sufficiently
serious to warrant radical changes'.[39]

No government will allow the customer-first focus of public services
to decline. It is now part of the DNA of provision. But few ministers rel-
ish the idea of telling voters that they can no longer expect to receive
the services to which they have become accustomed and that they need
to do more for themselves. One idea, copied from the United States and
based on behavioural science studies, has been to persuade or 'nudge'
consumers into reaching the same conclusion, namely that public services do not have unlimited budgets and that choice means taking on
more responsibility themselves. The Coalition agreement in May 2010
said: 'There has been the assumption that central government can only
change people's behaviour through rules and regulations. Our government will be a much smarter one, shunning the bureaucratic levers of
the past and finding intelligent ways to encourage, support and enable
people to make better choices for themselves'.[40]

The Coalition set up a unit in the Cabinet Office in July 2010 called
the Behavioural Insights Unit, soon dubbed the 'nudge' unit with the
aim of finding 'intelligent ways to encourage, support and enable people
to make better choices for themselves'. Its brief was to help the deficit-
reduction programme by changing behaviour that might lead to less
recourse to public services such as cutting the number of missed hospital appointments or smoking to assist health budgets or encouraging
prompt payment of tax and court fines through text messaging.[41]

For example, £2.5 billion a year is spent on dealing with smoking-
related illness but only £150 million on smoking cessation programmes.
The idea is that the public will themselves contribute to deficit reduction by taking more responsibility for their behaviour and lifestyle,
while still continuing to exercise their power as consumers. The unit
noted: 'By understanding how people react and behave in different situ-
ations, we can design policy to go with the grain of how people behave
rather than against it, both improving outcomes and respecting people's

autonomy'.[42] In September 2012 the unit claimed to have 'identified' savings of £300m since its launch and was exporting its expertise by working with the New South Wales government in Australia.

Maintaining and enhancing consumer-centric services and choice will continue to be at the heart of public sector provision and drive reform. Governments and providers however must increasingly adapt this policy to reduced levels of spend, managing down public expectations while placing more onus on the individual to choose their level of service within a limited budget.

Conclusion

Customer-focused services and choice are now an accepted part of public sector provision and information technology has helped frontline services become more efficient and more geared to the needs of customers.

Users of public services however still need a benchmark of how well their services are being managed. Some users, with low expectations, may be satisfied with services that turn out to be performing below average. It is vital, especially with the growing focus on personal budgets, that users receive accurate information in order for them to make informed choices and they also need to be aware of alternatives.

There is a well-developed market of private and voluntary bodies providing public services but the public sector as commissioner cannot simply step away because it is no longer a direct provider. It needs to ensure that the market is regulated, competitive, pluralistic and that users are informed to make their own choices.

One of the weaknesses of the public sector is in meeting the needs of the whole individual, rather than that of a particular transaction. For example, lifestyle changes such as birth, marriage, death or moving house involve several points of contact with public sector providers.

Equally as part of having responsibilities with rights consumers have to understand the limits of public sector provision due to budget restraints and to manage downwards their own expectations of what the state and its suppliers can provide.

Part III

Reforming the Key Public Services

8
Whitehall

Virtually every prime minister since the 1980s has expressed strong views about the effectiveness of the civil service. While respecting the intellectual capacity of senior Whitehall officials, prime ministers have expressed frustration at what they perceive as the civil service's lack of urgency, vision and ambition, its reluctance to innovate, its bureaucracy, poor technical skills especially in procurement and resistance to change. Ever since public sector reform has been on prime ministers' agendas, Whitehall has been top of their target list.

As a result there has been a succession of initiatives to 'modernise' the civil service, many of them however with little long-term impact. In one four-year period 2005 to 2009 there were 90 reorganisations within central government. These were accompanied by vigorous target-setting including Public Service Agreements, efficiency studies, Capability Reviews and an ongoing shared service programme all aimed at improving performance and driving down costs. Yet the same problems persevered through successive governments. The Institute for Government noted in 2012 that previous reform efforts showed 'a combination of muddled thinking, a failure to appreciate the constraints of parliamentary accountability and a quasi-federal departmental structure, vested interests, but, above all, a lack of clear political priorities and will'.[1] The PASC noted: 'Too often civil service reform seems to have become an end in itself for Whitehall, instead of a means of delivering a wider public service reform agenda'.[2]

The PASC also noted the failure of successive reform plans when it concluded:

> Many attempts to reform Whitehall and the civil service have ended in failure or have simply petered out ... the civil service has been

subject to frequent reform initiatives of limited success under successive governments. The intention behind these reforms has been to 'modernise' the civil service in terms of greater efficiency, better service delivery and improved capacity...Ministers want, and the public interest demands, a more innovative and entrepreneurial civil service which fosters and retains expertise aligned to the policy or major project lifetime and can work across departmental boundaries to address cross-cutting issues. Numerous civil service reform initiatives so far have failed to deliver these outcomes on a consistent basis.[3]

But why was this? MPs on the PASC attributed it to 'failure to consider what the civil service is for, what it should do and what it can reasonably be expected to deliver'. For the civil service is a complex organism dealing with a multitude of different problems and answering to ministers with their own often short-term agendas in the full glare of publicity. Civil servants work in a highly charged political environment, a media goldfish bowl, in which every action is scrutinised on a daily basis. New ministers, who generally have no choice over the civil servants they work with often arrive with a suspicion they are about to be 'stitched up' by the system, a view reinforced by their own political advisers, the 'Spads' (Special Advisers) who accompany them into office. Whatever reforms senior civil servants are expected to introduce to their own structures they must still answer to ministers who may have their own more short-term agendas and little interest in the minutiae of organisational change. Frequently a new policy and strategy can be drawn up only for a Cabinet reshuffle to change the minister and the strategy to be shelved. As the respected Institute for Government notes:

> Because departments rely on ministers for direction on policy, their core mission can be ambiguous and fluid. Departments also have multiple stakeholders and conflicting goals with no single measure of value against which to prioritise. As a result, rather than focusing on improving performance against a clear set of indicators, change in departments tends to be driven by new policy priorities, crises and ministerial dissatisfaction with the status quo.[4]

There has certainly been no lack of attempts to change Whitehall. In every decade since the 1960s it has undergone radical upheaval, in particular with the creation of executive agencies, first launched under Thatcher as Next Steps Agencies and continued through successive governments as arm's-length organisations running public services but managerially and financially distinct from Whitehall. But the results have been mixed. As the Institute for Government noted in November 2012:

'The current generation of leaders has experienced a huge degree of change in the last 30 years. Departments have been created and abolished, changed names and swapped functions. Major national industries have been privatised and formerly core functions have been outsourced and commissioned externally. Arm's-length bodies (ALBs) have proliferated and been put on the quango bonfire several times over. And the Civil Service has adapted to serving multiple governments simultaneously as a result of devolution. Yet, the core of the Civil Service in Whitehall departments also remains easily recognisable from the *Fulton Report* (1968), *Next Steps* (1988) and *Modernising Government* (1999)'.

The result adds the IfG study, has been that 'paradoxically, Whitehall is both a place of constant change and deep inertia. Whitehall does not lack experience of change and reorganisations. Departments are constantly adapting to new ministers and different policy priorities with numerous reorganisations as a result'.[5]

Over the years the civil service has widened its recruitment pool, hiring top management from outside the civil service hierarchy, especially from local government and the private sector, to bring in more experience of delivering services rather than advising on policy. It has coped with successive governments demanding reform without their having a clear vision of how it should be implemented. The short-termism of ministerial government has meant reform programmes being started only to dissipate as ministers move to other departments. Despite the Cabinet Office and Number 10 supposedly being the drivers of change in central government, neither have always had the capacity to provide strong direction right across departments with the result that reform programmes falter, much to the frustration of politicians and their advisers. The problem was compounded under the Coalition with the high turnover of Whitehall permanent secretaries; by December 2012 of those who had been in post in May 2010 only two remained. But the weakness is often as much with the government of the day as with the civil service machine. The PASC blamed ministers for failing to provide clarity and direction to civil service heads about their ambitious plans to decentralise Whitehall while also insisting departments cut budgets by a third and warned that their reform plans could fail as a result.[6]

Yet compared internationally the Whitehall machine still comes out well despite being routinely criticised. One study of central government administration in the United Kingdom and eight other countries regarded as similar, namely the United States, Canada, Australia, New Zealand, Germany, France, Sweden and Finland, found the United Kingdom 'compared well' against a basket of indicators. It performed however less well when it came to how the public perceived its services.[7]

The civil service today has its roots back in Victorian Britain, its remit set out in the Northcote-Trevelyan report in 1854 which described its key assets as 'permanence, political impartiality and meritocracy'. In 1919 the Haldane Report called for more formalised departmental responsibilities, in 1919 the Bradbury Report created a new establishment branch of the Treasury to oversee pay and civil service organisation and in 1961 the Plowden Report called for a more professionalised civil service. In 1968 the Fulton Report proposed more emphasis on managerial skills by the civil service with an opening up of the fast track recruitment beyond public schools and Oxbridge. In 1987 the Ibbs Report recommended an expansion of the Next Steps Agency programme of arm's-length bodies freed from the civil service machine. In 1999 the *Modernising Government* initiative under Blair proposed better policy-making, better services and better management. In 2004 the Lyons and Gershon reviews respectively proposed a downsized civil service with more functions moved outside London and efficiency-savings targets (see chapter on the Treasury).

Tony Blair later complained: 'The problem with the traditional Civil Service was not obstruction but inertia'.[8] John Major recalled a meeting of mandarins in his autobiography:

> One by one the members of the Cabinet and their permanent secretaries were invited to explain what more they could offer up in the way of public service improvement. Some departments, notably transport, the Home Office, education and the DTI, needed to be led several times to the fence before being ready to jump. And then only reluctantly with the whip on their back.[9]

Margaret Thatcher believed the permanent secretaries 'had come to think of themselves mainly as policy advisers forgetting that they were also responsible for the efficient management of their departments'.[10]

She decided to appoint an outside businessman, Sir Derek Rayner, to set up an Efficiency Unit that 'would tackle the waste and ineffectiveness of government'.[11]

Her hostility to what she regarded as Whitehall's lack of energy manifested itself early on in her first term. She later recalled: 'Whatever the short-term difficulties I was determined at least to begin work on long-term reforms of government itself'.[12] As one Whitehall expert Peter (now Lord) Hennessy noted: 'As an institution the civil service was seen as one of the great obstacles – part of an inflated public service/state industries sector with overmighty trade unions to match – to the creation of a more dynamic enterprise society'. Rumours of her attitude 'spread fast through the Whitehall grapevine' in the spring of 1979.[13]

Thatcher described a meeting of 23 permanent secretaries on 6 May 1980 as 'one of the most dismal occasions of my entire time in government' adding:

> I enjoy frank and open discussion but such a menu of complaints and negative attitudes was enough to dull any appetite I may have had for this kind of occasion in the future. The dinner took place a few days before I announced the programme of civil service cuts and that was presumably the basis for complaints that ministers had damaged civil service 'morale'. What lay still further behind this, I felt, was a desire for no change. But the idea that the civil service could be insulated from a reforming zeal that would transform Britain's public and private institutions over the next decade was a pipe-dream.[14]

Tony Blair was to repeat a similar complaint. He rejected a view prevalent among some of his colleagues that after 18 years of Conservative governments the civil service had been politicised and imbued with Tory ideology. Instead, as with Thatcher, he argued that its prime weakness was lack of drive. He wrote later:

> In Labour mythology the Civil Service is made up of closet Tories.... In this scenario the senior mandarins are forever poised to strike down the progressive action a Labour government wants to take...Wholly contrary to the myth, they were not the least in thrall to the right-wing Establishment. They were every bit as much in thrall to the left-wing Establishment. Or, more accurately, to a time and a way and an order that had passed, a product of the last hundred years of history.[15]

Blair's autobiography in 2010 was sprinkled with barbed observations on the abilities of the senior civil service. In one passage he referred to a popular TV satire about cynical Whitehall mandarins made in the 1980s and generally regarded as so timeless that it was recreated as a play in 2011 and later a TV comedy again. He wrote that while the Sir Humphrey character in the TV series, *Yes Minister*, was a parody, 'he was the closest parody could get to fact'.[16] Later he added: 'The Civil Service had and has great strengths. It was and is impartial. It is, properly directed, a formidable machine. At times of crisis, superb. Its people are intelligent, hard-working and dedicated to public service. It was simply, like so much else, out of date. Faced with big challenges it thought small thoughts'.[17]

Blair's Chief of Staff Jonathan Powell also took a jaundiced view, writing in his account of government:

> It is not just the mindset of civil servants that is the problem; it is also the skill set. The upper reaches of the Civil Service are still staffed with policy advisers when what is needed are project managers ... The Civil Service is akin to a monastic order where people still enter on leaving university and leave on retirement. Their attitudes change slowly and their powers of passive resistance are legendary.[18]

While there had certainly been no lack of effort to change the civil service during these years, successive governments still complained of the same alleged Whitehall weaknesses; a lack of business skills, a departmental silo mentality, a risk-averse culture, an over-emphasis on policy experience as a route to promotion rather than managerial or professional expertise. A Commons select committee in September 2011 commented: 'Despite successive programmes of reform and some undoubted and successful change and modernisations of the civil service, ministers remain dissatisfied with and disconnected from the outcomes'.[19]

When the Coalition took power in 2010 civil service reform still remained one of its key pledges despite all the previous years' efforts to change Whitehall culture. There was however one difference: the civil service from 2010 faced dramatic change alongside a cut of a third in Whitehall spending.

New Prime Minister David Cameron earmarked Whitehall reform as a key priority. His philosophy was that government must be scaled back, decentralised to its lowest feasible level and that the civil service must be radically changed to fit its new status as a downsized operation with new providers from the third and private sectors taking an increasing role. While still, like his predecessors, insisting that the civil service needed changing, Cameron distanced himself from the New Labour reform agenda by maintaining its target-based approach was counter-productive. Instead, he argued, the public would act as 'armchair auditors' monitoring government performance with business plans providing a guide to what people might expect from their administrators. This, he implied, would create a sustainable impetus for improved performance without the stop-start, target-driven approach of his predecessors.

In 2010 Cabinet Office Minister Francis Maude set the tone when he told civil servants: 'We still have a culture where you can preside over an inefficient status quo with impunity; however try something new that might improve things but doesn't, and it's never forgotten'.[20]

Civil servants however were not to be necessarily blamed for their predicament. According to Maude, the Cabinet Office minister whose job it was to drive the reform agenda in Whitehall, they were at one end 'the jewel in the constitutional crown' and at the other 'frustrated by bureaucracy and red tape, by numerous layers of management, and by a culture that tends to value the generalist over the specialist, and process over outcome'.

In his first major policy-setting speech to civil servants at a Westminster conference in July 2010 Maude, a former Treasury minister under John Major, outlined Whitehall's faults and how the Coalition intended to address them. Most of his complaints had a familiar ring, having been expounded by other ministers and prime ministers over the previous decades. Saying that 'caution too often trumps innovation', Maude added: 'We need a civil service genuinely transformed – smaller, more dynamic, innovative, agile and open. A workplace where good ideas get heard and acted on, and every employee can reach his or her full potential. The good – objectivity, honesty, integrity, impartiality – we must keep. The bad – sluggishness, rigidity, insularity – must go'.

The new minister named seven key proposals for change, namely a smaller civil service, a flatter management structure, more integration between departments, a more enterprise-driven culture, more recognition of the importance of professional and commercial experience rather than just policy, greater expertise in procurement and project-management skills and more performance management.

Management structures, he said, 'need to be less hierarchical and more streamlined, with reporting lines much shorter' while there should be more opportunities to work across Whitehall. The minister told the civil servants at the conference:

> People should be able to move around more easily within the service. The senior civil service is in theory a centrally managed resource. In reality it isn't. Talent isn't always matched to where it can be best used. And the fast stream graduate entry should be centrally managed also, so they expect to move around in the induction and training years. The graduate entry into many other professional services organisation would typically have four six month postings with a range of different experiences and challenges.

And despite the Fulton Report in 1968 planning to open up the civil service this 'was never delivered' according to the minister and as a result it was still 'a class-riven service'. He added:

> Yes we insist rightly that no one can occupy a top job without some serious management exposure. But it remains the case that departmental permanent secretaries are overwhelmingly drawn from the ranks of policy officials. Nowhere else would this be the case. In no other big budget environment would you expect there never to be a top executive drawn from the finance or commercial stream. Nowhere else would strategy and policy consistently trump operational delivery in the competition for the top slots. This must over time change. Ministers need to forego their apparent insistence on having policy experts as permanent secretaries. There must at some stage come a time when at least as many permanent secretary slots are filled from outside the policy stream as from it. Then we will genuinely have what has been talked about for so long: genuine parity of esteem.[21]

Indeed a civil service head with a background outside Whitehall – in local government – was appointed in January 2012.

Plans for public service reform were later set out in the Open Public Services White Paper in July 2011 which envisaged decentralisation of power from the centre to the local level and 'instead of seeking to run services directly the role of the central state is being redefined as overseeing core standards and entitlements'.[22] It was another year before the publication of the Civil Service Reform Plan described by the Cabinet Office as 'the first stage of a continuing programme of reform'.

However, these changes had to occur against an unprecedented backdrop of a third cut in Whitehall administrative budgets and a sharp drop in civil service numbers, down by 54,000 in 18 months to 2012 to some 260,000, the lowest level since 1939. Whereas civil service numbers under Thatcher were cut by 10% between 1980 and 1984 it took the Coalition just 18 months to achieve the same percentage. This was unprecedented even by international comparisons. Institute for Government research showed that even the Swedish government, renowned for solving its budget crisis in the 1990s, had avoided making structural changes to its civil service due to the uncertainty it would create and the consequent threat to its fiscal plans. The Institute for Government, writing in November 2012, suggested the Coalition's plans were more akin to the Canadian experience in the 1990s when the federal government restructured departments, adding: 'Neither approach is right or wrong The cuts present major risks and challenges for Whitehall, but also an opportunity to address deep-rooted weaknesses and, potentially, to emerge more capable and effective in future'.[23]

Another criticism of Whitehall is its 'silo mentality'. In a report on implementing reform the PASC highlighted a key weakness behind government efforts to reform the civil service, namely the lack of a powerful, strategic centre that ministers can draw on to drive through change. In the hierarchy of Whitehall the Cabinet Office, despite its claim to be 'sitting at the very centre of government' with a remit to 'make government work better' and to ensure the civil service is equipped to support ministers, is low down the pecking order. The big domestic policy departments, the Treasury, health, education and the Home Office act as fiefdoms under powerful secretaries of state. The PASC report added: 'In the absence of leadership from the Cabinet Office, departments are carrying out their individual programmes with limited coordination and mixed levels of success. Without clear leadership or coordination from the centre, setting out, in practical terms, how the reform objectives are to be achieved, the Government's reforms will fail'.

But the PASC blamed politicians for lack of direction, adding:

Ministers seem to believe that change will just happen. It is essential that the Cabinet Office take leadership of the reforms and coordinate the efforts in individual departments and across Whitehall as a whole. The scale of the challenges faced by the civil service calls for the establishment of a world class centre of Government, headed by someone with the authority to insist on delivery across Whitehall.[24]

The Institute for Government commented:

> Breaking the deeply ingrained cycle of siloed working requires committed leadership from the Head of the Civil Service, Cabinet Secretary and Civil Service Board. It will require: identifying the biggest opportunities for reform and sustainable savings; making changes to current Treasury rules and processes; and actively supporting those in departments to challenge existing priorities and siloed behaviour.[25]

Taking on board criticisms that the reform agenda lacked direction the Cabinet Office opted to hire a new director of civil service reform, the former chief executive of Kent County Council, reporting to the head of the civil service in September 2012. The appointment drew comparisons with an earlier effort to bring in an experienced outsider to help deliver reform when a former council chief executive was hired to head up Blair's new Office of Public Services Reform in 2001. The unit was quietly disbanded five years later.

Reform case study (1): Procurement

One of the constant weaknesses of which the civil services is regularly accused is its lack of procurement skills, highlighted in a report on efficiency by Sir Philip Green published in October 2010 and commissioned by the prime minister. Sir Philip concluded there was considerable 'inefficiency and waste of government spending' much of it to do with poor data and process and furthermore said senior civil servants agreed that 'it is impossible for the civil service to operate efficiently with the current processes in place'. He highlighted inefficient procurement, lack of centralised purchasing, lax control of the buying process and poor negotiation skills.[26]

His comments surfaced later in the Cabinet Office Civil Service Reform Plan produced in June 2012. It too concluded: 'Overall, the culture and behaviours of the Civil Service must become pacier, more flexible, focused on outcomes and results rather than process. It must encourage innovation and challenge the status quo and reward those who identify and act to eradicate waste'. And it added bluntly: 'No one's career suffers from persisting with an inefficient status quo, while those who innovate can feel like they are putting their future at risk'.[27]

The Civil Service Plan aimed to set out Whitehall's direction until at least 2015. It envisaged a 23% reduction in staffing, better training and skills in procurement, more focus on innovation and, more unusually, buying in outside advice, a skill the civil service hitherto always regarded as its particular strength, or what the plan report called 'a monopoly', complaining that 'policy is often drawn up on the basis of too narrow a range of inputs and is not subject to rigorous external challenge prior to announcement'.[28]

A consistent criticism of Whitehall has been its mixed record in procuring big projects from private sector suppliers, either being out-witted by canny negotiators when it comes to efficiency savings or taking on huge liabilities for the taxpayer. The Coalition admitted as such in its 2012 Civil Service Reform Plan which stated that 'only around a third of major projects have been delivered on time and to budget. This has led to taxpayers' money being thrown away, ser-vice and infrastructure improvements being delayed or denied, and the Government's commitments not being met'.[29] It set up a Major Projects Authority in 2011 to oversee Whitehall's biggest projects sup-ported by a Major Project Leadership Academy to develop procurement skills.

But these weaknesses had been identified as far back as 1999 when Sir Peter Gershon's report *Review of civil procurement in central govern-ment* called for greater commercial skills in Whitehall. Since then the demands for procurement expertise have increased but the skills have not kept pace. Consistent critics are the NAO and the PAC as the NAO recognised when it commented in a 2009 report that both 'have con-sistently identified cases of problem government projects involving a lack of public sector commercial skills and experience'. The NAO con-cluded that 'value for money has often been compromised by a lack of commercial skills and experience'.[30]

The PAC more bluntly said Whitehall's record of purchasing IT was 'a recipe for rip-offs' and that the government's inability to know whether or not departments were being overcharged had led 'to the waste of an obscene amount of public money'. It said there the market was an 'oligopoly of large suppliers' and the government lacked in-house IT expertise to deal with it.[31]

David Cameron referred to 'the enemies of enterprise' in a speech to party members at the Conservative spring conference in March 2011. It was regarded in the media as an attack on civil service inertia and resis-tance to innovation. In fact he was alluding more to the way Whitehall contracts are awarded by civil servants invariably to the large firms rather than the small because of the complexity and expense of the procurement process rather than to any deliberate block on outsourcing itself. He added:

> We are taking on the enemies of enterprise. The bureaucrats in government departments who concoct those ridiculous rules and regulations that make life impossible, particularly for small firms... The public sector procurement managers who think that the answer to everything is a big contract with a big business and who shut out millions of Britain's small and medium sized companies from a massive potential market.[32]

But Cameron's comments exposed a paradox in ministerial attitudes to reforming public sector procurement of goods and services, worth some £220 billion annually of which central government's share is 30%. On the one hand, ministers want Whitehall to spread its buying largesse across as many small firms as possible so as to boost jobs and business; yet on the other ministers complain that the multitude of different contracts means varying prices and Whitehall should therefore centralise its procurement to get the best deal from a small number of big suppliers by using its bulk-buying power. In 2010 the NAO complained that the public sector was paying a wide range of prices for the same commodities with, for example, a 116% variation between the lowest and highest prices for the same grade of stationery or 169% for computer monitors and recommended more collaborative purchasing to drive down prices.[33]

So what should it be? A myriad of smaller businesses offering different prices to different parts of the public sector or an oligopoly offering highly competitive deals because they are selling to one or two giant public sector purchasing consortia? On this, the jury remains out as far as ministers are concerned, irrespective of governments. Politicians want to be seen to be helping small businesses, yet on efficiency grounds centralised buying from a small pool of large suppliers means only large private companies can afford to offer the economies of scale.

Reform case study (2): Whitehall reorganisation

Structural change is difficult, causes upheaval and in the short-term, loss of focus, and it is the short-term that most concerns ministers whose tenure is measured in two- to three-year cycles. An NAO analysis of 43 Whitehall reorganisations found 77% of them had taken up considerable senior management time in handling the change process itself.

In the case of three newly created Whitehall departments, it took three to four months to agree the size of their new budgets.[34] Apart from the controversial health reforms abolishing primary care trusts the Coalition government tended to avoid large-scale structural change in the government machinery because of the instability it generates.

Governments also have a poor record on attempting to change Whitehall. All too often this has involved only moving around the furniture – sometimes literally – with little evidence of proper project management, budget control or improved outcomes in delivery. The NAO found that between May 2005 and June 2009 there were over 90 reorganisations, which it described as the 'allocation and reallocation of functions and responsibilities within and among central government departments and their arms length bodies'. Most of the cost lay in redundancies and pay increases to staff, IT and property. Since 1980, 25 departments had been created, 13 no longer existing, while in comparison during this period the United States created only two new departments. Of the 51 reorganisations it analysed the NAO estimated the total cost at £780 million and the annual cost at £200 million.

Yet despite this spend these reorganisations failed to demonstrate value for money since their objectives were 'vague' and costs and benefits were not tracked. Monitoring of costs and expected savings was poor with no proper procedure for setting up business cases. There was no requirement to set reorganisation budgets so that costs were hidden and no evaluation of benefits. Project management frequently took place after the reorganisation process had begun. The NAO concluded: 'The value for money of central government reorganisations cannot be demonstrated given the vague objectives of most such reorganisations, the lack of business cases, the failure to track costs and the absence of mechanisms to identify benefits and make sure they materialise'.[35]

Bearing in mind the poor record of even minor reorganisations the prospect of undertaking transformational change across central government is one which ministers are, and will be, reluctant to consider; yet it is difficult to see how without it Whitehall can cope with the long-term challenge of a reduced role and slimmer budgets. The PASC warns that incremental change will no longer be sufficient. The challenge is how to initiate transformational change without destabilising the civil service at a critical period. For as the PASC concluded in its study of Whitehall reform:

> The civil service has prided itself on reform through gradual change, building on past initiatives and adjusting to the priorities of each

new government... We consider that incremental improvements of this sort will not be sufficient to meet the scale of change implied by both the decentralisation agenda and the structural impact of a reduction by one-third of the administration budget of Whitehall. This will require considerable structural organisational reform of the civil service.

In other words, the reform agenda needs to be not less ambitious, but more.[36]

One solution has been the transfer of Whitehall functions to executive agencies or arm's-length non-departmental public bodies with the hope that greater operational independence will lead to more managerial innovation while still within the public sector umbrella. The NDPBs, although derided as 'quangos', have been a helpful tool for ministers wanting to create distance between themselves and agencies delivering complex services. They enable ministers to 'remove themselves from direct responsibility for policy implementation and quasi-judicial decisions and at the same time gain the informational and political benefits of incorporating outside expertise in the policy process'. They are also 'an indispensable part of the modern state'.[37]

Quangos are a useful stick with which opposition parties can attack governments for allegedly swelling unaccountable bureaucracy. Reducing them is more challenging. The Coalition announced in October 2010 that of 901 NDPBs 192 were to be abolished, 118 merged into 57 bodies and 171 restructured and backed this with a Public Bodies Act, passed in December 2011. Research in 2012 however found that most of those earmarked for abolition were 'very small advisory bodies', that many had spent nothing in 2009/10 and that 'the vast majority of the large and powerful quangos have not been affected'. Redundancy costs, contract termination and pension liabilities also reduced any of the claimed savings. Furthermore the Coalition also created new NDPBs as part of its public sector reform programmes including the Office for Budget Responsibility, the National Crime Agency and Public Health England.[38]

The PAC was also sceptical about the savings of £2.6 billion that the Cabinet Office claimed would arise from the abolition of arm's-length bodies. It said that some of these savings were cuts rather than reduction in administrative costs, that there was insufficient evidence to support costs of redundancy and pensions and that ongoing £400m costs of some of the NDPB functions transferring back to Whitehall departments were not taken into account. The Cabinet Office revised its initial estimate of £425m in transition costs to between £600m and £900m and admitted to the PAC it would take time to identify the final costs of the programme. As ever, it will be long after the alleged savings claimed by ministers have been announced – and they have moved on or out of government – that the real savings will become apparent.[39]

Reform case study (3): Shared services

Similar organisational obstacles arose during the process of forcing Whitehall departments to share, and thereby reduce, back office costs such as HR, IT, finance, payroll and asset management. On the surface the idea that these corporate services, which the public never sees and which only exist to provide infrastructure backing to the frontline services they do experience, should merge rather than be replicated through each Whitehall department seems eminently sensible. Local government has been a leader on sharing services. In the private sector, the NAO has noted, savings of 20% are usual with a less than five-year return on investment. Certainly governments expect efficiency and lower costs from merging back office functions which can be released to the frontline.

But they have not been easy to achieve in Whitehall and millions of pounds have been spent with poor or little return on investment. Implementing shared services across Whitehall has been a key target since the early 2000s and especially since the Gershon Efficiency Review in 2004 identified the potential for savings. In 2007 the NAO however said, 'slow progress' was being made and there was still 'substantial untapped potential for securing savings through shared services'.[40]

Five years later when the NAO revisited the subject these 'substantial' savings were still an ambition while the costs had soared. In the seven years since the shared services programme had been evolving, £1.4 billion had been spent on developing five shared service centres with £159 million of estimated savings from them by 2010/11. Against these supposed savings two of the centres estimated that their real net costs were £255 million and only one had actually broken even in the previous five years. These five centres had been expected to cost just £900 million to build and instead overran their budgets by £400 million. Costs were put down to complex software systems and processes and lack of engagement across central government. The NAO stated: 'It is our judgement that many of the benefits generated could have been achieved by other means or with lower investment'. And it added: 'Our analysis shows implementation projects have been expensive, with lengthy anticipated and actual break-even periods ranging from four to eight years. Typically, shared service centres in the private sector target and achieve less than five years for break-even'. The NAO concluded: 'The shared services initiative has not so far delivered value for money for the taxpayer ... By creating complex services that are overly tailored to individual departments, government has increased costs and reduced flexibility. In addition, it has failed to develop the necessary benchmarks against which it could measure performance'.[41]

The Cabinet Office reviewed the shared services agenda based on its own July 2011 paper *Strategic vision for shared services* which proposed two centres managed by the Cabinet Office operational from 2014. It estimated that of the £1.5 billion annual Whitehall spend on HR, payroll, finance and procurement between £67 million and £128 million a year could be saved under its new proposals requiring an investment of between £44 million and £95 million.[42] The NAO in its earlier March 2012 report doubted these figures saying, 'there is little evidence to assess how far the Government can make these savings from shared services'. Even the Cabinet Office admitted that its 'assessment of the risks is that they are very significant, high impact and highly likely, even after mitigation. The financial impact of these identified risks are not factored in to their estimate of savings and, in addition, we have identified further risks to the project'.[43]

The PAC also expressed scepticism, remarking in its own report shadowing that of the NAO that 'December 2014 is an ambitious deadline and we are concerned that the Cabinet Office is being unrealistic about their capability to meet it. Previous government attempts at implementing shared service centres on a similar timescale have failed'.[44] In the light of the already huge cost of the shared service centres the jury has to be out.

A similar lack of connect between reform and outcomes occurred with new business plans announced in 2010. As part of opening government to public scrutiny the Coalition ordered business plans in 2010 to be drawn up by each Whitehall department. Announcing them on 8 November, David Cameron said they created 'accountability to the people' and would mean that 'reform will be driven not by the short-term political calculations of the government, but by the consistent, long-term pressure of what people want and choose in their public services'.

But a year later the Institute for Government announced: 'Outside Whitehall, few people are aware of them. Neither Parliament, the media nor other intermediary groups have made more than limited use of the information that they contain'. It maintained that 'outcome measures' were not linked up to 'reform priorities and added: 'The ministerial ambition to deliver "click through" business plans where users could go from top level priorities to detailed actions and outcomes is still a long way off'.[45]

Reform case study (4): Capability Reviews

It has not been easy to measure whether the various reform initiatives in Whitehall have actually led to any marked improvement in performance. One example was the Capability Review programme. This was set up in 2005 by the then Civil Service Head and Cabinet Secretary Sir Gus O'Donnell and as one of only five such schemes in the OECD countries aimed to create 'a step change in the capability of the civil service' by using external review teams of five, including two from the private sector and one from local government, to benchmark performance in Whitehall departments, then afterwards monitor progress. The 'model of capability' was divided into ten elements across three sections, leadership, strategy and delivery and an assessment made against each element. The concept drew on successful 'peer review' programmes initiated by local government and was described by the NAO as the 'first to assess systematically the organisational capabilities of individual departments and to publish results that can be compared across departments'.[46]

By 2009, 22 departments had been reviewed and 16 re-reviewed. In a Cabinet Office progress report in December 2009 Civil Service Head Sir Gus O'Donnell said, 'I have seen the programme significantly improve the capability of the Civil Service, across all departments', and announced he was 'very pleased' with this success, though he admitted that the service 'needs to continue to adapt in faster and smarter ways'. Of the areas identified as requiring urgent development in the first Capability Reviews, 95% 'had been addressed' by the second review. The progress report quoted the Home Office Permanent Secretary David Normington as saying his department had 'improved dramatically' while Leigh Lewis, permanent secretary at the Department for Work and Pensions, said the Capability Review process had 'helped the department to strengthen its record of delivery and its policy and analytical ability'.[47]

But the reviews were accused by auditors of being too internally focused on management improvement, without any obvious link to improved outcomes in frontline service delivery. This was highlighted in an NAO report earlier in 2009 on the Capability Review programme which was far less optimistic about improvements than the mandarins. The NAO said it could not determine whether the programme represented value for money 'because the information currently gathered does not prove a clear link between departments' actions and improved performance' and nor was it clear where it was leading. The reviews, it alleged, had no link between departments' reported performance, had only a limited coverage of how departments delivered complex arrangements with other departments and the 270 other agencies and non-departmental public bodies, did not benchmark against organisations outside the civil service and did not focus on middle-management and frontline staff but mainly on senior management. Indeed, said the NAO, departments could show no 'clear evidence of impact on outcomes'.

Nor was the programme cheap. The NAO said that the first round of reviews cost £5.5 million, equal to £324,000 for each of the 17 departments covered, and the second around £4.3 million or £226,000 per departmental budget. And while there had been some evidence of improvement, two-thirds of the 170 assessments in the first round (10 for each of the 17 departments covered) rated a department 'less than well-placed'. Overall, said the NAO, 'the picture was mixed' with common weaknesses being poor skills, leadership and understanding delivery models which it said 'confirms conclusions from our work over the years and of the Public Accounts Committee'. The NAO concluded: 'It will be possible to determine value for money only when departments demonstrate that specific improved outcomes, including better public services, are linked to actions taken in response to Capability Reviews'.[48] Much later, in 2012, the NAO's head Amyas Morse told a Commons select committee: 'I thought that the capability review started out hopefully, but in my view it got softer as it went forward, which was a real pity. That was a wasted opportunity. Next time, please let us not start tough and get soft'.[49]

In the light of the critical NAO review the Capability Review programme was amended in July 2009 to put more focus on delivering value for money, linking capability to outcomes, sharpening the focus on delivery and encouraging innovation and greater collaboration between departments. The third phase of the programme dropped external reviewers in favour of departmental-based teams.

Reform case study (5): A single portal

Another ongoing criticism levelled at the civil service is its 'silo' mentality, its over-departmentalised perspective and inability to cut across
organisational boundaries. In 2006 a visionary report by Sir David
Varney (commissioned by the then Chancellor Gordon Brown) envisaged a time in the future – Varney cited 2020 – when all public services,
locally and nationally, would be accessed through a single portal. His
report on how the civil service might be transformed concluded that
'providing joined-up services designed around the needs of the citizen
or business will yield efficiency savings by reducing duplication across
the public sector' and said 'this ought to be the public service aspiration
for Government'. It remains an aspiration.

Varney envisaged services built around themes, citizens engaged more
fully in developing services, better data sharing and robust performance management, none of these especially controversial though by
no means easy to implement as indeed he recognised. His report cited
examples where bereaved families or those on benefits had to deal with
a myriad of overlapping public agencies. Some of these problems were
still being examined through government-inspired 'whole place' pilot
studies seven years later. In his proposals for 'channel optimisation',
the process whereby public service providers offer users a choice of type
of contact, telephone, Internet or face-to-face, there has been progress
driven by technological change.

In a fanciful paragraph Varney looked ahead to 2020 when frontline
services would be completely integrated, citizens would access public
services through their local area portal which would trigger both local
and national services and when 'behind the scenes central and local
government coordinate a network of public bodies, private and third
sector partners to provide seamless access to these services'. In practice,
as he realised, this was 'a long-term goal requiring a fundamental shift
of models of current service delivery'.[50]

To some extent the government's Directgov site set up in 2004 aimed
to provide such an online portal though primarily to provide advice
and contact information by folding government websites into its own.
Varney optimistically predicted that by 2012 Directgov would be 'the
primary electronic channel to citizens for government and is a place
citizens can turn to for the latest and widest range of public services'.
It would achieve this, he added, by 'providing a single electronic des-
tination to meet the vast majority of citizen needs for government
informational and transactional services'. By 2011 Directgov had cost

£128 million since its launch and in 2010/11 had 187 million visits. But the NAO said it was difficult to quantify savings or ascertain what proportion of the public used Directgov though at the time of its report in December 2011 it had over 30 million visits a month. In practice social media rendered Directgov, which became gov.net in 2012, increasingly outdated.[51]

But the structure of government itself militates against working across departmental boundaries and spending cuts have made Whitehall departments even more jealous of protecting their own budgets. As Varney noted: 'It is often difficult for departments to reach agreement to fund cross-cutting initiatives between Spending Reviews and, as departments will have already allocated their budgets to departmental priorities, they are often reluctant or unable to contribute to the kind of common venture that is essential for efficiency savings or service transformation'.[52]

Despite years of change the civil services still struggles to adapt to changed circumstances. One long-standing politician with inside experience of Whitehall and government concluded gloomily:

> My 45 years in politics have shown me that successive governments of all colours have failed to address the reality that Whitehall departments – both ministers and officials – too often pull in different directions. They can be resistant to change, take too long to make decisions, devise policy in ivory towers and create uncertainty through repeatedly changing tack.[53]

Conclusion

Prime ministers and governments criticise the civil service for being cumbersome, unresponsive and slow to change but are often unclear about what they want from it. Cabinet ministers also have short-term horizons which make it difficult for Whitehall departments to embark on longer-term reforms. Ministers also adopt silo mentalities with their departments which run counter to efforts by Number 10 and the Cabinet Office to create more corporate, joined-up government. But criticisms of the civil service have been consistent through successive governments since 1979, namely that Whitehall has not evolved sufficiently quickly to adapt to the changing world, that it lacks procurement skills, is too inward-looking and too focused on policy rather than delivery.

The proliferation of non-departmental public bodies has been frequently criticised by opposition politicians but efforts to reduce them are more difficult. Claims by the Coalition of major savings by reducing the number of NDPBs have been questioned by auditors.

Attempts to drive through changes have led to structural reorganisations of Whitehall departments that often fail to deliver their targets and end up as net costs rather than savings. The civil service now faces the challenge of both reforming itself while downsizing.

9

The National Health Service

The United Kingdom's National Health Service faces perhaps the most demanding decade since its creation. Despite avoiding the scale of spending cuts suffered by other parts of the public sector since 2010 such as local government, the NHS faces budget rises way below healthcare inflation. Demand pressures from a population which is both growing and ageing, greater numbers of patients with long-term chronic illnesses and constantly developing medical technology are expected to add 4% a year to NHS costs for the next decade. With expected budget increases of 0.1% a year, this means the NHS needs to *reduce* its costs by 4% a year just to stand still. Yet since it was formed in 1948 the NHS has *increased* its costs by an average annual 4% and even higher in the decade to 2010. As one analysis warned in 2012, 'After 2014/15, to avoid cuts to the service or a fall in the quality of care patients receive, the NHS in England must either achieve unprecedented sustained increases in productivity, or funding will need to increase in real terms'.[1]

The NHS, free to its UK users, arouses passionate debate unlike any other part of the public sector. Its detractors argue that it is inefficient, monopolistic, driven by its professional staff interests from consultants at the top through to its nurses and unionised porters, top heavy with bureaucratic management, centralised, unresponsive to patients and a huge drain on the taxpayer. Its supporters maintain that the NHS is unique in being free at the point of use, is more efficient than insurance-led health services and driven by the needs of its patients not private sector providers.

What is not disputed is that the NHS is one of the largest public sector organisations in the world with 1.7 million staff. In a typical day over 835,000 people visit their GP or practice nurse, some 50,000 visit accident and emergency departments, 49,000 have outpatient consultations and 94,000 are admitted to hospital for an emergency. The NHS in England is the biggest part of the system employing some 1.4 million staff and treating 3 million patients each week. The NHS in Scotland, Wales and Northern Ireland employ some 155,300, 85,250 and 65,000 people respectively (although funded centrally from national taxation, NHS services in England, Scotland, Wales and Northern Ireland are managed separately although they remain mostly similar and are regarded as belonging to a single, unified system).[2] In 2011/12 the NHS spent £121 billion according to the Treasury (£102 billion in England), a fifth more than in 2007/8, most of it allocated by primary care trusts on commissioning healthcare from GPs, hospitals and other providers. Total spending on the NHS doubled in cash terms in the previous decade with the NAO estimating this was the equivalent of real-term annual increases of 6%. Against this, demand rose by 5.5% over the same period.[3]

The decade to 2010 saw huge increases in spending on the NHS and an increase in the number of employees by some 300,000. But while health services improved productivity declined, as staff and salaries rose and the taxpayer was landed with expensive long-term debt from PFI hospital projects.

Demand, particularly among the elderly and those with long-term illnesses and disabilities, continues to grow and if clinical services are to continue being provided free without crippling the taxpayer then cost reductions must be found elsewhere, partly but by no means only through efficiency savings. As an MPs' report noted: 'This challenge can only be met through service redesign and reconfiguration'.[4] The NHS, facing budget squeezes and major restructuring, cannot afford to repeat the errors of the boom years of investment. It needs to focus on reducing its greatest costs, especially in elderly care and through merging budgets with local authorities that are responsible for care services, using technology to assist greater homecare-based services and maintaining a tight rein on overheads, especially workforce costs. The challenge is not only to reconfigure services to ensure greater home-based care but to ensure funding when local authority care budgets are being reduced by spending cuts.

The NHS, brilliant in its principle of providing a free service to all funded by national taxation, has nonetheless been a financial challenge for governments – or rather, taxpayers – ever since it was introduced in 1948. But understandably the public continues to be resolutely wedded to the principle of free healthcare and resistant to any attempts to introduce other forms of revenue such as charging or opening up provision to more private sector providers. As public policy commentator Nicholas Timmins noted in his critique of new health legislation in 2012: 'Suspicion over the profit motive runs deep, even if at the same time polling shows that most of the public does not mind if they are treated in public or privately run facilities so long as their NHS care remains free at the point of consumption'.[5] Conversely the public are also reluctant to see taxes rise in order to cover the costs.

Yet the public and the media also hold governments to account for operational failures within the NHS because of its status as a national public service. Ministers are then on one hand in the unenviable position of ensuring that the NHS is efficient, productive and responsive to the needs of patients with the constant fear of being blamed for its failings if it is not, while on the other having to find the means of funding healthcare without increasing the tax burden and ensuring that it remains free at the point of use.

Solving this conundrum has been at the heart of health reforms that successive governments have introduced in the past half century. For a key challenge for governments is that while they desire to devolve NHS decision-making, put more power into the hands of GPs who are closest to their patients and let hospital trusts run their own affairs, they are also expected by the public to ensure a national level of minimum standards which often requires top-down direction. The Blair government in particular applied targets to reduce waiting lists and waiting times, or mortality rates from diseases like cancer, across the NHS to iron out variations in performance.

The thread that runs through NHS reform from the late 1980s onwards is the idea of the market as a mechanism to make healthcare provision more efficient, more flexible and more responsive to patient demand. Although Labour devoted considerable attention to and investment in NHS reform from 1997 to 2010, the Coalition government launched a major restructuring of its own through its Health and Social Care Act 2012. But what makes this latest round of NHS reforms more challenging than those previously is that the health service is in an environment of squeezed budgets set to last for the foreseeable future coupled with rising demand. An alarming challenge is the impact of more elderly patients with chronic and expensive long-term diseases such as dementia, which is likely to overshadow any reform efforts to improve elective care.

The NHS had to find annual 4% efficiency gains adding up to £20 billion by 2014/15 to be re-invested back into healthcare delivered through its Quality, Innovation, Productivity, and Prevention (Qipp) programme even though the government was committed to protecting health spending. The two-year pay freeze to 2013 contributed the single largest share of the savings reflecting the NHS's high labour costs. The government also believed it would save £4.5 billion by 2015 by abolishing the strategic health authorities and primary care trusts as part of its restructuring of the NHS. Lessons from past restructurings which have involved organisational upheaval and redundancies tend to show that savings end up being much less than anticipated. But as usual it will be well after the event that the real financial picture will be clear.[6]

Early analysis of the £20 billion efficiency savings suggested that most of them were down to the impact of pay freezes and internal accounting such as reducing tariffs paid by PCTs to trusts. But it is not easy to make permanent savings by reducing hospital beds and staff unless the number of patients is also permanently reduced. One solution is to step up community-based care for the elderly to reduce their demand on hospital beds; indeed a fifth of the efficiency savings is expected to come from transformational change like integration with adult care services run by cash-strapped local authorities. The NAO, in analysing the first year of meeting the efficiency targets, commented: 'The quality and productivity gains needed do not lie within individual NHS organisations but at the interfaces between primary and secondary care, between health and social care, and between patients and the NHS. At the heart of this is transforming "patient pathways", leading to the integration of services and, in some cases, the integration of organisations'. But the NAO found 'no evidence of a shift in staff from the acute to the community sector' while 'spending on community services as a proportion of total NHS spending was the same in 2011–2012 as in 2010–2011 (8.4 per cent)'. It added: 'Most providers (86 per cent) reported that differing financial incentives between organisations are a major barrier to service transformation. Similarly, almost all primary care trust clusters (96 per cent) reported that organisational barriers (including differing financial priorities) between acute and community services are a major or minor barrier to transforming services'. The NAO concluded sceptically that 'for the NHS to be financially sustainable and achieve value for money in the future, it will need to quicken the pace of service transformation and make significant changes to the way health services are provided'.[7]

In this chapter we see where in the key areas of productivity, procurement, PFI and the costly National Programme for IT millions of pounds of investment has been often poorly managed despite, and occasionally because of, government's efforts to make the NHS both more efficient and yet more responsive to patients' needs. These experiences will help determine whether the latest plans for reform can avoid the mistakes of the past. A key concern for the NHS in the next five years is whether it can undergo structural reorganisation with all the costs and upheaval this entails at the same time as it drives through £20 billion of efficiency savings and dismantles the centralised IT programme without damaging frontline services. On past record the prognosis does not look good. As Nicholas Mays and Anna Dixon conclude in their detailed King's Fund study of recent health reforms:

> Policy sometimes struggles to adapt to a changing context, while the politicians who conceive of and enact reforms have often already moved on by the time the consequences of their actions become visible. However, over the next decade, the impact of the financial situation the NHS finds itself in is likely to overshadow any consequences of further market reforms.[8]

The financial prognosis for the decade of health funding from 2012 is alarming. One gloomy Nuffield Trust analysis provides three scenarios. The first scenario assumes that spending remains broadly flat in real terms, which in the case of the NHS in England means a deficit of £28 billion to £34 billion by 2021/22. The second, more optimistic, scenario assumes that spending increases in line with GDP economic growth projections from the Office for Budget Responsibility (themselves subject to revision) in which case the funding gap would be £12 billion to £14 billion by 2021/22 as well as annual 2% savings incorporated into these figures. The third, even more optimistic, scenario imagines that health spending continues to rise with the historic average of 4% a year for the NHS. Only in the last case would there be no shortfall but considering downbeat Treasury projections for health spending in the next few years the research analysis says this scenario is 'highly unlikely'.[9]

As so often with the auditing of public sector reform programmes, measuring their success or failure invariably occurs well after they have taken place and it is too late to influence their outcomes. The challenge is to get the reforms right in the first place. This is difficult, as other health services overseas have found, for the problems of the NHS are not unique as a health service. As Nicholas Timmins noted in his 2012 report for the Institute for Government and the King's Fund:

> There have been huge battles over health reform in other countries, including those with social insurance systems. France, for example, saw strikes by doctors and nurses over reform in the not so distant

past. In the US, which has the lowest level of tax-funded health care among leading Western democracies, 'Obamacare' has been bitterly divisive. There, even attempts to introduce NICE-style organisations aimed at restricting spending to cost-effective care, have led to allegations that 'death panels' are being formed. In other words, reforming the delivery of health care is just difficult.[10]

Reform case study (1): Market-led reforms in the NHS

The Conservatives were and are, unfairly or not, seen by the public to be ambivalent about the principle of the NHS as a provider of free healthcare. Their attempts at reform have been met with accusations they want to dismantle the NHS, bring in private sector providers and introduce charging. John Major recalled in his memoirs: 'The NHS has always been unfairly a sort of political quicksand for the Conservative Party...The public were always doubtful that the Conservatives really believed in the NHS. In fact we do – I did anyway'.[11] In opposition David Cameron went out of his way to emphasise that a Conservative government would uphold the principle of free healthcare on demand and would even protect the NHS from spending cuts.

The NHS was one area of the public sector where Margaret Thatcher stepped warily such was her fear of a public backlash if she were seen to be dismantling the concept of a free service. In her memoirs she recalled:

> I believed that the NHS was a service of which we could genuinely be proud. It delivered a high quality of care, especially when it came to acute care, and at a reasonably modest unit cost, at least compared with some insurance-based systems. Yet there were large and on the face of it unjustifiable differences between performance in one area and another. Consequently I was much more reluctant to envisage fundamental changes than I was in the nation's schools. Although I wanted to see a flourishing private sector of health alongside the NHS I always regarded the NHS and its basic principles as a fixed point in our policies.[12]

Such was her acute political antennae to the public's suspicion of changing the NHS that she squashed a Treasury proposal to increase and extend charging as it 'would have discredited any other proposals for reform'.[13] Later she commented: 'Any reforms must not undermine public confidence'.[14]

This did not change her view that the NHS was an inflexible monopoly dominated by its employee interests and needed more effective cost-controls. She regarded it as 'a bottomless financial pit' and added: 'If more money had to be provided I was determined that there must at least be strings attached'. She later recalled: 'We clearly had a long way to go before all the resources of the health service would be used efficiently for the benefit of patients', and later added: 'Dedicated its staff generally were, cost conscious they were not. Indeed there was no reason why doctors, nurses or patients should be in a monolithic state-provided system'.[15]

Although the 1983 Griffiths Report was to set the general principles of sound management in the NHS, the real reforms only occurred towards the end of Thatcher's term in office, taking effect after she had departed. In particular she became attracted to the idea of forcing efficiencies through the health service by the introduction of an internal market. In 1986 she became aware of 'renewed interest in the economics of health care' and noted that 'Professor Alain Enthoven of Stanford University had been advancing ideas about creating an internal market in the NHS whereby market disciplines would be applied even though a full-scale free market would not'.[16]

The government even considered the idea of funding the NHS through a health stamp rather than general taxation but quickly discarded it. She later recalled: 'The objective of reform was that we should work towards a new way of allocating money within the NHS so that hospitals treating more patients received more income. There also needed to be a closer, clearer connection between the demand for health care, its cost and the method for paying for it'.[17]

In January 1988, by which time Thatcher had already been prime minister for nearly nine years she decided to launch a review into the NHS and a White Paper *Working for patients* was published in January 1989 outlining the idea of an internal market. She later declared that her aim was to reform the administrative structure of the health service guided by four principles, namely high medical standards of care free for all, the greatest possible choice for patients, responsibility for medical decisions or budgets to be made 'at the lowest appropriate level closest to the patient' and in a barb to producer interests, any reforms to lead to genuine healthcare improvements not just salary rises for employees.[18] No government since, irrespective of political background, has deviated from these key principles.

Thatcher later recalled: 'By the autumn of 1988 it was clear to me that the moves to self-governing hospitals and GPs' budgets, the buyer/provider distinction with the (health authority) as buyer and money following the patient were the pillars on which the NHS could be transformed in the future'.[19] All of these principles were to run through consequent NHS reforms, although not all were successfully implemented. But as one commentator was later to write: 'In the context of the first thirty static and declining years of the NHS, these reforms were quite radical. But they were hardly revolutionary'.[20]

The NHS and Community Care Act 1990, introducing an internal market for the first time, became law from April 1991 by which time John Major was prime minister. The new system separated the roles of purchaser and provider with health authorities being the purchaser of services on behalf of patients in theory from any provider, though in practice mainly from the public sector. Hospitals, as purchasers, became trusts while GP practices became fundholders with their own budgets for non-emergency treatment. In principle the idea was that providers would have an incentive to be efficient in order to increase business. Major later recalled:

> We followed through Margaret Thatcher's reforms to break the monolithic structure of healthcare provision that had endured for four decades and put in its place a system of self-managing hospital trusts, encouraging – though not compelling – GPs to become fundholders, looking after their resources on behalf of the patients. Unlike the old centrally-planned system which had allowed backlogs to build up, the reforms raised standards and allocated resources according to real lives, real experience and real needs on the ground.[21]

Echoing the complaints of his successor in dealing with public sector professional interests, Major called the process of introducing the changes 'a noisy business' adding:

> The BMA [British Medical Association] defended the way things had always been done without reference to the palpable failings of the system. Always we were harried by the suggestion that the creation of the internal market was a covert step on a path to full privatisation of the NHS. It was not but we had no answer to the charge other than simply to say it was not.[22]

His successor Tony Blair was also a critic of the existing NHS structure. Like Thatcher he regarded it as monolithic and inflexible with little incentive to innovate. Blair believed that competition and private sector expertise would change this inertia, writing later about his frustration that 'competition even in the event of a hopeless service was literally banned. So the different bits could negotiate with each other but if they were unhappy there was not a lot they could do'.[23] He added: 'For a public service, even one like the NHS, in the negotiation of contracts for buildings, IT equipment, technology, it is like a business. When it cuts costs, as it should if it can, it is like a business. When it employs or fires people it is like a business. When it seeks to innovate, it is like a business'.[24]

Initially opposed to Major's market-led reforms, Blair later adapted and refined the concept in 2000, three years into his government, when the NHS Plan was published. The Plan, 'a ten-year vision for reforming the NHS' (in England as responsibility for the NHS in Wales and Scotland passed to the Assembly and Parliament respectively in 1999) envisaged that a 'significant increase in NHS budgets would drive systemic change leading to improvements in the quality of care and increased NHS productivity'.[25]

It was divided into three stages, the first about improving the workforce, infrastructure and waiting times, the second about widening choice and creating better financial systems and the third from 2008 onwards using the increased resources to transform services and improve value for money. Having better paid and better qualified staff was also a key aim of the Plan through new contracts from 2004 while 303 (later to become 152) primary care trusts from 2002 became the commissioners of services with part of their budgets devolved to GP practices, or practice-based commissioners. The aim was to give patients a wider choice of provider, increased autonomy for hospitals and payments for treatment linked to activity or Payment by Results (PbR). In theory with money following the patient through PbR, the most efficient providers would benefit persuading the others to improve. New foundation trusts, free from direct government control, would be created from 2003. In short, the target was to create more efficiency, quality, responsiveness, output and equity of care. The changes represented 'a major attempt to improve an iconic public service using market-led incentives'.[26]

But importantly for Blair as he later wrote:

The door was edged open for the private sector. The concept which, in time, was to result in foundation hospitals was introduced. And the whole terminology – booked appointments, minimum guarantees of service, freedoms to innovate – spoke of a coming culture of change, orientated to treating the NHS like a business with customers, as well as a service with patients.[27]

There were strong arguments against the marketisation of NHS care. Critics said then and do now that healthcare cannot be treated like groceries or hotel rooms, that market failure is likely to be higher, that there are few providers, and that patients themselves are not informed to make choices about such specialist services. Furthermore, the idea of the market has often been compromised by politicians themselves who faced with the logical outcome of the market, namely that the inefficient go out of business, then object because a failing hospital happens to be in their constituencies or because voters do not want to lose a small, inefficient hospital.

In their analysis of the market reforms under Conservatives and New Labour Mays, Dixon and Jones from the King's Fund wrote: 'The assumptions made by the proponents of the market reforms were not universally shared and many parts of the reform package were extensively debated. A number of commentators questioned whether a greater choice of provider was really deemed important by patients arguing that patients would prefer good quality local services'.[28]

There was also criticism of the government's new General Medical Services contract with doctors from 2004 for underestimating the effect of higher pay for GPs and consultants (see below). In theory the new staffing contracts were supposed to introduce more flexible working and improve care; in practice they increased costs. Blair was to admit this in his memoirs writing: 'There were errors in implementation. We paid more for the consultants' and GPs' contracts than strictly necessary'.[29]

Foundation trusts were launched in 2004 with the proviso that they could control their own affairs, were financially and clinically viable and had a management capable of running them as autonomous bodies. The programme continued through successive governments and by September 2011 there were 139 leaving the remaining 114 NHS trusts open to receive foundation status by 2014. But by 2011 the latter were already struggling under the impact of budget squeezes. The PAC noted that 80% were in financial difficulties – an increase from 49% in 2010, the previous year – while 'two thirds acknowledge they have performance and quality challenges' and 'a particular problem is the quality of leadership'.[30]

But the biggest impact on the NHS since its creation was the huge increase in funding for a decade from 2000, a luxury that few post-war governments had before or have had since. Between 1997 and 2010 NHS spending more than doubled in real terms.[31] In 2000/2001 the NHS budget was £60 billion increasing to £102 billion in 2010/11, a rise of 70% in the decade following the NHS Plan in 2000.[32] In 1997 public sector UK healthcare spending as a percentage of GDP was 5.3%. In 2000 it was 5.3%. By 2009 it was 8.2% (although it needs to be noted this last percentage partly rose because healthcare costs continued to increase while GDP fell following the credit crunch from 2008). During this period 1997–2009 private healthcare as a percentage of GDP rose only modestly from 1.3% to 1.6%. Total public and private healthcare spend in 2009 of 9.8% of GDP was almost equal to that of the 12 more prosperous EU member states.[33]

This funding boom enabled patient services to dramatically improve with lower waiting times and improved outcomes as investment poured into infrastructure, equipment and staffing enabling supporters of the reform agenda to argue that the changes were working. But critics, supported by figures from the Office of National Statistics, in turn maintained that the spending increase actually masked declining productivity with increased fixed costs through extra staffing and higher pay.

Nevertheless thanks to the huge increase in spending, the health service as far as the public was concerned underwent a major improvement. Waiting times were down, new hospitals were built or refurbished through PFI projects and between 2000/1 and 2009/10 the number of patients admitted across all NHS hospitals in England rose by 31% to 14.5m from 11.1m annually. The average number of staff per hospital bed increased by 5% between 2006/7 and 2008/9. Significantly at the same time, in an ominous sign of rising demand ahead, the number of patients aged 75 and over went up by 59% reflecting underlying rising costs from an ageing population.[34]

Blair's successor Gordon Brown was less enthusiastic about market-led reforms in public services. Brown's biographers later wrote; 'The initiatives that had defined the Blair years from academies to foundation hospitals were noticeably absent ... Brown had deliberately set out at a calmer pace, rebuilding relationships, especially in health'.[35]

But the fiscal crisis in 2007 leading to a sharp fall in UK GDP meant that as a proportion of GDP healthcare costs escalated in the following two years from 6.8% to 8.2%. The economic downturn also spelled the imminent end of large-scale investment in the NHS even though spending would continue to rise at about the level of healthcare inflation. In November 2009 the NHS chief executive signalled that the NHS and Department of Health (DoH) would have to deliver £15 billion to £20 billion of efficiency savings in the four years to 2014/15.

So by 2010 as the New Labour era ended, how successful were its health reforms? In their critique Mays and Dixon comment: 'The English NHS was still some distance away from functioning as a fully fledged provider market for publicly financed care. The system continued to be run by a closely managed hierarchy'. The number of new providers was low, hospital managers identified GPs rather than the supposedly empowered patients as more important for deciding referrals and 'focussed their marketing accordingly' while waiting times and financial targets continued to be more important in setting standards than the impact of the market. Overall, there were successes in reduced waiting lists and waiting times, better survival rates for cancers and cardiovascular diseases and a rise in public satisfaction with the NHS but these were not necessarily to do with market-led reforms. In particular, the major rise in staff costs led to a fall in productivity. The authors concluded: 'The scale of the market-related effects was modest compared with the overall improvements in the performance of the NHS from 1997 associated with other policies, such as service modernisation and targets, and these effects were realised in a benign period of strongly growing NHS spending'.[36]

In opposition Conservative leader David Cameron, conscious of the voters' attachment to free-on-demand healthcare not to mention his own positive experiences of the NHS through its treatment of his severely handicapped son, had pledged to protect the NHS from spending cuts. As prime minister from 2010 he stuck to his pledge on paper although in practice pressures from ever-increasing demand meant NHS managers having to find savings.

The biggest change to the NHS was the controversial plan outlined in the Health and Social Care Act 2012 to abolish the ten strategic health authorities and 152 primary care trusts and hand over their commissioning responsibilities to consortia of GPs, or clinical commissioning groups, overseen by an NHS Commissioning Board. It was called 'by far the most contentious change to the way the service functions since Kenneth Clarke's original introduction of the purchaser/provider split in to the NHS in 1991'[37]. A new economic regulator will monitor choice and competition, now open out to 'willing providers' from the private and voluntary sectors. In addition public health duties transferred to local government in April 2013 with local health and well-being boards promoting integration of health and social care and public health. The government believes it will give GPs more control over commissioning the right health services for patients as well as save in managerial costs.

The Bill, introduced in a record 60 days after the Coalition government was created, had a turbulent passage through Parliament during

2011/12 facing criticism from virtually all professional groups within the health sector that it would destabilise the NHS and incur huge redundancy costs just when the NHS needed to focus on cost savings. Its optimism that a greater variety of providers, especially from mutuals and social enterprises, will be willing and able to supply health services, was also questioned. As Mays, Dixon and Jones warned: 'Looking ahead to a tighter funding environment, the coalition government's ambition to see a greater plurality of provision, the mutualisation of public services, and the transfer of all publicly owned providers to foundation trust status seems unlikely to be realised ... NHS-funded care is likely to continue to be largely provided by publicly owned providers'.[38] Public policy commentator Nicholas Timmins warned in his critique of the Act that if it fails 'this will be the fifth or sixth successive failure in 20 years to get commissioning and the purchaser/provider market really to "work" and deliver undoubted and big benefits'.[39]

Reform case study (2): Productivity in the NHS

The Health and Social Care Act was unusual in that it was not brought into being to address an immediate crisis in the NHS. As Timmins noted:

> The Coalition government's upending of the NHS in 2010 came not amid an NHS financial or performance crisis but after the longest period of sustained spending increases in its history. Waiting times were the lowest they had ever been. International surveys of health systems, while being clear that the service still had its problems, nonetheless put the NHS high in the league tables on many measures.[40]

Indeed in the World Health Organisation's annual comparison of healthcare across the world, the United Kingdom came out reasonably well. Its 2012 figures (referring to the year 2009) put the United Kingdom's per capita spend on health at 16th in the table of European and former Soviet Union countries, below France and Germany. But whereas from 2000 to 2009 these countries saw a drop in government spending as a percentage of the total health budget the United Kingdom's rose from 79.2% to 84.1%.[41]

But was this investment matched by proportionate increases in productivity, an important measurement considering that the next decade will see standstill budgets in the NHS? For a major principle of public sector reform is to increase productivity levels – although health productivity is not easily measured. The NAO describes it as the ratio between the volume of resources going into the NHS (inputs like staff and clinical supplies) and the quantity of healthcare provided by the NHS (outputs or healthcare adjusted for quality). It explains: 'If inputs rise faster than outputs, then productivity goes down...Productivity is focused on the measurement of inputs and outputs that are directly in the control of the organisation that produces them, rather than the outcomes that are not wholly within their control. For instance, a hospital can control the time a patient waits for an operation, but cannot fully control their long-term health'.[42]. Statisticians also grapple with how quality improvements are measured such as how time spent reassuring patients can be factored into productivity estimates.

The Office for National Statistics is regarded by the NAO as providing the most authoritative measure of productivity in its productivity index although even this is by no means absolute and does not easily measure, for example, changes in quality. However, the NAO and ONS remain the principal sources of evaluating productivity.

The ONS estimated that from 1997 to 2009 healthcare productivity fell by 2.7%, an average of 0.2% a year due to the inputs growing by 88.8% but the outputs only by 83.8%.[43] In the 13 years to 2010, spending on the NHS doubled in real terms while the ten-year NHS Plan in 2000 envisaged that increased investment in the NHS would be accompanied by increased productivity. This, as judged by the ONS and NAO, has not in practice occurred, with major implications for the future management of costs at a time when real terms spending is heading downwards.

Much of the surge of spending on the NHS between 2000 and 2010 went on increased staffing and pay. In particular, new contracts with consultants, GPs and with other staff through the Agenda for Change programme enacted from April 2004 onwards led to increases in pay and staffing levels without a commensurate uplift in productivity. The aims of the new contracts were first set out by the DoH in a business case to the Treasury; they specified increased productivity, an extension of patient services especially in deprived areas, improved rates of recruitment and retention and better care through payments by results. The DoH estimated that Agenda for Change, which aimed to encourage new ways of working through a simplified pay system, would deliver up to 1.5% a year in increased productivity.

But even by 2006 a Health Select Committee report estimated that the new contracts 'cost the NHS significantly more than was predicted', called the government's original estimates of the cost as 'hopelessly unrealistic' and concluded: 'In the last 5 years the NHS has received the largest ever growth in funding. Unfortunately, largely because of large increases in the number of staff employed combined with large pay rises, the rise in spending has exceeded the unparalleled rise in income'. The report said that since 1997 there had been a 77.65% increase in the number of senior managers and 45% in clerical and administrative staff. The 2000 NHS Plan had envisaged 20,000 more nurses and 2000 more GPs whereas in fact the numbers of GPs had risen by more than double that figure and the number of nurses by 54,000. Furthermore of the 56% extra spend on staff in 2005/6, 47% was due to pay increases.[44]

As one critic, health academic Nick Bosanquet, wrote in 2007:

A vast amount of funding and new staffing was poured into a system which had a very weak capacity to manage or to use new funds in an effective way. In the event the funding was mainly spent on new employment contracts and on increased staffing... This was one more sign of the lack of synchronisation between the plans at the centre and the actual decisions taken locally.[45]

In a critical June 2008 report looking back on the new contract with GPs, which had started in April 2004, the PAC said that while partner GPs had seen average pay rises of 58%, GP productivity actually fell by 2.5% in the first two years. While services certainly improved, the extra funding into general practice meant the level of productivity fell. The PAC said the new contract cost £1.8 billion more than planned as incomplete data on the cost of services provided by GPs led the DoH to underestimate spending in the first three years while access to GP services had 'not improved significantly'.[46]

In their analysis of the health reforms under New Labour, Mays and Dixon conclude:

The fall in measured productivity was largely due to the big increase in NHS funding, leading to more staff and higher wages that were not compensated for by increases in measurable output... These increases overwhelmed in scale any potentially positive impact of the NHS market reforms. Furthermore, in most of the period there was little emphasis on raising productivity in return for the additional resources. Instead, the focus was on increasing spending and staffing levels per capita so that they were closer to the European average through old-style input planning.[47]

A decade after the NHS ten-year plan was launched the NAO in 2010 issued its own analysis of the change in hospital productivity following the increase in NHS funding over this period, since acute and foundation hospital trusts made up 40% of all NHS spending. Significantly it quoted the DoH's insistence that the extra funding was to 'meet the key public expectations and would not initially be matched by a commensurate increase in outputs'. The report quoted the ONS's earlier conclusion that overall NHS productivity had fallen by 0.2% a year since 2000 and 1.4% a year in hospitals. The NAO said new staff contracts 'are not always used effectively to drive productivity', there were variations in costs and understandably managers were more focussed on meeting national performance targets rather than increasing productivity.

The NAO report concluded:

The past decade has seen consistent, significant increases in hospital funding. This was designed, in part, to deliver more productive behaviour. However, hospital productivity has fallen. The Department's design and the NHS's implementation of national initiatives were predominantly focused on increasing capacity, quality and outcomes of healthcare whilst maintaining financial balance, rather than on realising improvements in productivity. Whilst hospitals have used their increased resources to deliver many of the national priorities, hospitals need to provide more leadership, management and clinical engagement to optimise the use of additional resources and deliver value for money.[48]

In May 2010 consultants McKinsey, in a study commissioned by the DoH in 2009, estimated that greater efficiencies in the NHS could save £13 billion to £20 billion over the succeeding three to five years. This included £6 billion to £9.2 billion from provider costs and £2.7 billion to £4.1 billion from moving care to out of hospital alternatives (which of course shunts the costs elsewhere, in particular to social care).[49]

Reform case study (3): The PFI in the NHS

In the two decades to 2010 the PFI acquired a major role in the procurement of major government projects, especially hospitals. Private consortia design, build and manage facilities for the lifetime of a contract, usually 30 years, in return for annual payments at the end of which the facilities return to the public sector. Governments liked PFI as it transferred risk to the private sector, enabled infrastructure projects to be developed off balance sheet and therefore not on public spending figures and injected private sector project management skills into design and servicing.

But PFI also saddled the public sector with inflexible long-term fixed payment costs. As the UK economy headed into recession from 2007 and levels of public spending became increasingly unsustainable as tax revenues and GDP declined so PFI costs came under scrutiny. Although private finance has always been more expensive than government borrowing, the financial crisis widened the gap further as bank lending costs rose. In 2009 the PAC advised the DoH and other departments with PFI contracts to renegotiate with PFI investors and contractors 'to secure better deals for the taxpayer'.[50]

By 2010 as the decade of annual public spending rises ended, the spotlight fell on the huge liabilities incurred by PFI. In 2010 the NAO, examining the 70 PFI hospitals costing £900 million a year with a capital value of £6 billion, found most were well-managed and achieving value for money. But it also warned that the ability to reduce PFI annual charges was limited, a looming concern considering the amount of savings the NHS was expected to deliver.[51]

In August 2011 the Treasury select committee questioned the fundamental premise of PFI, noting that it was considerably more expensive to fund than traditionally procured projects and that because PFI debt did not appear in government deficit figures Whitehall departments had little incentive to monitor its costs. The CBI, defending PFI, told the committee that PFI had directed investment into rebuilding infrastructure like hospitals that would otherwise not have received it through conventional funding.[52]

The PAC reported that the DoH had identified six hospital trusts as unviable because of their PFI charges. Those acute trusts then in the pipeline for foundation trust status but concerned about their finances identified PFI charges as one of their three major worries. It warned:

> Long term (PFI) deals reduce the [DoH]'s ability to establish a level playing field of financially sustainable, autonomous trusts. In many cases efficiency savings alone will not be enough to make unviable trusts financially sustainable. The Department faces a particular dilemma about how to manage the debt of these hospitals as their long term financial commitments make reconfiguration more difficult.[53]

In a separate report the PAC also criticised governments for using PFI, then standing at 700 projects with a further 61 in the pipeline, 'as the only form of financing available without clearly proving whether it is value for money' and added: 'The use of PFI has been based on inadequate comparisons with conventional procurement which have not been sufficiently challenged'. It maintained tax revenue was being lost because PFI investors used offshore arrangements even though the Treasury factored in tax revenue in its cost-benefit analysis of PFI projects. The report said, the public sector had 'insufficient information' on the returns made by PFI investors and no mechanism for sharing in the gains when investors sell their shares. It added, it was difficult to ascertain the true costs of PFI because of departments and investors 'hiding behind commercial confidentiality' while public sector procurement skills remained variable 'and there were examples of projects clearly lacking in commercial awareness'. The Treasury claimed that it would find £1.5 billion in savings from PFI projects across England although the PAC warned this must not come simply from cutting services.[54]

In November 2011 the Treasury announced a review of PFI with the aim of finding a better deal for the taxpayer through other forms of raising finance that would be cheaper and more flexible. Its report in December said, 'the government shares some of the commonly identified concerns that PFI contracts can be too costly, inflexible and opaque'.[55]

In February 2012 the Treasury select committee, reporting on responses to its report in August 2011, bluntly stated that 'a great deal of public money may have been misallocated or wasted' due to PFI. The Office for Budget Responsibility asked to assess PFI liabilities as if they were part of the government's debt, estimated they would add another £33 billion or an extra 2.3% of GDP as at March 2010.[56] In October 2012 the PAC noted that: 'A number of trusts in financial difficulty have PFI contracts with fixed annual charges that are so high the trusts cannot break even. Paying these charges is one of the first calls on the NHS budget and the Department is liable for supporting all PFI payments because it underwrites the Deed of Safeguard given to contractors. It already expects to have to find £1.5 billion to bail out seven trusts facing problems with PFI repayments over the remaining life of their contracts – equivalent to £60 million a year'.[57] The PFI regime has since been revised (see chapter on the Treasury).

Reform case study (4): Procurement of health supplies

The NHS is a huge purchaser of supplies; in 2011 its 165 hospitals spent some £4.6 billion on 'consumables' such as medical, clothing and other supplies, representing a quarter of non-pay spending and 10% of total spend.[58] In theory their buying power should enable it to drive down prices. In practice, as elsewhere in much of the public sector, there is wide variation between the highest and lowest prices paid as hospitals decide their own purchasing arrangements. Yet even modest improvements in use of resources can lead to hundreds of millions saved annually. NAO analysis shows that of 66,000 medical and other items purchased by hospitals researchers found a variation in price paid of 10% and estimated that had they all been purchased at the lowest rate, then £150m could have been saved.[59]

Sample research by the NAO into 61 hospital trusts in 2011 which dealt with 17,000 suppliers found that £7m could be saved in the purchasing of A4 paper alone if the number of orders was reduced to the level provided by the best performing 25% of trusts. The 61 trusts between them bought 21 different types of A4 paper, 652 different types of surgical gloves and 1,751 cannulas (tubes). One trust bought 13 types of glove, another 177 types. The NAO estimated that by amalgamating small purchases into fewer, larger orders, hospitals could save some £500m a year, almost 10% of the total annual spend. Its sample analysis of contract notices published in the Official Journal of the EU in 2009/10 showed that 378 different notices for 'medical consumables' were placed by hospitals and other health purchasing bodies costing between £14m and £84m to administer. This was despite the target of the DoH's Qipp programme, launched in 2009, to save £1.2 billion by 2014/15, the then nine Collaborative Procurement Hubs set up in 2005/7 to streamline purchasing and the NHS Supply Chain which provided a bulk-buying service for hospitals.

The NAO concluded that fragmenting purchasing meant that NHS procurement of consumables was 'poor value for money'. It also warned that with all hospitals becoming foundation trusts and therefore released from DoH control there needed to be ways they could be accountable for their procurement practices.[60]

Reform case study (5): The NHS IT Programme

The record of governments in successfully completing major public sector IT projects is, to say the least, variable. The hugely ambitious IT programme to transform the NHS's information processes proved to be an expensive fiasco.

The DoH first launched the National Programme for IT in 2002. It was then the largest civilian IT project in the world with an estimated cost of around £11.4 billion over the first ten years. The programme was designed to reform the way the NHS in England used information, and hence to improve services and the quality of patient care. The programme was soon several years behind schedule and a progress report by the NAO in 2008 concluded: 'The scale of the challenge involved in delivering the National Programme for IT has proved to be far greater than envisaged at the start, with serious delays in delivering the new care records systems'.[61]

A succession of reports by the NAO and PAC chronicled the mounting costs and slippage of the National Programme. In May 2011 the NAO, in examining a core part of the programme, the £7 billion planned centralised care records system, concluded: 'We are seeing a steady reduction in value delivered not matched by a reduction in costs. On this basis we conclude that the £2.7 billion spent on care records systems so far does not represent value for money'. In July 2011 the PAC issued its own verdict on the care records system, which aimed to ensure that by 2010 every patient would have an electronic record capable of being transmitted between different parts of the NHS. The PAC said such a goal was now 'beyond the capacity of the [DoH] to deliver' and would now never happen. It said costs had escalated yet the DoH was unable to show what had been achieved for the £2.7 billion so far spent and had 'not got the best out of its suppliers' despite paying them £1.8 billion since 2002. It said the DoH now recognised a one-size-fits-all system 'was a massive risk and has proven to be unworkable' and the difficulties were compounded by lack of consultation with clinical staff from the outset which could have identified problems earlier and helped define specifications. The PAC was also highly critical at the time it took the DoH to provide information to it and the NAO, with a statement on the programme's benefits up to March 2010 promised by the DoH by summer 2010 finally arriving nearly a year later in May 2011 by which time it was also a year out of date. This was despite the fact that Connecting for Health, the NHS organisation responsible for managing the programme, had 1,300 staff and had spent £820m on central programme management. The report, as indeed had the NAO's in May, also raised concerns about the effects of NHS restructuring, the abolition of Strategic Health Authorities, responsible for implementing the National Programme, and the legal position of hospital trusts taking on liability for existing contracts and systems.[62]

A review by the Major Projects Authority in May 2011 concluded that while there had been 'substantial achievements' covering two-thirds of the £6.4 billion so far spent by March 2011, the programme 'has not and cannot deliver to its original intent'. The DoH announced in

September 2011 that it was accelerating the dismantling of the National Programme for IT on the grounds that 'it is no longer appropriate for a centralised authority to make decisions on behalf of local organisations'. The DoH added: 'We need to move on from a top down approach and instead provide information systems driven by local decision-making. This is the only way to make sure we get value for money and that the modern NHS meets the needs of patients'.[63]

Conclusion

The NHS remains unique in being totally free and while this marks it out as one of the most progressive health services in the world it also brings with it challenges in maintaining quality while driving down costs. While successive governments since 1979 have been committed to a free NHS they have also attempted with mixed success to make it more responsive to users, more cost-efficient and more market-led. Most of the improvement in the quality of care from 2000 to 2010 was down to increased spending but this extra investment was not matched by a proportional increase in productivity.

The combination of spending cuts and rising demand, especially in adult care, make the need for the NHS to make efficiency savings and reduce overheads even more pressing. But a weakness in previous efforts to change the NHS has been a focus on structural change leading to extra costs and upheaval and questions remain about whether structural reform of the NHS from 2013 onwards will increase productivity or add on further costs.

Nonetheless the challenges the NHS faces are familiar to other health services abroad which also struggle to maintain costs and productivity.

10
Local Government

The diversity of the United Kingdom's local government, with its 433 different authorities and 10,000 parish and town councils, has been a challenge to reformist ministers of all political parties. The fact that a few councils embrace change and new ideas does not automatically imply their less dynamic colleagues will immediately follow. Pulling a Whitehall lever does not, unlike the centralised NHS, mean every council reacting in precisely the same manner. Local government is not the local agent of the state. Each council has its own priorities, traditions and relationship with the communities it serves. As one Labour local government minister once joked: 'If reforming the NHS is like changing the direction of an oil tanker, then reforming local government is like turning round a flotilla of small boats'.[1]

But local government has been unique compared to the rest of the public sector because its political managers, its councillors are elected. It enables them to claim equality with MPs and government ministers as regards their respective democratic mandates, and for councillors to maintain they deliver their services tailored to the needs and views of their voters and residents rather than the priorities of central government. Councillors are also often leading figures in their own local constituency parties to whom the MP and minister answer, thereby confusing the hierarchy of central above local government.

This has as a result made the task of reform more dependent on the will of local political administrations and less on that of government ministers. It has not prevented reform but it has made it more complex for government, especially when tackling changes to local political management, an unpalatable task for those MPs and ministers whose local parties also happen to be in charge of their local councils.

Local government reform, as driven from Whitehall down to local level (in the case of Scotland, Wales and Northern Ireland local government is answerable to the Scottish and Welsh Governments and Northern Ireland Assembly), is prompted by five key influences.

Firstly even while councils have their own democratic legitimacy, they are still recognised by voters as part of the public sector and therefore the domain of central government. High-profile failings in children's services have led to public and media demands for ministerial intervention. MPs in their constituency surgeries regularly hear complaints from their constituents about some or other apparent failing in their local council, which tends to colour their own perception of local government.

Secondly, party politics influences parliamentary attitudes to local government. If an MP is from the same party as the administration running his or her local council then the MP will expect the council to be performing well so it does not adversely affect the MP's re-election chances. Conversely if the council is run by a party different to that of the MP then the MP is likely to highlight weaknesses in the council's performance as a way of attacking the opposition and helping their re-election.

Thirdly, since central government until recently was funding 75% of local government through grants or redistributed non-domestic rates (the latter until spring 2013 when councils were allowed to keep half of their non-domestic or business rate income) with council tax providing just a quarter of income, ministers expect councils to be efficient and well-run, politically and managerially. They, and indeed the public, expect consistent standards in service delivery, especially in social services and education which represent together some two-thirds of local government spending. Furthermore investment in local government was on an upward trajectory between 2000 and 2009. Between 1993/94 and 2008/9 local government revenue spending more than doubled in cash terms or 58% in real terms. In 2011/12 spending on local government services in Britain was £142.7 billion.

Fourthly, ministers want local government to help them deliver their social and economic agendas and become frustrated when local political leaders fail to rise to the challenge. Both Labour and Coalition governments were attracted by the concept of directly elected mayors as a way of creating strong local leadership, though in practice the electorate was indifferent.

Fifthly, as was shown by the Audit Commission's monitoring regime, the comprehensive performance assessment regime in England (which did not cover Scotland, Wales or Northern Ireland), local government's service delivery has been inconsistent. While there have been efficient councils of all political hues, there have at the other end been well-publicised failures and in between councils of average performance.

Governments therefore have expected, and will continue to expect, that local government, funded mainly centrally by the taxpayer, must maintain high standards of political leadership, management, performance and delivery. At the same time ministers want to ensure that this occurs without their being seen to be overtly centralist or interventionist as councils are still independent entities liable to resent direct interference. Ministers therefore have used a mix of stick and carrot to induce reform, encouraging initiative within a framework of external inspection. Paradoxically, this operates against a backdrop of public ignorance about the true cost of local government services. Most people believe that their councils run predominantly environmental services such as emptying bins, cleaning streets and filling potholes, which while a core function for district councils are only a small part of the responsibilities of all-purpose and county councils. Two-thirds of local government spending goes on education and social services with the former, through academies, increasingly independent of local authority control. The biggest financial headaches for councils, namely adult care and the cost of looked-after children, are virtually invisible to the bulk of residents.

As with reform in other parts of the public sector there is a thread which runs through from previous governments to the present. Labour pursued the concept of 'double devolution' or 'devolution to your doorstep' meaning that while councils received more powers they in turn were expected to devolve their own powers to communities. In reality few powers were delegated to councils and further devolution to the doorstep was stymied by the difficulty of identifying the communities supposed to receive it.

The deal by which central government promised to devolve powers to local government in return for the latter also devolving powers downwards to local groups was summed up by the then communities and local government Minister David Miliband, later foreign secretary and failed candidate for the leadership of the Labour Party in 2010, losing to his brother Ed. David Miliband told the National Council for Voluntary Organisations' annual conference in February 2006 that reform of local government was 'the double devolution of power from the central government to local government and from local government to citizens and communities' and that it would take 'the partnership between state and the third sector into a new phase'. He added: 'Devolution is a deal. It is conditional on local government taking on new powers from central government, but then sharing power with citizens, neighbourhoods and the third sector, not hoarding it'.[2]

It was a view that was taken by the Coalition government, albeit with different terminology. Its ministers called it 'localism' and argued that reducing the state meant not only central government devolving powers to local government but the latter further handing powers to other local community and residents' groups even to the extent of their providing ex-council services.

To show faith the Coalition scrapped the body monitoring local government performance, the Audit Commission, maintaining it was up to councils and their electorates to determine their policies and performance, not external bodies, and privatised the auditing function. It backed up this approach with the Localism Act 2011 which introduced a 'power of general competence' giving councils the freedom to innovate. It also gave community groups new powers to take on council services or assets and to challenge poor service delivery. But there was a catch; the government's longer-term aim was to reduce central grant funding and enable councils to develop their own revenue streams such as extra business rate from new inward investment.

Local government also faces a fiscal challenge, namely a huge rise in demand for its services, especially from adult social care but also from children's services and waste disposal at a time when its budgets have been sharply reduced. The recession increased demand for its services in housing, benefits, looked after children and social services just at a time when its budgets were being sharply cut. In June 2012 the Local Government Association warned that a £16.5 billion deficit by 2020 caused by soaring adult social care costs would make it almost impossible for councils to provide other services like leisure or libraries as efficiency savings could not fill the gap.[3] Sceptics argued that localism therefore merely meant the government shunting the responsibility for making difficult spending decisions to councils. For it also made local government the biggest loser in the Spending Review of 2011–2015 with a cut of 28% in grant funding over the four-year cycle, much of it 'front-loaded' in the first two years. In its view, budget constraints created their own incentive for reform without the need for external pressure. Coalition ministers also contradicted their own commitment to localism by issuing edicts to councils on issues which were entirely the latter's remit such as the frequency of bin collections, salary levels for senior managers and whether or not they should publish their own quarterly magazines.

As part of 'transparency' the government ordered councils to publish all items of spending over £500 from January 2011 hoping that this would create 'armchair auditors' out of local residents who would monitor performance and spending, acting as self-appointed regulators and providing local accountability. In turn the sector, through the Local Government Association, developed its own peer monitoring regime.

Labour's attitude to local government had been a combination of respect for its delivery abilities when working well and a desire to regard it as a partner in governance, albeit as a junior operating on central government's terms, but frustration at its slowness to change and scepticism at the calibre of its politicians. In contrast the Coalition strategy was to remove many of the central regulatory burdens that constrained local government and to give it more powers. The Coalition's argument was that regulation, far from promoting reform, was actually impeding it and that allowing councils to decide their own priorities was more conducive to creating change. However, this 'carrot' approach was also accompanied by a very large 'stick', namely that huge cuts in local government grant funding would force councils to initiate reform simply to balance their budgets.

In essence Labour's approach was to increase spending on local government accompanied by a rigorous programme of centrally determined inspection to drive through reform. The Coalition's strategy was to allow local authorities more freedom but to reduce grant funding to the point where local authorities had no choice but to introduce reforms themselves in order to balance budgets. The mantra across the local government sector was that only transformational change could enable councils to deliver services on lower budgets.

Governments tend to be driven by three key priorities when delivering local authority reform, namely the need to:

- improve the quality of political and officer leadership;
- bring in a more pluralist delivery of services by using the voluntary and private sectors; and
- enhance councils' democratic role.

Under Labour these were underpinned by a vigorous inspection regime and an interventionist approach. Under the Coalition the driver for change was the fiscal imperative which it argued would incentivise councils to deliver transformation in their organisations.

Central government's ambivalence to local government, offering it some concessions on the one hand and yet maintaining a centralist control over its finances, is replicated in its attitude to how councils should be positioned in the local institutional hierarchy.

On the one hand, ministers maintain that local authorities, because of their democratic mandate, should be the community leaders in their areas, working with partners in the private and voluntary sectors for the good of their areas. The Lyons Report in 2006/7 talked about local government's role in 'place-shaping'.[4]

The Audit Commission refined its inspection regime, the Comprehensive Performance Assessment into the Comprehensive Area Assessment. This moved away from inspecting councils as stand-alone organisations to judging them in their role as community leaders and therefore through the performance of their local partners for which they had to take some responsibility. To emphasise this wider role the Coalition gave councils new strategic responsibilities for improving local public health through the Health and Social Care Act 2012 (see chapter on health).

But ministers simultaneously saw an enhanced role for local groups that did not have the democratic legitimacy of local government but still carried a substantial role in local governance such as the voluntary sector, and faith, residents and tenants' groups. The Conservatives called this concept Big Society. But Labour too had been keen in government to see more community engagement in the shaping of services believing that the public was as equally well-placed to decide local priorities as councils.

Reform case study (1): Local leadership

Local politicians in theory should run local government on a strategic level. Chief executives in theory should deliver the politicians' agenda and manage their organisations. Weaknesses occur when council leaders fail to give strategic direction or insist on the wrong one or become involved in detail that should be the preserve of officer management. There is a further impediment to the running of a successful council, namely that the leader and chief executive fail to establish a working partnership in which each recognises the territorial domain of the other.

Reformists of local government understand the vital role of councillors but have often been frustrated by their leadership abilities. Labour ministers in government after 1997 were sceptical about the calibre of councillors, not least their own and especially those in the old Labour heartlands, the northern metropolitan councils, Wales and Scotland, many of whom were seen as old-fashioned, union-dominated and ideological in approach.

The Labour sceptics or 'modernisers' believed that local authorities lacked both political and managerial leadership, decision-making was

slowed down by an antiquated committee system and councillors inter-
fered with detail without paying sufficient attention to strategic and
corporate issues. They saw the profile of councillors as being unrepresentative of the population at large, with too many of them retired or
not in work.

Labour saw local government in the wider context of the public sector, in need of reform to make it fit the requirements of a pragmatic,
non-ideological, customer-driven and technologically enabled service.
The mantras were 'modernisation' and 'what matters is what works'.
The challenge was how to initiate reform and maintain continuous
improvement when local government itself was such a mosaic of different organisations, each with their own local traditions and anti-centrist
sympathies.

In particular Labour was sceptical about local government's core rai-
son d'etre, namely its democratic mandate. The declining turnout in
local elections was one obvious sign of this weakness. But the 'modernisers' also saw lack of political leadership itself as a problem. They
were impressed by the directly elected mayoral model of local leadership as used in the United States which they saw as creating both a
strong decision-making executive and a direct link between leader and
voters. They believed that the public were much more enthusiastic for
more streamlined, delivery-led councils than the current council leader-
ships themselves and directly elected mayors therefore were more likely
to respond to the modernisation agenda. David Cameron too was also
impressed by the idea of powerful local leaders with a direct mandate
from the electorate who could bypass council bureaucracies.

In recent years governments have toyed with the idea of creating
powerful directly elected mayors to expedite decision-making and create strong local leadership. The 2000 Local Government Act's plans to
bring in directly elected mayors soon foundered on lack of interest by
the public, a perennial problem with the mayors agenda. The Act stipulated that mayoral systems could only take place following a referendum
and a 'yes' vote and that at least 5% of the electoral register was required
to sign a call for a referendum. Many council leaders of all parties were
opposed to directly elected mayors, including the big cities.

In the end there were 34 referendums between 2001 and 2007 of
which only 12 backed, and led, to elected mayors, none of them the
leading provincial cities – and one or two like Mansfield or Bedford
(since then a unitary) being small urban districts – although two London
boroughs, Newham and Lewisham, did elect them. The only big city to
introduce an elected mayor system was London with the new Greater

London Authority created through separate legislation. In Wales there was just one referendum with a rejection of the elected mayor model while the new legislation did not apply to Scotland. Hopes of seeing Manchester, Birmingham, Sheffield or Liverpool going down the path of Chicago or Lyons came to nought. There was no obvious pattern of performance or turnout among the elected mayor councils, each of them being governed as much by unique local circumstances and personalities as by the mayoral system itself.

The Coalition made its own attempt to roll out elected mayors in May 2012 with referendums in ten major cities but this too met with indifference by the electorate and nine cities rejected the idea with only Bristol in favour. The government was blamed for failing to explain to a sceptical public why there was a need for another system of local governance at a time when voters were increasingly cynical about elected government generally.

Reform case study (2): Performance monitoring

Local government has various parts of its functions scrutinised, in particular education, housing and social services. However, the bureaucratically sounding Comprehensive Performance Assessment (CPA) was unusual for examining the corporate heart of the local authority, an area hitherto off-limits for inspectors. For it was only with the introduction of the CPA inspection regime in England in 2002 by the Audit Commission that council corporate management and the political/managerial interface faced real external scrutiny for the first time.

The late and in most places unlamented CPA replaced a burdensome system of performance indicators called 'best value' backed by best value reviews which proved obtuse for most of the public and bureaucratic to administer. The CPA instead examined key council services and listed every local authority as either excellent, good, fair, weak or poor, later moving to a star system of four down to zero. Although it was criticized for over-simplifying complex organisations and failed to seize the public's imagination like the school league tables the CPA had a major impact on local authority performance, especially corporate. The Audit Commission concluded: 'Over the time we implemented CPA, council services improved significantly and CPA is acknowledged to be one of the catalysts for this. CPA evolved in response to improving performance of local government, rising public expectations and changes in the operational and regulatory environment'.[5]

The CPA was aimed initially at the 150 upper-tier councils and later rolled out to all English districts from 2003. For the first time its results would be published annually as a league table with the best performing councils at the top and the worst at the bottom. Ministers' real targets were not just the handful of 'basket cases' at the bottom but the substantial number which were average. Indeed the original categories were to include one called 'coasting' but this was replaced by the more anodyne 'fair'.

The CPA, although controversial at the time, proved to have a major impact on corporate performance. Its categories, 'excellent', 'good', 'fair', 'weak' and 'poor' could be clearly understood by the public, council staff and in particular councillors. The assessment was based on points covering education, social care for children and social care for adults, the environment, housing, libraries/leisure, benefits and use of resources as well as a score for overall service provision.

But what was different was that the CPA also built in 'a new corporate assessment of councils' ability to improve' which 'identifies the strengths and capabilities of the council as well as where more support is needed'. As the first report noted: 'The CPA framework measures the effectiveness of the whole council … its focus is on the leadership, systems and culture that lead to improved services'.[6]

The CPA's focus on the corporate function of each authority rather than just its key service departments for the first time placed the cabinet – that is, the executive – and the leader in the spotlight. It also exposed poor relationships between leader and chief executive as well as in the top tier of managers, the corporate management team. In effect the CPA showed that a local authority, just like a private company, was dependent for its success on its top management team, in this case cabinet, chief officers and chief executive.

The methodology at first had some flaws. But from now on no leader or chief executive could be unaware of their authority's CPA or what its goal was for the next year's results. Some chief executive and political careers were impaired, even ruined, by CPA results while those of others were enhanced. As one ex-chief executive noted: 'The fear of being deemed poor or weak was also a driver for performance improvement and some heads rolled'.[7]

The league table results also offered a clear direction of travel for performance. In December 2002 when they were first published, there were 22 'excellent' councils and 13 'poor'. By December 2004 there were 41 'excellent' and just one rated 'poor'.

In 2005, by which time the 'harder test' (as termed by the Audit Commission) had been introduced with star ratings ranging from four down to zero there were no councils in the bottom category at all and 47 in the top. Four out of five were either three or four star councils.[8]

For both central and local government it was evidence of improvement with each being able to take credit. An official survey of public satisfaction with council services in 2006/07 commented: 'Satisfaction correlates with measures of performance such as the CPA – better councils achieve higher levels of satisfaction'.[9] As one government department with limited dealing with local government noted in July 2007: 'The performance of local authorities as measured through the CPA has improved greatly in recent years'.[10]

And in the long-term the CPA provided statistical proof that local government's performance had improved and that it was therefore well-placed to take on a wider public service role. This was important when the emphasis on local service delivery began to move away from organisations to the 'place' itself with local government as a local leader and 'place-shaper'.

But CPA had strong critics within the sector – and not all of them were from poor-scored councils – their view being that it was up to a council to decide its priorities and to make its own mistakes. The CPA also led to an increase in chief executive salaries as councils increasingly began to seek out the limited number of candidates with strong CPA results. This was to expose the sector to accusations of hosting 'fat cat' salaries when public spending took a sharp downturn from 2010/11 onwards.

In 2007 accepting that CPA had run its course, the Audit Commission unveiled the CPA's successor, the Comprehensive Area Assessment (CAA), to launch in autumn 2009. The new CAA reflected the 'place-shaping' agenda with councils now also judged by the performance of public sector partners within their locality along with input from HMI Constabulary, Ofsted and the Care Quality Commission. The CAA was therefore potentially more onerous for councils in that they were compelled to take a role in driving up the performance of partners for which they were not directly responsible.

The move from best value to CPA and CAA showed some recognition by government that micro-management of performance was not the most productive way of driving up improvement. Partnerships and place rather than on single organisational improvement reflected the changing mood among politicians from all parties for light-touch assessment but it was too late to save the inspectors. The then Opposition

Conservatives announced, as part of its 'post-bureaucratic age' assault on regulation, that they would scrap the CAA altogether on the grounds that it was a costly and unnecessary burden on councils. Not only did they scrap the CAA, weeks after forming the Coalition in May 2010, they then abolished the Audit Commission itself in August 2010.

Unlike the civil service, there is no managerial fast-track training scheme to provide the chief executives of tomorrow. Most have risen up through the local government ranks, beginning their careers in professional disciplines such as legal, finance or education before moving into strategic management. A few come from outside local government, mainly Whitehall, and the private and voluntary sectors.

The transformation agenda, driven by the sharp downturn in grant funding from 2010, has placed new demands on senior managers to deliver ambitious change programmes while cutting management and staff costs.

Earlier pressures to improve managerial performance were driven by the CPA which created a demand from councils for chief executives who presided over high-performing councils, and councillors became risk-averse to hiring candidates outside this pool. In turn this pushed up salaries as an Audit Commission analysis of 190 English single-tier and county chief executive appointments between 1998 and 2007, *Tougher at the top*, noted. It found that key reasons were 'an emerging consensus that effective political and managerial leadership are fundamental in creating high-performing local authorities' along with greater accountability through the CPA and the increased and varying demands on the post. An increase in turnover was down to 'the greater accountability for performance provided by CPA'. In addition poor scoring authorities were 'twice as likely to lose their chief executive to retirement or termination of employment as good performers, and are significantly more likely to recruit an existing chief executive'. However, it found no evidence that outside candidates were any better than internal promotions in delivering improved CPA scores.[11]

The demise of the CPA and then the CAA in 2010 may have removed external performance monitoring pressures from top management but this was swiftly overtaken by the need to deliver transformational change if severely reduced budgets were to be balanced from 2012 onwards and then beyond from 2015. This has led increasingly to the creation of shared management teams and services to reduce overheads, primarily in two-tier areas at shire district level between districts, though there have been examples of county and districts and London boroughs sharing services.

The transformation agenda also calls for a fundamental reappraisal of councils' service priorities, the means and costs of providing them and their use of technology to improve frontline delivery. In particular it includes a reduction in management tiers, teams and costs.

Reform case study (3): Enhancing councils' democratic role

Local and central governments have all grappled with the conundrum of the lack of diversity among councillors across all parties. Although there have been outstanding female and ethnic minority leaders in local government most councillors remain white males, middle-aged or elderly and retired. The most representative – the young single, working age, young parents, ethnic – are often absent precisely because of family and work commitments. Many councillors also argued that the emasculation of local government meant it was unattractive to people wanting to make a difference because it held so little power.

But it was little use ministers castigating local government for being unrepresentative when most local parties found it difficult persuading people to stand in local elections – unlike the picture for aspiring MPs.

Either way little effort was made by government to make it easier for potential candidates. The *Municipal Year Book 2013* showed little change in the gender ratio over the preceding eight years, with 14,565 councillors in England, Scotland and Wales compared to 6,241 female councillors. For chief executives the figure was 301 male and 94 female.[12]

Back in 2006, aware that the problem remained unresolved even as the nation, especially in the big cities, had become increasingly more cosmopolitan over the previous decade, the government set up a commission under a former London borough leader and doctor Dame Jane Roberts to examine ways of making councillors more representative. Its final report in December 2007 made a long list of recommendations but full-time salaried councillors or cabinet members was not one of them. The conclusion was that being a councillor was compatible with full-time work while being on the cabinet was compatible with a part-time job.[13]

The disparity between the age and gender profile of the average councillor and the general public was not the only reflection of a weakening democratic mandate for councils. Both local and central government were also concerned about the declining turnout in local elections which they partly blamed on the unpalatable process of voting. If people did not have to make a special trip to a local village hall or school but instead could vote at their local supermarket, online or via texting, went the argument, then turnout would surely rise.

In fact the process remained unchanged, apart from the introduction of different voting systems in Wales, Scotland and the London mayoral elections. Attempts to bring in postal voting were soon mired in a couple of high-profile local corruption scandals while electronic voting remained an unfulfilled dream.

Labour also introduced a new regularity regime, the Standards Board, to ensure high ethical standards by councillors. Although it eventually devolved many of its functions down to councils the Conservatives regarded the board as a supreme example of unnecessary external intervention and abolished it when they formed the coalition government in 2010.

Many reformists also argue that local government is made inefficient and lacks leadership because of its structure, with a hybrid system across England of unitary, metropolitan, county and district councils. They believe that the most efficient structure is one in which only all-purpose councils exist, responsible for all services in their area, thereby providing economies of scale and strong local leadership. In particular they argue that shire district councils, part of a two-tier system with counties, are too small and should either be subsumed into unitary councils or merged.

But reforming council structures is always hugely controversial among councillors and MPs, irrespective of parties. In the 1980s the Thatcher government had abolished metropolitan county councils and the Greater London Council. In the 1990s the Major government undertook a sweeping restructuring across the United Kingdom. But while unitary councils replaced the two-tier systems in Scotland and Wales, reorganisation in England soon became mired in controversy, primarily because ministers decided to embark on a consultative exercise which enabled lobbyists from particular tiers or councils to harry their MPs at a time when the then Major government had a tiny Commons majority. The process in England caused much enmity between districts and counties and a loss of focus on service provision. It also created headaches for ministers and government Whips trying to maintain party discipline. MPs of all parties often have constituency boundaries loosely co-terminous with district councils, the tier most likely to lose out when new unitaries are created because they are the most numerous, and MPs tend therefore to lobby ministers on behalf of their districts. Nor are there any votes in reorganisation. In the end, although new unitaries were created, much of the existing two-tier system remained and the experience so scarred Conservative ministers that they vowed never to revisit the issue, preferring to encourage councils to merge voluntarily.

Labour ministers in 1997–2010 decided to keep their options open. There was a strong body of opinion in Whitehall, the private sector and even in local government, especially among senior managers, that the two-tier system in England with its separate shire districts and 34 counties, was out-of-date, eclipsed by the huge growth in computer technology. There was also a view that the 1990s changes had been a missed opportunity to create a uniform unitary system across England Proponents of reform argued that technological change now made economies of scale more urgent and that it was no longer viable for shire district councils to each create their own IT systems for handling their call centre services such as benefits and tax administration and customer relationship management systems as well as their own internal 'back office' services like payroll, IT, human resources and finance. A number of major private sector suppliers were now offering to take on 'back office' services and run them from regional centres, further diluting the divide between tiers of local government. Although there were short-term start-up costs in terms through redundancies, there was the prospect of long-term savings in less senior staff and greater efficiencies.

Labour neither ruled in nor ruled out plans to create a completely unitary system of councils across England such as already existed in Wales, Scotland and London. Eventually in 2007 it agreed the go-ahead to bringing in nine unitaries in six counties from 1 April 2009. Of these, five, Northumberland, Wiltshire, Durham, Shropshire and Cornwall, were based on former counties.

The Conservative opposition – by then the dominant party in local government – took the view that reorganisation was a diversion and that districts connected well with the public. In one of its first acts as a government the Coalition in spring 2010 halted plans for new unitaries in Devon, Suffolk and Norfolk and announced there would be no reorganisation.

Similar attempts to create regional structures were also problematic. The Labour government of 1997 devolved powers to a Welsh Assembly and a Scottish Parliament and created the Greater London Authority and nine English regional development agencies.

Labour's goal was to create re-invigorated regional government formed of powers partly devolved down from the government offices and partly upwards from the county councils like economic development and planning. The regions in theory would provide both a revitalised local democracy and an engine for regional economic growth outside London, one of the key targets of both Blair and Brown governments. An attempt to introduce elected regional assemblies failed after voters turned the idea down in the North East of England in 2004.

The Conservatives, and the Coalition, opposed regional structures for taking away powers from local government, especially strategic planning, regarding them as contrary to localism. In 2010 the Coalition abolished the RDAs and instead created 39 sub-regional local enterprise partnerships in England formed of councils and businesses and encouraged city regions and other networks of local authorities.

Reform case study (4): Competition

Local government was among the first parts of the public sector to feel the icy blast of Thatcher's drive to open up services to external competition. Her government argued that in-house providers, the Direct Labour Organisations, were inefficient and dominated by trade union and 'producer' interests. Beginning with legislation in 1981 councils were compelled to market test a succession of services, initially blue collar like building and highways maintenance, then refuse and street cleaning, catering and cleaning and later in 1992 back office services like IT and payroll. Although Labour subsequently abolished the compulsory element, it still insisted that services must provide 'best value' and that there would be no return to in-house monopolies. As a result market testing has remained a feature ever since of local government service provision and the introduction of enforced tendering, controversial at the time, proved to be among the most long-lasting of public sector reforms. It compelled councils to focus on ensuring that their in-house teams were efficient and productive and usually led to tougher control of workforce costs and better financial management of service arms. Critics however maintained that it was not sensible to award contracts on the basis of price alone while privatised labour-intensive services like cleaning and catering saw wages of already low-paid staff fall.

Nonetheless external provision has been the feature of council services ever since. Local authorities may be responsible for ensuring that services are provided; but they do not necessarily have to deliver services themselves. They can commission services from other providers such as the private and voluntary sectors or social enterprises. The Coalition also encouraged the use of employee partnerships, or mutuals, as a way of providing specialist local services and it was keen to see more local services provided on a voluntary basis.

While Labour historically has preferred services to be run by in-house departments, many Labour councils use private suppliers, especially if they promise to bring jobs into the localities from other parts of their organisations. While some of these suppliers are in manual services like refuse collection and vehicle maintenance, others enter into strategic partnerships providing a large range of back-office functions like IT, payroll, personnel and facilities management.

Progress has not always been consistent. Although Labour abolished the compulsion to tender services in 2000, councils were nonetheless expected to constantly test them against the private sector market and if necessary outsource if provision could be more efficient or offer better value. In November 2007, the Audit Commission produced a report criticising local authorities' failure to exploit private sector markets in various services by testing them as a benchmark for cost and quality purposes. Pointing out that over £50 billion a year, half of all annual council expenditure, was 'potentially subject to competitive pressure' and that there were further gains to be made in both cost and quality, the report concluded: 'The pre-conditions for using competition most effectively are not widely in place'.

Members and officers, it added, did not always 'adopt a pragmatic approach to using market mechanisms' and lacked procurement skills or knowledge about markets. It reminded councils that 'the concept of contestability has also been introduced to the public service reform agenda in recent years. The government's model of public service reform incorporates competition and contestability, increased pressure from users and improved capacity to deliver'.[14]

A later report in January 2008 also criticised councils' management of large, long-term strategic partnerships with private suppliers. Noting that three of the earliest such contracts had been terminated early, leaving councils with extra costs, it said that even in those continuing, 'benefits from economies of scale and transferred learning between sites have been slow to emerge'.[15]

Yet local government has consistently been pragmatic about service delivery. Some Conservative councils have taken services back in-house while some Labour councils have outsourced theirs. Whereas the issue of more private sector involvement in the NHS and police continues to be politically controversial, in local government it has long been recognised as a feature of the delivery landscape. The Coalition has also attempted to encourage more diversity by granting councils 'a power of general competence' allowing them in theory to be more entrepreneurial and develop local partnerships without facing legal obstacles.

The shared service agenda, so difficult to develop in central government, is much more prevalent in local government though less than some private sector providers desire. Technology enables councils to streamline their back offices and provide more sophisticated frontline services. Some two-thirds of local authorities conduct their basic transactions online, thus reducing the costs in staff time spent in telephone or face-to-face communication and allowing them to focus on more complex inquiries such as in social care which require personal attention. The success of shared services in local government is recognised by Whitehall. The 2012 Civil Service plan noted that 'local authorities provide a good example of sharing strategic and executive functions across IT, human resources, finance, and even sharing chief executives'.[16]

However, the idea of regional centres providing basic council services from council tax collection to refuse collection for a wide variety of councils remains an aspiration. But there are plenty of shared services in various guises, some covering large-scale strategic services between councils and private sector partners, others just one or two services like building control, human resources or environmental health. A dozen district councils also share their senior management teams to reduce salary costs.

Reform case study (5): Fiscal reform

UK local government is among the most centralised in Europe with two-thirds of its funding coming from central government and advocates of greater independence argue that this makes it passive, only being pro-active when ordered to by Whitehall. In Sweden, in contrast, over 70% of local spending is from local taxation while in France it is half. Supporters of localism argue that giving councils more fiscal powers will make them more dynamic and entrepreneurial and that reform will therefore come from within rather than be imposed.

Coalition ministers responsible for local government claimed that they were 'localist', scrapping external bodies like the Audit Commission and the Standards Board along with ring-fenced grants and granting new legal powers in the form of a general power of competence. But the deal was local government would have to operate on a substantially reduced budget, finding new ways of providing and funding local services in partnerships.

In its approach to local government finance, Labour displayed a reluctance for fundamental reform, avoiding decisions likely to stir up public controversy and preferring instead to make minor amendments to fiscal policy. At one stage, when it commissioned a far-reaching review into local government finance, the government appeared committed to finding a long-term solution to the vexed question of how to fund local services. Instead, when the review was published its more contentious clauses were ignored by ministers.

Concern about the balance between local and national funding is not new. In 1974 under the Labour Government, Sir Frank Layfield was asked to report on ways of improving the system of local government funding. His report in 1976 which asked for a solution as to whether accountability for local services lay locally or nationally was never answered and was anyway overtaken by events, first the national economic crisis and then a change of government in 1979.

Over two decades later, Labour was committed to maintaining the tight fiscal policy of the previous Conservative government, at least for its first term in office after which from 2001 onwards public spending rose significantly.

But central government had less control over council tax which began to rise annually well above inflation. Local government argued that tight grant settlements against a backdrop of above-inflation rises in costs in areas such as children's and adult care services forced it to recoup the balance from local taxpayers. But ministers were irritated by the rises, especially after 2001 when grant settlements became more generous, increasing by 39% in real terms from 1997 to 2007. There was a fundamental issue at stake regarding English local government finance, namely finding a satisfactory balance of funding the proportion of local authority net budgets which came from central government grant and the proportion from the local taxpayer (excluding income from local charges such as swimming pools). Since the nationalisation of the business rate in the 1980s, the only source of local revenue until 2013 was council tax which represented about a third of total local authority income.

The fiscal imbalance meant councils, irrespective of which party was in control, were completely dependent on government grant which many councillors argued made a mockery of local democracy. It also meant council taxpayers having to foot the bill for rising costs in social services which were a national, rather than local, problem. Education was a different picture since the budget was ring-fenced and 'passported' by councils to local schools while education budgets after

2001 were to rise annually well above the level of local government funding.

Labour commissioned former Birmingham City Council Chief Executive Sir Michael Lyons to look into the balance of funding. His review in 2007 was an opportunity to make a fundamental decision on how best to fund local government services in the future, especially in the light of the latter's supposedly rising stock in Whitehall. But ministers' reactions to the final report in March 2007 showed that fundamental reform was not on the agenda. Lyons called for an end to capping, a rebanding of council tax through a revaluation and the return of business rate to councils, the last of which was later implemented in part by the Coalition in April 2013 But ministers were clear that local government would continue to be funded mainly from the centre, capping would continue and business rate would remain nationalised.[17]

Whitehall and its ministers are frequently nervous about granting local government too many fiscal powers. They fear it will take away their control of public spending or lead to big increases in council budgets over which they have little control. Some departments, in particular education, would ideally prefer to bypass councils altogether and indeed do so with free schools and academies. Yet the upper echelons of Whitehall and non-departmental public bodies are filled with ex-council chief executives which make a statement about the high regard in which senior council managers are held in government. For council managers are used to delivering services while civil servants are used to delivering policy.

The Coalition however took on board some of the Lyons Review. It was reluctant to see a revaluation of council tax because of the political storm it would inevitably cause and it was opposed to capping as an interventionist measure instead substituting local referenda to determine council tax rises as a way of keeping them down. For its first two years the Coalition froze council tax by funding increases of up to 2.5%, then 2%.

But the Coalition did relocalise part of the business rate from April 2013, for the first time since it was nationalised under Thatcher, allowing councils to keep 50% of their business rate income. It also introduced other fiscal powers for councils to benefit from new development such as Tax Increment Financing and the Community Infrastructure Levy. Ministers hoped these and other fiscal initiatives would encourage economic development. But this was against a backdrop of severe cuts in grant-funding to local government from 2011 which would overshadow efforts to give councils more financial independence. The Coalition also signalled its faith in local government by transferring responsibilities for public health from the NHS to councils. Less welcome for the latter was responsibility for administrating council tax benefit from April 2013 as the government announced these benefits would have to be cut by 10% or £500m a year.

Another experiment with new funding streams has been with social impact bonds in which providers are paid on results, the risk being taken by their investors. In November 2012 Essex County Council, which had a high number of children in care, awarded a contract to a provider to support some 380 adolescents at risk of going into care. Success in the five-year programme will be measured by the reduction in days spent in care by the adolescents as well as reduce offending and improved school results. If the targets are met then investors can expect returns of 8 to 12%. If they are not met then the council pays nothing. But as the cost to the council of keeping children in care can be as high as £180,000 a year, the potential savings are huge. As children who have been in care also form a disproportionately high percentage of the prison population then longer-term savings to the taxpayer are even higher.

Reform case study (6): Pooled budgets

Among the public sector local government has experienced the highest percentage of spending cuts since 2010, at a time when demand for its services, especially in adult care and children's services, has been increasing. Dire warnings that the soaring coast of adult care will make it impossible for local authorities to provide any other services by 2020 have given an impetus to local government to find other means of sharing costs.

As noted above, there has been a move towards merging management teams and sharing services but the most ambitious ideas concern sharing services with other parts of the public sector with a view to reducing long-term demand, especially in those areas such as welfare, health and youth justice which straddle different funding streams. The Coalition's healthcare reforms recognised that socio-economic issues cross several departments when it transferred public health responsibilities from the NHS to local government in April 2013, arguing that public health is less a clinical issue and more to do with housing, environment, leisure, diet and employment, the remit of the local authority.

In its last year in office, the Labour government developed the concept of 'Total Place' in which public funding for a defined area, usually a local authority, is regarded as a single pot rather than a variety of funding streams. In this ideal scenario, public sector silos are demolished, the multitude of different agencies currently engaged in working with, say, problem families is streamlined down to one or two, and there is a focus on early intervention to reduce longer-term costs. A classic example of this is the foresight of one health trust which helped fund its local authority highways budget to salt pavements in winter thereby reducing the number of elderly people slipping on ice, breaking bones and ending up in hospital requiring expensive care. Another is ensuring that elderly patients discharged from hospital are cared for at home so they do not end up either in expensive residential care or back in hospital. A third example is providing a housing and employment support service for young offenders so they do not commit more crime and return to prison. These initiatives may seem blindingly obvious to the public but they are hugely challenging for the public sector to achieve.

The Total Place programme, initiated through Department for Communities and Local Government (DCLG) in 2009 but strongly backed by the Treasury, gathered a head of steam with pilot local authority studies identifying substantial savings, and more detailed roll-out plans were outlined in the March 2010 Budget. One of the pilots, Birmingham City Council, which completed a financial mapping of the city's entire public sector budget, concluded that the public sector was good at dealing with symptoms but bad at tackling causes. As an example, it found that 93% of the city's unemployment spend was on out-of-work benefits but only 7% was on helping people to find jobs and in health, while 96% of spend was on treating illness only 4% was on keeping them well. It added: 'Users find services disjointed and confusing. Whilst partners often focus on the same individuals and communities, activity and infrastructure can be duplicated and not properly connected'.

Its groundbreaking study found that the total public sector spend in the city in 2008/9 amounted to some £7.3 billion or £7,200 for each inhabitant of which half was the city council's budget, £1.9 billion was spent on health and £700 million on welfare benefits. When applying these budgets to themes irrespective of providers, health and well-being took up the lion's share at £2.1 billion followed by children and young people at £1.7 billion.[18]

The national programme was kicked into the long grass when the Coalition won the May 2010 election and in a typical example of ministerial short-termism, the programme was scrapped. Needless to say, because its principles were not only eminently sensible but also offered huge long-term savings, the Total Place agenda was resurrected a year later and renamed as 'community budgets'. Further pilot studies took place and four more detailed 'whole place' studies involving Whitehall officials as well as local public agencies were then completed in local authority areas in Greater Manchester, London (Hammersmith & Fulham, Kensington & Chelsea and Westminster City councils), Essex, and Cheshire (Cheshire West and Chester).

These 'whole place' studies reported in winter 2012 and their findings showed huge potential savings. The Cheshire West and Chester pilot estimated savings of £26 million over five years through integrating health and adult care. Essex believed it could save £127 million by reducing reoffending by 5%, while Greater Manchester anticipated savings of £183 million over five years by implementing a support and control budget for young adults at risk of offending, based on a pilot study in Manchester and Salford.[19]

As examples from the DCLG of how costs might be reduced, in Greater Manchester it is estimated that 750,000 hospital bed days a year are occupied by older people with multiple long-term conditions, costing £800 million to £1.2 billion annually. Two per cent are aged over 85 but they account for 10% of emergency admissions and 18% of all hospital bed days. If these can be reduced then immediate savings can be achieved. Similarly the three west London boroughs in their 'whole place' pilot found that 20% of residents who had the highest health and social care needs accounted for nearly 80% of spend on these services. This represented almost £25,000 for a person with very high needs compared to £250 for people with very low needs. Essex has 29,000 incidents of domestic abuse causing costs of £86 million in the county every year. Four in five victims visit GPs before going to police. Essex County Council's plan will see a single hub streamlining the current system where 1,000 locations, 116 phone numbers and over 80 agencies deal with domestic violence, bringing agencies together with common goals and aligned budgets. Its focus on prevention and early intervention will save over £100 million by reducing reoffending and domestic abuse. Westminster, Kensington and Chelsea and Hammersmith and Fulham found that half of those given short sentences were likely to reoffend within a year. That group totals 9% of all offenders but two-thirds of all prison admissions and releases. The councils are planning a bespoke service to co-ordinate help that is expected to save £25 million.[20]

Ironically, quite separately from the pilot studies, former Conservative Cabinet Minister Lord Heseltine in autumn 2012 delivered a report on boosting regional economic growth in which he recommended merging some £49 billion of employment and economic development-related government funding for local areas into a single pot. He explained in his report *No Stone Unturned* that this would include 'significant parts of the skills, infrastructure, employment support, housing, regeneration and business support budgets held by central government. Local leaders would have flexibility to spend the budgets on priorities relevant to local circumstances as agreed with central government'.[21] The Coalition, accepting his idea, did however launch its 'City Deal' programme from 2012, giving local authorities in regional cities and other areas more powers over budget-setting in return for displaying commitment to promoting new businesses. By spring 2013, 28 areas were part of the City Deal scheme representing 71% of the English population.

Conclusion

Local government was one of the first parts of the public sector to undergo enforced market testing from the early 1980s. Although politically controversial at the time compulsory competitive tendering had a major impact on improving productivity and led to a culture in which market testing of services became normal even without compulsion. Private sector involvement in delivery, as supplier and partner, has been an accepted feature of the landscape ever since. The introduction of the CPA regulatory regime with its league tables in 2002 also helped improve corporate and political management. The rise of increased consumer expectations about local services coupled with technological change has meant more customer-focused, computer-based frontline services.

The development of a more cross-cutting approach to service delivery using single funding pots has been piloted through the 'community budgets' agenda. Although breaking down departmental silos remains a challenge, the potential for huge savings long-terms means this agenda must be a priority for both local and central government.

11
The Police

For years insulated from the management and productivity initiatives prevalent in the rest of the public sector, the police from the early 2000s and more especially from 2009 with their budgets reduced have found themselves subject to similar reform pressures.

The language of public sector change – transformation, leadership, better procurement, cuts in back office costs, partnerships, customer focus – is now part of the lexicon of policing. In addition funding cuts have spelled the end of increasing officer numbers and created pressure on forces to use private sector resources for back office support so as to release uniformed officers for frontline duties, a culture change that has not been without political controversy. Finally, the introduction of directly elected police and crime commissioners and the abolition of the police authorities in 2012 as a way of creating a direct link between the public and the police must be seen as part of the reform agenda, described by the government as the 'most radical change in policing in 50 years'.[1]

The police are expected to maintain frontline services, that is, neighbourhood and response-led activity, with less money, funding the difference through more efficient business processes, better management and a stronger focus on driving down staff costs. In particular the spending downturn and cuts of 20% in the police have forced politicians and chief constables to reappraise the consensus view that hiring more police officers is the only way of dealing with crime. The argument now is how to cope with fewer officers, managed more smartly and productively, their skills applied to where they are most useful. In turn non-uniformed and cheaper staff, increasingly from the private sector, take on the back office and administrative support services such as telephone answering, building and vehicle maintenance, prisoner guarding or data storage. Supporters of the concept of police as commissioners, such as exists in the NHS and social care, argue that the police continue to retain control, but the services are provided more efficiently and at lower cost by private suppliers. Some supporters of reform, such as former Metropolitan Police Commissioner Lord Blair, maintain that without the use of the private sector to provide support services, police visibility will only decline as cuts take effect. He warned in May 2012: 'The fears being expressed about the private sector are entirely misplaced; actually its involvement is the only way to ensure the police do not withdraw from the streets into their cars and offices which is what 20% cuts would do unless policing arrangements are modernised'.[2]

The result is chief constables are expected to act like the rest of the public sector in driving through efficiencies and initiating transformational change even while ensuring that the police maintain the confidence of the public in tackling crime, both major and low level. They cannot, like the private sector or even other parts of the public sector, simply drop a 'product line' because it is no longer sensible to pursue such as chasing up minor acts of vandalism. To the public preventing anti-social behaviour is an indication that the police are doing their job. Furthermore with crime linked to socio-economic issues over which the police have no control, measuring productivity and meeting performance targets are more challenging. These contradictions make the task of reforming the police more difficult than in changing other aspects of the public sector.

The police command a unique role as a public service provider on whom citizens rely to maintain law and order while politicians are careful not to denigrate their role or reduce their effectiveness. While police forces accept they will be questioned on specific operational issues the idea that they might also be challenged about broader organisational weaknesses similar to those existing in other parts of the public sector such as poor management, inflexible working practices, dominance by professional interests and lack of consumer focus has been in the past difficult for them to accept. As one criminologist commented when describing the reforms of the early 1990s: 'Many within the police service believed they would always be protected from the reforms meted out to other public services'.[3] HM Chief Inspector of Constabulary Sir Ronnie Flanagan noted in his milestone 2008 report on policing: 'Our knowledge base about productivity is less developed than in other sectors, as this has not been an area of high priority'.[4]

Yet government policy in the past 15 years has been driven by the view that far from being insulated from reforms being applied to health, education or local government, police forces need to experience the same managerially led, culture changes because they too are public sector bodies. Most police force income is from central government grant, with a proportion raised locally through council tax. Indeed governments have often been frustrated by the sense that the police are oblivious to the customer-centric focus of public services, that they operate on a 'we know best' basis, that they regard low-level crime such as anti-social behaviour as unimportant even though it is consistently a top priority for the public and that their management structure is inward-looking and unresponsive to change. Despite increased government funding in the decade to 2009 along with increased police numbers, complaints from the public about lack of police presence on the streets or in preventing ASB persist. On average only 11% of total police strength is visible and available to the public at any one time.[5]

This disillusion with the police certainly partly explains the radical decision by the Coalition to abolish police authorities outside London and replace them with directly elected (salaried) police and crime commissioners from November 2012, reflecting a disenchantment with the previous governance structure and the accountability process. The government's paper *Policing in the 21st century: reconnecting police and the people* maintained that the police had become disconnected with their communities and driven by national targets.[6] The new directly elected police and crime commissioners, set up under the Police Reform and Social Responsibility Act 2011, have the power to set budgets, appoint the chief constable, suspend a chief constable or order him or her to retire and must set a police and crime plan and answer to local police and crime panels. The government believes, as it does with elected city mayors, that direct accountability by commissioners to their public will focus police forces on responding to the latter's priorities especially in tackling anti-social behaviour. However, the low voter turnout of 15% at the elections for the new PCCs, many of whom stood on party political platforms, in November 2012 does not suggest the public believe that more politicians are the solution to making the police more accountable.

But the police are also in a difficult position, caught between the populist pressures that influence governments particularly in law and order and the need to prioritise particularly when budgets are tight.

The role of the police has changed dramatically in the past three decades. A Home Affairs select committee noted in 2008:

'The role of the police in the 21st century is broader than it has ever been, owing to a sharp rise in crime levels during the second half of the 20th century, the classification of increasing numbers of incidents as criminal offences, the impact of changes in society and technological advances on patterns of criminality, and growing police involvement in multi-agency approaches to public protection'.[7]

In fact because of the growth of specialisms such as counter-terrorism and organised crime only 43% of the police officer workforce is allocated to response and neighbourhood policing – the part of the service that the public sees and experiences.[8]

The police barely featured while reform was taking shape across the public sector in the 1980s. Indeed, Mrs Thatcher's government was grateful for their role in dealing with picket line violence during the bitter miners' 1984/85 strike and with inner city riots. But towards the end of her term in office even her government was becoming frustrated at what it regarded as the inflexible and hierarchical working practices of the police forces and the fact that despite increased pay and numbers, crime continued to rise and productivity remained stagnant. Criminologist and historian of the police, R. I. Mawby, commented:

Following more than a decade of government support to (and use of) the police it became apparent that it was increasingly exasperated by the apparent inability of the police to control crime and by the apparent lack of effective management of the service observable to its critics ... even Mrs Thatcher was prepared to consider radical change to improve the quality of the service.[9]

Her successor John Major took the view that the police ought to be included in the reform process, like education, health and local government, recalling: 'I was also keen to raise police efficiency – which was not always all that it might be – so police forces were brought into the ambit of the Citizen's Charter and given performance indicators'.[10]

The new Home Secretary was Ken Clarke (later Justice Secretary in 2010), who had already been involved in market-led reforms in previous ministerial roles at health and education. Clarke commissioned Sir Patrick Sheehy to look into police pay and responsibilities. The Sheehy report in 1993 proposed dramatic changes to pay and pensions including ten-year fixed-term contracts renewable thereafter every five years, bonuses linked to performance and severance for surplus officers as part of a strategy to increase productivity across the police and reduce staff overheads.

Mawby comments: 'The market solution proposed by Sheehy was based on a view within the Inquiry team that the police service was mismanaged, highly wasteful and bureaucratic and that of all public services was the most in need of major reform'.[11] Needless to say the police rejected it, the Police Federation holding a mass rally at Wembley Arena which attracted, according to the federation, 23,000 off-duty officers (though less by other accounts). Tony Blair, who addressed it as Shadow Home Secretary, was later to remark of this rally that the Police Federation was 'by far the most well-drilled union I ever came across'.[12]

Clarke however pressed on, producing a White Paper on police reform with new national performance and measurement standards against which forces would be monitored and stronger police authorities. The aim was to encourage the police to devote more time and resources to fighting crime and to bring in management practices and comparative performance data that were increasingly being applied to other parts of the public sector. He also reviewed police governance arrangements, in particular the sometimes uncertain lines of accountability between police authorities, police chiefs and the Home Office.

The result, the Police and Magistrates Act 1994, introduced after Clarke had moved on to become chancellor, made chief constables responsible for their own budgets along with new performance management indicators and created police authorities composed of co-opted councillors, appointees and magistrates replacing the previous local authority police committees. It also included only part of the Sheehy recommendations on pay such as the abolition of the housing allowance. The police, through the federation, the Association of Chief Police Officers and the Police Superintendants' Association, lobbied hard against the reforms, perhaps unsurprisingly. John Major referred to 'the terrific rearguard action from the system' when strengthening the Police Inspectorate.[13]

Seventeen years later a study into police pay which was critical of the Sheehy proposals noted that they 'provoked such severe opposition from police officers that the Government at the time decided that, since its higher priority was the reduction of crime, the most controversial of Sheehy's recommendations should not be implemented'.[14]

In opposition as Shadow Home Secretary, Tony Blair had coined the phrase 'tough on crime, tough on the causes of crime' to show that New Labour was both in favour of strong policing and tackling the socio-economic roots of crime. In government from 1997 he was also clear that the police must not be immune from reform either, believing the Major government changes were only the start. In his memoirs Blair wrote: 'In crime and welfare policy I figured the Tories had not really thought it through and had only begun to think radically at the end of their time'.[15] The Police Reform Act 2002 set chief constables annual performance targets and allowed the Home Secretary to order police authorities to dismiss under-performing police chiefs and to insist on meeting performance targets.

In 2007 former Northern Ireland Police Chief Sir Ronnie Flanagan was commissioned to review policing in England and Wales and aimed to present a guide to how forces should adapt to the demands of twenty-first century policing. He recognised the increased pressures on the police and the need for forces to adapt. He asked whether the response to the growing complexity of modern policing should be to 'specify every outcome and control and bureaucratise every aspect and process, from the centre to the force and within the force from the chief constable to the constable, in an attempt to cover every risk and meet every demand' and concluded that 'such a response would fail to acknowledge that a fundamentally different, more dynamic model is essential'.[16]

But Flanagan also predicted that less money would mean a focus on productivity and that forces would 'have to look at how they can use their resources more efficiently' adding: 'This is the essence of improving productivity – it is about doing more with the same resources – making them go further by improving their deployment to deliver better outcomes'. He regarded the then targets as too easy, being fixed to an historic baseline which meant many forces were 'incentivised to 'coast' rather than to excel ... as private consumers we do not go out of our way to buy an average product. We aim to buy the best that we can afford and this principle should apply equally, if not more so, to the public sector especially in light of the additional investment in policing in recent years'.[17]

Demands on the forces have continued to increase with police responsibility covering a diverse range of issues from counter-terrorism and civil emergencies to criminal gangs and community policing. There are tensions unique to police forces. On the one hand, their task is to catch murderers, rapists, terrorists, bank robbers and burglars while on the other they are expected to devote resources to dealing with graffiti and low-level anti-social behaviour. On the one hand, they must maintain harmonious relations with communities and avoid aggravations such as stop and search even if this might prevent crime; on the other, they will be blamed if crime then increases or anti-social behaviour is allowed to spiral out of control such as it did in the summer 2011 riots. Furthermore communities are not homogenous. Middle-class areas may regard graffiti and vandalism as important while a police force may feel tackling violent crime in more deprived areas is more deserving of their attention. The police cannot operate outside their communities as an alien force. They must both protect them, in all their ethnic, age and income diversity, and be accountable to them. As Sir Ronnie Flanagan's report into the police noted: 'The public must always be the single most important aspect of policing. Not just because their protection, trust and confidence are the key outcomes that policing must achieve but, crucially, because it is only by engagement with the public that the police service can truly know where its targets and priorities should be'.[18]

The paradox is that on the one hand the police are run by local forces yet on the other they are subject to national performance indicators. Governments claim to want to give police chiefs more powers to make them run their forces more efficiently and respond to the priorities of the communities they serve and know best; indeed having police commissioners elected directly by the public is an extension of this desire. Yet governments also demand that centrally set performance targets are met and if necessary will impose them.

The police have a rare esprit de corps, bound together by shared common threats and a view that as a result decent pay, good working conditions and generous pension entitlements should reflect the facts that their job is uniquely dangerous compared to other professions. The nature of their work means their organisational methods cannot be so readily examined in public, even though 80% of police spending is on the workforce, for fear they might be used for criminal use. But police are also part of the public sector and funded by the taxpayer who demands that the police are efficient, well-managed, perform their duties, work with other agencies in partnerships and are not dominated by their own professional, 'producer' interests. This requires strong management capable of adapting to change, not previously always apparent in a rigid hierarchy whose senior personnel have been drawn from within the ranks and are steeped in the culture of the force. For as Sir Ronnie Flanagan noted:

> Policing is far too important to be left to the police alone. It is a public service and one that can only be effectively carried out with the support and consent of the public. Using and developing this engagement with the public is one of the most important challenges in modern policing and it is a challenge that must be met at all levels.[19]

Reform case study (1): Police numbers

The spending downturn from 2010, as with the rest of the public sector, followed almost a decade of year-on-year increases in both funding and personnel. The police budget rose from £6.45 billion in 1994/5 to £13.7 billion in 2008/9 (£16.6 billion with pension and national costs) while the police workforce increased by over 124,000 between 1969 and 2010. Treasury figures show spending peaked at £17 billion in 2009/10 and in 2011/12 was £16.5 billion.[20] Spending on police officers including pensions was £7.8 billion in 2008/9, up by 29% since 1997/98 while during the same period the number of officers increased by 14%. Spending on police staff including community support officers was £3.2 billion in 2008/9, an increase of 92% since 1997/8. Police pay scale rates in 2011 were also typically 10% to 15% higher than other public sector workers and in some regions police officers were on 60% more than the median local earnings.[21]

During this period although crime fell the public remained both sceptical about crime figures and at what they regarded as the low visibility of the police despite their record numbers while critical studies also showed that increased staffing had no automatic benefit on increased productivity. Part of the problem is the way police are deployed. To increase the number of trained officers in order to then allocate them to back-office or administrative duties is a poor use of their skills. A police officer costs some £54,400 including on costs compared to a police staff member at £32,000. Party political rows over whether greater use of the private sector should be made by police forces is about whether it is more efficient to use private sector suppliers for back office support so trained police officers can focus on frontline duties or whether the idea of private sector involvement in any form of police work is itself anathema.

With staffing representing 80% of policing costs it was inevitable that the focus of savings from 2010 onwards would be on numbers. Former Metropolitan Police Commissioner Lord Blair wrote in May 2012:

> Politicians of all parties have used the numbers of officers as a convenient shorthand to the public for increased spending on the police. Chief officers have been unable to break out of that position as budget increases depended upon employing more officers...Now however the coalition has inadvertently broken the consensus that created that stranglehold. Reluctantly and quietly ministers have

acknowledged that they can see no way to mask the service for 20% cuts and keep officer numbers at the same level.[22]

An auditors' report complained in 2010, 16 years after Ken Clarke's reforms were launched and when the decade of public sector investment was drawing to an end, that it was still difficult to audit value for money in the police stating: 'While funding has increased the scrutiny and challenge of spending has so far been poor. Public debate and political interest has focused more on increasing police officer numbers, with a simple equation that more is better...There is no evidence that high spending is delivering improved productivity'.[23]

The Flanagan report on the police in 2008 had been similarly critical of the numbers game noting: 'The debate about policing has often had too great a focus on inputs, such as the growth of police officer and PCSO (Police Community Support Officers) numbers, rather than a focus upon what those staff are actually doing and what outcomes they are supporting through their work'.[24] A Home Office select committee report similarly noted that 'there is no simple relationship between number of police officers and levels of crime...the reduction in the police workforce need not inevitably lead to a rise in crime'.[25]

The national media and politicians often regard police numbers as an indication of whether they are doing their job. In practice the size of a force has little bearing on its efficiency. Flanagan noted in his 2008 report:

> There has been an unhelpful party political debate around police numbers which has been taken as the sole measure of police success rather than one important contribution to the truly central question of the outcomes which policing can deliver...Maintaining police numbers at their current level is not sustainable over the course of the next three years...in recent times major political parties have recognised this fact, as well as the opportunities presented by workforce reform...we would not be making the most effective use of the resources dedicated to the police if police officer numbers were sustained at their current level.[26]

He believed that workforce reform had been 'delivered piecemeal and with a lack of consistency' and that it was unnecessary for trained police to undertake work which could be accomplished by less-expensive staff while pay should reflect performance not just length of service. He added: 'The number of officers we need is a careful balance between the risks we face, and ensuring that we don't simply have officers forming large standing armies for the majority of the time, deployed only if there is a major incident of some kind'.[27]

Three years later in 2011, by which time spending cuts were underway, lawyer Tom Winsor was asked to look into police pay and conditions, and he described the system as 'a barnacle-encrusted hulk that needs to be reformed in many respects'.[28] In his study of police pay Tom Winsor noted: 'Given that such a high proportion of their budgets is spent on pay, it is striking that Chief Constables and Police Authorities do not possess some of the most important instruments of management control and intervention which are almost invariably available in other organisations in relation to their workforces'.[29]

Tom Winsor also noted that while previous police pay reviews had been prompted by low pay and discontent within the ranks his was inspired by the need not only to reduce costs but 'because police pay and conditions have developed a degree of rigidity and a distance from modern management instruments and practices. These inhibit the ability of the police service to adapt to the changing needs of the public and the demands properly made of the police'. Stating that police pay was in need of 'fundamental reform' he proposed higher pay for key frontline officers and lower for those in less demanding roles along with a review of allowances and overtime payments, saving £217m by April 2014.

The Home Office select committee questioned how his 62 report recommendations for changing terms and conditions and reducing the pay bill might be carried out without damaging police morale just a time when budget cuts and structural change were also placing additional pressures. The debate is ongoing and forms part of a wider and equally controversial discussion about the use of the private sector in routine back office policing functions. The appointment of Tom Winsor as Her Majesty's Inspector of Constabulary in 2012 gives some indication that workforce reform in the police will continue to be a high priority.

Reform case study (2): Anti-social behaviour

With the increasing complexity of criminal behaviour to manage the police might be forgiven for regarding low-level crime as further down their list of priorities. But for the public and the media and hence politicians, anti-social behaviour – vandalism, street drunkenness, graffiti, pickpocketing, begging, teenage 'yobbishness' – is a high priority, indeed a measure of whether the police are in command of the streets. It was New York Mayor Rudy Giuliani who in his tenure, 1994–2001, developed the concept of 'zero tolerance', the idea that low-level crime leads to major crime and that preventing the former will help stop the latter from developing. In the United Kingdom the public and politicians soon became equally enthused by the idea and the police, who were and still are often criticised in the media for ignoring low-level crime, came under pressure to take it more seriously.

Tony Blair understood the public's concern. In his memoirs he recalled: 'Out and about around the country [ASB] was what people talked about. I felt it was a classic challenge of the modern world and our system had to be modernised to meet it'. But he also felt he did not win the argument 'in the way the argument was won about choice in health, or academies. But sometime or other a government will have to relearn the lesson'.[30]

In 2002 some 16,000 police community support officers were hired to patrol alongside police officers while Neighbourhood Policing teams were set up in 2005 to roll out neighbourhood policing in England and Wales and by 2008 there were 3,600 teams in the 43 forces. In his 2008 report Sir Ronnie Flanagan praised the initiative:

> Policing is not simply the preserve of the police. Modern policing is carried out in partnership with a wide range of local agencies, from councils to primary care trusts to schools. The success of Neighbourhood Policing demonstrates how productive this approach can be in building trust and confidence and combating so-called 'low level' crimes that can blight people's lives and causes significant harm'.[31]

But the Home Affairs select committee was still critical, noting: 'Public expectations of the police are not being met. The public want the police to be more active in dealing with minor crime and anti-social behaviour'.[32]

The HMIC comments that 'visibility of policing is a key issue' every time it talks to the public. Its survey of five forces found an inconsistent approach to ensuring that police were on duty when most needed, notably in the evenings when ASB was high, adding: 'This is despite increases in investment and a commitment to neighbourhood policing teams...and very clear evidence that for the public anti-social behaviour is important'.

Its survey found there were actually fewer police available on busy Friday nights than on quiet Monday mornings. Its further analysis showed that out of 143,835 officers in England and Wales just over 3.5% were on response duty on a typical weekday morning. It concluded:

'The fact is that general availability, in which we include neighbourhood policing and response, is relatively low. Several factors have combined to produce this "thin blue line" of which shift patterns, risk management, bureaucracy and specialisation are the most significant'.[33]

There will always be a conflict of priorities between dealing with high-level or low-level crime but the police must accept that preventing anti-social behaviour will also always be a priority for the public. Equally if the public want more visible policing they must be prepared to accept a greater role for non-uniformed, and if necessary private sector, staff in the back office to release trained police officers for the frontline.

Reform case study (3): Police productivity

The public spending downturn has focused police chiefs on their need to drive efficiencies while being expected to reduce crime, tackle terrorism and maintain public confidence. As the inspectorates noted in their July 2010 report on efficiency which claimed the police in England and Wales could save £1 billion: 'Forces need leaders who can drive the organisational changes needed to make savings from a transformational approach . . . Leadership is essential to delivering transformational change'. Yet it noted that less than a third of chief constables 'identify leadership skills as important in achieving savings' which is 'a barrier to forces meeting the challenge of getting better value for money'.[34]

The inspectorates' report outlined how the police could save £1 billion. It claims £90m can come from better management of staffing rotas and overtime, £20m from reducing management posts, £270m from 'changing the workforce mix', £100m in better procurement, and further savings by increasing the productivity and procurement levels of forces to that of the best performing forces.

But productivity is not easy to measure in the police force. The HMIC says that 'police productivity has never had an agreed definition: some focus on activities and products. A more persuasive interpretation would be to focus on fewer victims and reduced crime'. This, it adds, bears an 'uncanny resemblance' to police founder Sir Robert Peel's first instruction in 1829 that 'the absence of crime will be considered the best proof of the complete efficiency of the police'.[35] Furthermore some crimes are linked to socio-economic issues over which the police have little influence.

Attempts to monitor police efficiency and productivity through national inspection and performance targets have had mixed success although or perhaps because, as with so much of the public sector, Labour under Blair created a complex centrally driven, target-focussed regime.

For example, the Policing Performance and Assessment Framework was launched in 2004 and continued until 2008 with rankings from each force on how they tackled crime and how satisfied the public was, with gradings from 'excellent' to 'poor' such as existed then in local government. Flanagan noted:

> PPAF was a great leap forward because it was based on robust comparative data and the domains largely reflected where most effort was directed, with the exception of Protective Services. It did bring significant benefits and was an important part of the process of focusing on the outcomes policing should be delivering and the ways in which performance can be improved.[36]

Against this was criticism that it was too rigid, did not take into account local conditions and created perverse incentives. In 2006 the Home Office announced it was replacing PPAF with a new system of performance assessment, the Assessment (later renamed Analysis) of Policing and Community Safety (APACS) which took a wider look at the role of other public agencies in policing.

In contrast the Home Office select committee in 2008 heard evidence that Home Office indicators caused perverse incentives. One example of the absurdity of targets was one called 'offences brought to justice' which made no allowance for the nature of the crime, whether murder, taking weeks to solve, or a formal warning for cannabis possession which took 20 minutes. In 2005 the police were set a target of contributing towards bringing 1.25 million 'offences to justice' each year by 2007/8. Of the 1,447 offences brought to justice in the year ending March 2008, 7.1% were warnings for cannabis possession. The targets were causing trivial offences to be brought to court because they added to the total and sensibly were later adjusted to include only serious offences.

The Home Office select committee said: 'The current system of measuring police performance has distorted operational priorities, criminalised many individuals for trivial misdemeanours, and prevented forces from focusing on what is important locally'.[37]

The Flanagan report was also critical of the performance regime. He called Activity Based Costing which aimed to link input costs to output but which was unduly bureaucratic 'a costly exercise'. Forces also had to submit efficiency plans to the Home Office which were monitored to see if they included real savings and met agreed targets. Flanagan said they created 'a wasteful bureaucracy' and concluded:

Centrally derived targets have generally been found by forces to be extensive and onerous. While crime has gone down, public confidence has only marginally improved. ACPO [the Association of Chief Police Officers] regard top-down direction as inefficient, creating anomalies and disincentives. Their view is that properly scrutinised localism with much fewer national priorities would improve matters. The national media tend to characterise policing issues and crime as being within the gift of solely national solutions, thereby escalating problems to the door of government.[38]

The monitoring regime also created its own bureaucracy. In 2009 alone 2,600 pages of guidance were issued to officers setting out how their work should be done while there were 100 processes in the criminal justice system requiring 40 interventions by police, staff and specialists at an estimated cost of £2.2 billion a year. It found that in a burglary case from the point of reporting through to court appearance, 30 different people were involved in the process while a randomly chosen case of common assault took 242 days to pass through the system generating five copies of case papers across three IT systems. The effect was to draw police away from community policing, the visible face of their work, into bureaucracy.[39]

A joint Home Office/inspectorates' value for money report in 2010 claimed that its efficiency programme QUEST had delivered 'impressive results' including £1.6m in productivity gains caused by less time spent solving crimes and £1.37m in reduced incident desk queuing. But these figures are difficult to quantify. Equally difficult to quantify are the savings expected from the Coalition's abolition of the National Policing Improvement Agency.

The study noted that 60% of the police workforce was based in seven functions, namely response, neighbourhoods, CID, control rooms, criminal justice units, intelligence and traffic and that therefore forces 'must focus on these biggest functions as a central part of their work to increase productivity'.[40] It added: 'Ministers are clear that efforts to save money in order to balance budgets must not come at the expense of a reduced level of service to the public … police authorities and forces in England and Wales must meet both challenges; they must balance budgets and sustain delivery'.[41]

The report used the language of public sector reform in calling for business process improvement, better procurement, more efficient deployment of police, a cut in back office costs, a reduction in overtime payments and more frontline productivity and it set the tone for future reform when it insisted that 'there must not be a reduction in either the level or the quality of the service the public receives; indeed both must rise'.[42]

Reform case study (4): Reducing back office costs

A particular weakness, by no means unique to the police, is IT procurement, exacerbated by having 43 different police forces. The 2008 Flanagan report criticised the structure saying that Airwave, the national police communications system, 'is an example of an initiative that demonstrated service wide benefit but was met with considerable resistance. The lack of ability to compel forces to adopt this new technology meant it took almost 10 years to implement a project which is now demonstrating real benefits'.[43]

MPs in 2011 described police IT as 'not fit for purpose to the detriment of the police's ability to fulfill their basic mission of preventing crime and disorder' and said the Home Office should make 'revolutionising police IT a top priority', especially following the abolition of the National Policing Improvement Agency which was responsible for police IT. A new police IT company owned by the police and crime commissioners aims to fill the gap. MPs were also sceptical that the Home Office, inheriting the NPIA's non-IT procurement services, would be any better at squeezing out better deals as 'central government does not have an encouraging record on achieving efficient and effective procurement'.[44]

But whereas in local government and to a lesser extent in the NHS, private sector involvement in back office service delivery is acceptable it continues to remain controversial in policing. Indicative of this was the exploratory work between West Midlands and Surrey police forces and private sector partners in 2011/12. Opponents, notably the unions, argued that this was opening the door to privatising the police while supporters maintained it was about making the back office more efficient, just as in the rest of the public sector, in order to target resources on frontline policing. Former Metropolitan Police Commissioner Lord (Ian) Blair took to the media to complain at the way the debate revolved around the sterile private v public argument, writing: 'The police service is grasping that private sector companies can deliver routine functions at a much lower price and higher standard than individual forces can'.[45]

West Midlands Chief Constable Chris Sims told a sceptical Home Affairs Committee that the forces had spent a year researching into how the public sector used private suppliers and that their aim was to have access to the best technology in order to make their operations more effective. There was certainly private sector interest since the forces had received 264 responses to their OJEU procurement notice. He added: 'At the end of the day we may transform the service that the public of the West Midlands and Surrey get'. Surrey Chief Constable Lynne Owens told the MPs:

> At the moment, the police service has huge quantities of technology, but it isn't quality technology. If you report a crime as a victim and you want to track your crime through the process, in the same way you could a parcel, you can't do that through either of the computer systems that the force currently uses. For the frontline officer on a Friday and Saturday night, we both have officers who witness an incident and make an arrest. They then have to go and seize CCTV, they have to bring it back to the police station, they have to log it in, they have to view it, they have to draw evidence from it and only then can they question offenders.[46]

But hostility to the proposals forced the police forces to put the idea on hold although both had drawn up a shortlist of six providers. In November 2012 the newly elected West Midlands police and crime commissioner postponed the plans.

Conclusion

The police, while part of the public sector, until the 1990s escaped many of the reform pressures facing other areas because of their unique responsibilities in fighting crime and the unique demands on police officers. However, as investment poured into police forces from 2001 onwards governments in return called for greater productivity, higher performance, more professional management and greater workforce flexibility. But target-based performance regimes proved bureaucratic and counter-productive.

The police have also had to respond to public pressures for more visible customer-focused frontline services, particularly in tackling low-level crime. The expansion of community support officers has enabled trained police to focus on dealing with higher-level crime while ensuring neighbourhood level presence and there are attempts to outsource more back office functions to the private sector. The Coalition embarked on structural reform to create greater accountability to the public by abolishing police authorities and creating directly elected police and crime commissioners. The appointment of the author of a controversial report into policy pay and productivity as the head of the HMIC signals that police reform continues to be high on the government's agenda.

12
Welfare

Welfare is a hugely complex system which successive governments since the 1980s have reformed with mixed results in reducing long-term dependency and with little impact on rising costs. Welfare spend makes up over a quarter of all government spending, allocated through the Department for Work and Pensions, whose goal is both to financially support those who are unable to work through unemployment or illness and to ensure that they return to employment as soon as possible.

Between 1996/97 and 2010 spending on welfare increased by 40% in real terms despite a strong economy throughout most of this period, while in 2010 the Treasury stated that 1.3m people had been on out-of-work benefits for nine out of the previous ten years.[1] In 2012, £84 billion was spent on working age benefits, one pound in eight of public spending, including £10 billion on disability allowance.[2] The NAO noted in 2012 that 'welfare to work schemes in the UK have a history of inherent risk and limited success'.[3]

A major reason for the mixed record of reform is welfare's interaction with so many other aspects of socio-economic policy. Governments can change benefits and introduce new initiatives but have less control in the short-term over social issues. The level of unemployment reflects the state of the economy so the number of claimants rises and falls accordingly. In addition other benefit recipients such as single parents or those with longer-term medical conditions may find it difficult to work even when the economy is strong. A different, though often interconnected, group of claimants are those with low skills for whom work is either not available or not attractive because of its low pay or whose lifestyles are not conducive to the responsibilities of employment. Attempts to help such 'inactive' benefit recipients are entwined with education and social policy reform.

The fiscal downturn and change of government in 2010 has led to a radical rethink of the entire benefits system with the aim of more aggressively encouraging claimants back to work and reducing benefit costs. Opponents of radical welfare reform argue that while it is about reducing costs and improving the efficiency of delivery it is less about enhancing the service to customers, the recipients, and more about ensuring they cease to be customers altogether. Advocates of reform maintain that on the contrary they are striving to improve the service to the user just as reform elsewhere in the public sector aims to achieve. For their argument is that the current welfare system has let down users by being too complex to those who deserve it while locking others into benefit dependency, removing incentives to return to work and condemning them to a lifestyle of low self-esteem, poverty and ill health. Advocates of radical reform point out that families who are long-term recipients of benefit invariably crop up as clients in other parts of the public sector, notably social services, police and criminal justice. Reduce dependency on benefits, say the advocates of major reform, and savings will be made not just in lower welfare costs but also in other parts of the public sector as well as improved lifestyles for those who have returned to a life of employment.

What is not disputed is that the cost of providing benefits from housing and council tax to unemployment and disability allowances has soared in the last decade despite rising overall prosperity for most of that period. In 2010/11 the DWP, created in 2001, paid out half of its £151.3 billion spend involving 27 benefits to 20 million people (the other half being pensions). The amount paid to local authorities for housing and council tax benefit was also up over that period by £4.4bn to £25.8bn.[4] Most benefits are either contributory (payable to those who have paid sufficient National Insurance), non-contributory (payable to those in need such as carers or the disabled) and means-tested such as housing benefit and income support. One reason for the rise in costs is because the benefits system through housing and council tax benefit has become a top-up for low wages as better-paid industrial jobs have declined in favour of poorer paid service employment. Another cause of the rise is the sharp increase in house prices from the 1990s alongside a slowdown in new social and affordable housing leading to rising rents and hence rising housing benefits. The right-to-buy programme launched under Thatcher also reduced the amount of social housing stock held by local authorities. A third reason is that the rise reflects a minority of long-term claimants for whom welfare has become their only source of income, either through lack of incentive to work or lack of skills or both. A fourth is that the benefits system has become a means of lifting families out of poverty rather than merely providing a safety net. The NAO sums up the work of the DWP as aiming 'to relieve poverty by helping people find work, provide assistance during sickness and disability, and help people to support their children and plan for retirement'.[5] Critics of government efforts to reduce the welfare bill point out that this is dealing with the symptoms rather than the causes such as the lack of affordable housing and the escalation in house prices. Furthermore, benefits are invariably spent in the locality in which the recipients reside. Reducing benefits therefore further depresses local economies already suffering from deprivation.

Governments of all political hues have attempted to reduce the ballooning welfare budget with little success. Yet the original concept of the welfare state as outlined in the Beveridge Report in 1942 and developed during the 1940s envisaged it both as a safety net, a means to provide temporary income support for those who through no fault of their own were out of work, and a way of helping them back into employment. Beveridge proposed the introduction of national insurance and assistance and family allowances while stressing the importance of full employment. His report also warned that the long-term unemployed 'should be required, as a condition of continued benefit to attend a work or training centre, such attendance being designed as a means of preventing habituation to idleness and as a means of improving capacity for earnings'. As one welfare adviser to the Labour government wrote in 2007: 'Even in 1942, it was understood that it was not enough just to provide a safety net – the welfare state also had to support people back into work in an active labour market policy. The balance between active and passive policies has ebbed and flowed over the intervening sixty years'.[6] Most of the Beveridge proposals were introduced under the 1945–51 Labour government and over the following four decades were refined and changed.[7]

As the welfare state developed and its costs expanded inevitably there was media and political focus on the minority of families for whom dependency on benefits replaced employment altogether and often continued through successive generations. They were dubbed 'welfare scroungers' by the media and by the 1980s Margaret Thatcher had concluded there was some truth to this accusation and that the system itself was at fault. She later wrote: 'We were feeling our way towards a new ethos for welfare policy: one comprising the discouragement of state dependency and the encouragement of self-reliance; greater use of voluntary bodies including religious and charitable organisations ... and most controversially, built-in incentives towards decent and responsible behaviour'.[8]

It was apparent that those most likely to be on long-term benefits also had other personal and social problems, in particular low skills and poor educational achievement but also drug and alcohol addiction and criminal behaviour. The link between rising welfare costs, long-term benefit dependency and broken families was becoming clearer although Thatcher herself recalled there was an 'attitude that it was not for the state to make moral distinctions in its social policy. Indeed when I raised such points I was sometimes amused to detect ill-concealed expressions of disapproval on the faces of civil servants'.[9]

The key question was how the long-term unemployed could be helped back into work. Blair notably in his first term ordered his ministers to 'think the unthinkable' when it came to finding ways of reforming the complex web of welfare programmes and encouraging the unemployed back to work but backed away from radical reform after opposition from within his own party. In the following decade a booming economy leading to lower unemployment reduced the incentive to radically restructure welfare policy although there were successive initiatives aimed at reducing joblessness. One further contribution to 'thinking the unthinkable' was a study commissioned by the DWP into the welfare to work programmes by former businessman David Freud who advocated a more personalised, pro-active approach to encouraging claimants back into work supported by a greater private sector role. In his 2007 report Freud noted that while unemployment rates were low in the United Kingdom compared to other OECD countries there were 3.1m claimants who had been on benefits longer than a year of whom 95% were on 'inactive' benefits such as incapacity and income support. He concluded: 'The Government has tackled an inheritance of long-term dependency on unemployment benefits, but much more remains to be done on long-term dependence overall'. To meet the government's aim of 80% employment, the number of benefit claimants would have to reduce by 1.3m. Welfare policy would need to target all claimants with the aim of getting them into work including single-parent families, older people and those on incapacity benefit as well as almost half of those who had been unemployed for more than a year. He also recommended that the private and voluntary sectors should have a greater role in helping claimants back into employment and keeping them there with 'prime' contractors taking a lead role in each region. A further proposal was to create a single benefits system to reduce complexity and waste. Interestingly, considering many of these ideas were to be implemented by the Coalition government from 2011 in a year, he estimated it would take up to eight years for the recommendations to be rolled out. Freud called his ideas 'a major step forward in welfare reform' which aimed to reduce by 40% 'those trapped at the bottom of society' but most of his proposals were sidelined by the government.[10]

Brown's Chancellor Alistair Darling later admitted in 2011: 'We could have gone further in reforming the benefits system, particularly on disability and housing benefit. These were put in place, with the best of intentions, often many decades ago and have not been adapted to the circumstances of today. We made significant reforms but more were needed'.[11]

In 2011/12 the government's welfare bill amounted to £3,324 for every man, woman and child in Britain and 30 million people are recipients of some kind of benefit. Of the total some £12.2 billion went on child benefit, £5.1 billion on unemployment benefit, £31 billion on the sick and disabled and £41.8 billion on support for people on low incomes.[12] Social security as a percentage of total government spending was about 15% after the Second World War and about 27% in 2008/9.[13]

The benefits system also became hugely complex and as a result prone to fraud, inefficiency, error and waste through overpayments. In 2005 the NAO produced a study specifically on its complexity, noting that the Department for Work and Pensions administered 40 different benefits, allowances and grants, 'an accumulation of years of legislative change'. Between 2000 and 2004 there were six new Acts and 364 statutory instruments affecting the law on social security. There were 24 files of guidance on Jobseeker's Allowance alone and 14 volumes for Income Support. But while advocating simplification on the grounds of efficiency the NAO also warned that 'radical reform is a rare, costly, time-consuming, and potentially controversial act. Even when such reform is agreed, the process from consultation through to changes in primary legislation may take several years'.[14]

Increasingly, politicians and social commentators were taking the view that the answer to reducing welfare dependency was not only financial and that the home environment was also a major factor. There were in effect two sides to welfare reform. One was refining the system, simplifying the varying layers of benefits to enable they were taken up by those who needed them, especially the disabled and sick, while also ensuring a more personalised and pro-active focus on encouraging the jobless back into work. The other, far more challenging and long-term, was intervention in the lifestyles of families for whom benefit dependency was a way of life, with the aim of getting them off the taxpayer's books and back into employment.

The fiscal crash in 2008 leading to the crisis in public finances and a long-term cut in public spending refocused ministers' attention on how to achieve such aims while cutting welfare costs. The deteriorating economy also pushed up the number of jobless making the task of reducing the welfare bill more challenging while also making welfare reform as a result an even greater priority for the Treasury.

The new Coalition in 2010 announced its intentions both to simplify and reform the benefits system and tackle the dysfunctional families for whom welfare dependency was a way of life while sharply reducing costs. The June 2010 emergency Budget announced £11bn of welfare reform savings to be rolled out by 2014/15. The 2010 Spending Review promised optimistically that welfare costs would fall over the next four years and that included within this would be steps 'to tackle the culture of welfare dependency engendered by the current benefits system'.[15]

Reform case study (1): Universal Credit and the Work Programme

In response a series of changes was introduced to the welfare system. A White Paper on welfare reform including the creation of a single system for working-age benefits and tax credits called Universal Credit (UC) was introduced in late 2010 and subsequently formed part of the Welfare Reform Act 2012. The principle of UC is that it applies equally to those in work and out of work and therefore eases the transfer from one benefit to the other previously handled by different agencies. Some 7 million people on benefits worth £57 billion are expected to be affected by the new system, phased in between 2013 and 2017. It takes the place of Jobseeker's Allowance, Employment Support Allowance, housing benefit, working tax credit and child tax credit. Work and pensions Secretary of State Iain Duncan Smith described UC as 'the most radical redesign of the benefits system this country has ever seen' and the DWP said it aimed to 'secure a welfare state for the 21st century'.[16]

Other changes were more immediately controversial. In April 2011 a programme to reassess all Incapacity Benefit recipients was launched with the aim of moving them either on to one of the unemployment allowances or off benefits altogether. Changes to child benefit were also announced, phasing it out for higher earners. A cap was introduced on the amount of housing benefit that could be claimed with a maximum of up to £400 a week for a four-bedroom property, a change which espe-cially hit housing benefit recipients in central London where rents were far higher. Advocates of the cap said it was deeply unfair that welfare recipients could live in expensive housing funded by the taxpayer which those paying the taxes could not afford. Opponents said it was 'social cleansing' forcing families out of their homes and schools into cheaper areas.

The government also announced cuts to council tax benefit for 5.9 million recipients across Britain by devolving responsibility for allo-cating it to local government and building into its forecasts a reduction of 10% from spring 2013. Councils estimated the actual cuts to be more in the region of 15% to 20% with local authorities either having to make up the shortfall or devote more resources to collecting council tax.

In June 2011 the government launched its most radical and contro-versial reform, the Work Programme (WP), replacing all existing welfare to work initiatives in England, Scotland and Wales such as Flexible New Deal, Employment Zones and Pathways to Work. Introduced in just a year, compared to the average four years for other welfare to work schemes, it aimed to encourage the unemployed on Jobseeker's Allowance or Employment Support Allowance back to work with the help of private sector suppliers or 'prime providers' who were remuner-ated on a payments by results basis partly funded by projected savings on benefits. Providers would be paid 'outcome fees' of £1,000 to £3,500 for every person placed into sustained employment defined as either three months or six months depending on the person's category with further payments if the person continues in work. The WP's contract value over five years was worth £3bn-£5bn, aimed to process 3.5m claimants and initially used 18 prime contractors including 15 private, one public and one third sector across 40 contracts. The WP's goal was to achieve what had eluded previous governments, namely to increase the rate of return to work of those on its books to 36% compared with previous schemes such as Flexible New Deal at 25%, reduce the time spent on benefits and narrow the gap in re-employment rates between the easier and harder to help claimants. The DWP ambitiously estimated it would save £1.95 in 'social benefits' for every £1 spent, the result of increased employment, reduced crime and improved health.

The WP was an example of Whitehall moving, unusually, at breakneck speed to introduce a highly ambitious and innovative reform. Ministers told the DWP to implement the programme in a year, by June 2011 without any pilots, while previous welfare to work schemes had taken four years. The initial invitation to tender was published in December

2010 six months before the programme went live in June 2011. In comparison the DWP took 15 months to deliver the procurement of phase one of the Flexible New Deal.

Many of the WP proposals drew on the 2007 Freud Report, perhaps unsurprisingly since its author David Freud joined the Conservatives in February 2009, became a peer and then DWP minister in charge of welfare reform in 2010. But his 2007 report had envisaged a timetable of six years for rolling out a new system of provider contracts compared to the WP's timescale of 12 months. The NAO said that 'launching an innovative scheme to a very challenging timetable was a significant administrative achievement' and that the DWP used 'a streamlined approach to project management which meant that benefits from the WP will be realised earlier'.[17]

The downside to such speed was that weaknesses in the system would only be discovered after implementation as indeed the NAO warned in a report in early 2012. It expressed concern that the WP's original assumptions were optimistic with a forecast of 35% of referrals to providers being found work at a time when unemployment was rising. The DWP worked out the pricing mechanism for providers based on the likely return to work rate of participants including those who would have found work without the help of providers. But an analysis of the largest group of participants in the WP and the one most likely to find work estimated that their estimated back-to-work rate was more like 26%, while the DWP was assuming 40%. The state of the economy was also a risk factor, since original estimates had been based on economic growth projections based on 2002 to 2008 figures. There was a threat that if the assumptions were too optimistic then providers would find it too difficult to make a return and walk away. The NAO also maintained that insufficient analysis of previous welfare to work schemes had been undertaken and that some of their providers who had contracts terminated early had to be paid off (the NAO's unaudited estimate was this had cost £63m by early 2012).[18]

The first opportunity to analyse progression came with the analysis of the first year's results to July 2012 by the DWP and the NAO by which time the WP had cost £378 million in fees. These showed that of the 878,000 people who joined the WP, just 31,000 found a job that lasted for six months or more – 3.5% of the total instead of the government's target of 5.5%. The NAO however said that while the figures were below expectations it was too early to conclude they would never be met.[19]

Critics of the Coalition's welfare to reform initiatives argue that while their aims have merit in reducing complexity the timing is wrong.

To achieve their goals the reforms require two key elements, namely funding to ensure a smooth transition to the new system and a strong jobs market. Neither of these were present when UC and the WP were introduced. Furthermore, the reforms were brought in from 2013 onwards at breakneck speed with IT systems still unproven. For once Whitehall could not be accused of inertia yet because the welfare system directly affects millions of claimants any failings in the reforms present a huge risk in terms of human misery and political fallout.

Reform case study (2): Troubled families

Welfare reform is driven by two imperatives; the need to reduce costs and a view that it is morally wrong for one part of society to be abandoned to a lifestyle of benefit dependency at the taxpayers' expense in contrast to the Beveridge principle of welfare as a temporary safety net. Central to the latter is a sense that a hard core of welfare recipients is incapable of participating in society through work and that the system actively encourages them to remain dependent.

The approach was summed up by Prime Minister David Cameron when he set out views on further long-term welfare reform beyond the 2015 general election. In a speech in June 2012 he stated: 'The reform of welfare isn't some technocratic issue. It's not about high-level accounting to get the books in order. It's about the kind of country we want to be – who we back, who we reward, what we expect of people, the kind of signals we send to the next generation'.

Mr Cameron argued that the welfare system encouraged irresponsible lifestyles when he added:

> There are more than 150,000 people who have been claiming Income Support for over a year who have three or more children and 57,000 who have four or more children . . . quite simply we have been encouraging working-age people to have children and not work, when we should be enabling working-age people to work and have children. So it's time we asked some serious questions about the signals we send out through the benefits system.[20]

Cameron was not the first prime minister to make moral judgements about welfare recipients. In his memoirs Tony Blair noted: 'The right-wing phrase "the underclass" was ugly but it was accurate. These people at the bottom didn't have dysfunctional working lives. They had dysfunctional lives full stop'.[21] His government's view was that tackling the roots of family breakdown, namely poverty, would break the cycle of long-term deprivation. Under Labour considerable investment was poured into programmes to meet its ambition to eradicate child poverty by 2020, child poverty being defined as household income on 60% or below median income. There were sound financial as well as moral reasons for doing so; the consequences of poverty in terms of ill health, unemployment and criminal activity is estimated at £10bn to £20bn a year.[22]

A key part of Labour's welfare reforms was the introduction of tax credits from 1999 for low-income families – later to become working tax credit and child tax credit – to make work financially worthwhile and reduce child poverty. There was also support for parents through New Deal programmes and Sure Start for under-fives in deprived areas. But it became increasingly clear that the 2020 target would not be met without huge further spending which from 2009 onwards was no longer feasible. Furthermore as household incomes increased during the decade of prosperity so did the median income against which the government was measuring poverty. One expert described trying to meet the target as like 'walking up a descending escalator'. Nonetheless the targets were enshrined in the 2010 Child Poverty Act. Between 1999 and 2010, £134 billion was redistributed to families through tax credits alongside an increased emphasis on work being the prime route out of poverty. But the overall reduction in child poverty was disappointing, from 3.8m down to 2.8m in ten years. The percentage of children in poverty in 1998/99 was 34%, falling to 28% in 2004/5 before rising again to 31% in 2007/8 and falling to 30% in 2008/9.[23]

In 2010 Frank Field, the former Labour welfare minister whom Blair had once asked to 'think the unthinkable' about reform, was asked by the Coalition to chair a study into child poverty. Field's view was that tackling the roots of family poverty would in the long-term lead to savings in welfare in adulthood. His report in December 2010 also argued that financial poverty alone was not the only reason why so many children had poor chances in life with the home environment and parental skills being particularly strong influences. He wrote: 'While welcoming the Government's continued determination to counter child poverty, I believed that the results of this strategy were more modest than taxpayers hoped for, especially considering the huge sums invested in the approach. More worrying still, the stubbornly obstinate number of children in poverty showed that this strategy had stalled even before the recession'.

He believed that poor parenting and selfish parents focused on their own lives rather than their children's were as much to blame. He recommended that spending should be targeted at early years with affordable childcare from age two, local authorities should be able to access data from the DWP to identify families most in need (subsequently carried out in 2012) and parenting and life skills should be included in the school curriculum.[24]

Similar observations were made by the Centre for Social Justice, the think-tank set up by former Conservative leader Iain Duncan Smith, who was made work and pensions secretary in 2010 and steered the Welfare Reform Bill through Parliament. The CSJ said that the main drivers of poverty were not just financial but also 'family breakdown, educational failure, economic dependency and worklessness, addiction and serious personal debt' and recommended that these also become indicators along with income levels. It also noted: 'A son with a workless father is likely to experience between 8–11% more time out of work themselves between the ages of 16 and 23 . . . the number of households where no one has worked has doubled since 1997'.[25]

A separate study headed by a Labour MP which reported to the prime minister in July 2011 recommended a culture change in attitudes to spending, arguing that money spent on early intervention with troubled families and children would save millions in later costs. Recommending the expansion of a social finance market and incentives to invest in outcomes-based projects, it concluded: 'The provision of successful evidence-based Early Intervention programmes remains persistently patchy and dogged by institutional and financial obstacles. In consequence, there remains an overwhelming bias in favour of existing policies of late intervention at a time when social problems are well-entrenched – even though these policies are known to be expensive and of limited success'.[26]

But it was the riots in August 2011 that prompted the Coalition to come to the same conclusion as Tony Blair, that a minority of dysfunctional families was costing the taxpayer a fortune through the welfare, social services and criminal justice systems and that these families needed targeted action to reduce their burden on the state. Over the years varied terminology has been used by social commentators to describe these families all of whom are known to social services and often the police. They are the 'underclass' or 'families with multiple needs' or 'vulnerable families' or 'families with chaotic lifestyles' or 'priority families' or simply 'problem families'. Coalition ministers decided to call them 'troubled families' and identified 120,000 of them costing the taxpayer £75,000 each or £9 billion a year, mostly in multi-agency intervention. In December 2011 it set up the Troubled Families Unit based at the Department of Communities and Local Government under Louise Casey, former head of the Anti-Social Behaviour Unit at the Home Office when Blair was prime minister.

With a budget of £448m over three years drawn from seven government departments including the DWP, the new Troubled Families Unit operated through the 150 'upper tier' English local authorities (those with education and social service responsibilities). Through a payment by results model the unit pledged to remunerate councils up to £4,000 per family if they met certain criteria in helping turn round the troubled families in the area. These were described in DCLG guidance as households involved in crime and anti-social behaviour, children not attending school and with an adult on out of work benefits. Councils had to identify a third of such families in their area in 2012/13 and the remainder in 2013/14. Payment was outcomes-based and delivered if truancy, crime and worklessness targets were met. One early obstacle, namely that data protection rules meant details of adults receiving benefits even in the same household could not be given to other public sector agencies like social services, was swiftly removed. Organisers of the troubled families programme argued that long-term benefit recipients invariably had other social problems which needed to be addressed under the programme and they needed to know their details.[27]

The challenge of helping problem families is one which previous governments have taken up with mixed results. The difference with the current programme is its realisation that a multiplicity of agency interventions – criminal justice, social services, schools, housing, welfare – has so far generated huge costs and a bureaucratic apparatus of state support with little success. The troubled families programme aims to streamline such interventions through a single point of contact with a focus on those households needing practical help.

There are plenty of criticisms of the scheme. Some local authorities maintain they are already targeting these problem families and that this programme is merely the government providing a short-term fix until the general election. Others maintain that these families are too challenging to turn round and that the focus should be on those households who have run into temporary difficulties through unemployment but are receptive to help. The principal weakness of the programme is that while £448m is being allocated to help long-term problem families, millions of pounds elsewhere are being cut from housing and council tax benefit for households already struggling to make ends meet during the recession. The DWP envisages that its benefit changes will save £2.3 billion by 2015, five times the budget for the Troubled Families Programme while some two million recipients of housing benefit saw their payments reduced as a result of benefit cuts introduced from April 2013.[28]

Conclusion

Beveridge envisaged his welfare state as a temporary safety net not a permanent support for the workless or as a subsidy for low private sector wages. Welfare reform aims to return to this original concept and reduce long-term benefit dependency. Success has been mixed. The welfare system has become so complex that it is difficult for benefit recipients to move back into employment without losing income. But welfare demand continued to rise even during a strong economy and low unemployment during 2000–2010. The problem is that long-term welfare dependency is a socio-economic issue requiring joined-up responses from various Whitehall departments. Helping 'troubled families' who are welfare dependent is difficult and involves many different agencies.

But welfare represents a quarter of all public spending and governments want to reduce it even though a stagnant economy and higher unemployment creates greater demand. The Coalition's UC and WP are highly ambitious reforms, brought in quickly. If they achieve their goals of reducing welfare costs and long-term benefit dependency against the backdrop of a sluggish economy they will prove to be one of the most successful public sector reforms of the past three decades. But in the meantime thousands of families, many working, find their incomes falling because of welfare changes.

13
Education and Schools

The driver behind education reform is improving the education of the nation's children; how this is achieved becomes more contentious. Frequently incoming ministers believe that the answer lies in reforming the structure of education provision, in giving more freedom to headteachers to manage their schools as they think fit without the perceived interference of local authorities. Others regard the socio-economic educational divide as the key challenge to be addressed. Some governments believe that the obstacles to reform lie in the producer-driven interests from teacher unions to politicised governors. In May 2012 Education Secretary Michael Gove summed up 'opposition from vested interests' to his reforms as 'from those in trade unions who put adults' interests before children's, from those in local government who put protecting their power before fulfilling children's potential and from those who have acquiesced in a culture of low expectations'. His comments, whether fair or not, were by no means unusual for education ministers.[1]

Overall educational performance has increased in the past decade. In its annual report for 2010/11, Ofsted reported that 70% of state schools were delivering a good or better standard of education. Of the 5,727 schools inspected that year, 57% were delivering a good or outstanding education while 6% were judged inadequate, a slight drop over the previous year's 8%. In 2011, 69.8% of pupils taking GCSEs in England received A*–C passes. In 2008 the results were 65.3% and in 2007, 61.4%. In September 2012, Ofsted stepped up the pressure, insisting that the minimum expected performance from schools from then on would be 'good' as opposed to the previous 'satisfactory'. A new network of eight regional inspectors in England was set up in early 2013 to work with schools and colleges receiving a rating lower than 'good'.

In his annual report for 2011/12 published in November 2012, Ofsted Chief Sir Michael Wilshaw, a former headteacher, said that while overall 70% of providers were good or better 'in most assessments, a 7/10 mark might equate to "fair but could do better"'. He added: 'For an aspiring leading nation in a 21st century global economy, it has to be "not good enough; must do better"'. He maintained that strong leadership was essential, remarking:

> Most of our inspection findings are attributable to strengths and weaknesses in leadership, and leadership accounts for all the most important findings in this Annual Report. Wherever we find success, good leadership is behind it. Where we find inadequacy, questions must be asked of leadership, of governance, and of those accountable at a local and national level.

But all too often breaking the vicious cycle, the link between low educational achievement and family background, remains unachieved. For education, like health, is a highly political subject area where reform frequently arouses opposition on party political lines. Nonetheless despite at least a decade of investment in education and a focus on raising the standards of schools in poor neighbourhoods, deprivation continues to exert a powerful negative influence on educational achievement. As Ofsted noted in 2011: 'This variation in performance continues to have a significant impact on the life chances of many pupils, reinforcing inequality and reducing social mobility. Addressing this is one of the key challenges for the education system'.[2]

Yet as in the rest of the public sector this followed a decade of spending growth on education. In 2010/11, £87 billion was spent on education in the United Kingdom compared with £43 billion in 1987/88. In 2006 the United Kingdom's education spend as a percentage of GDP was 5.91% which compared favourably with the OECD average of 5.69%.[3] In 1991/92 public spending on education was 5.2% of GDP and in 2010/11, 6.2%.[4] The question for governments is how to address continuing weaknesses in under-achievement among pupils from disadvantaged backgrounds when spending will reduce. A common complaint from businesses is poor standards of education among school-leavers applying for jobs. Reform can loosely be divided into four areas, some given priority over others. The first is increasing educational attainment overall; the second, giving parents maximum choice of schools; the third, ensuring the brightest children are encouraged in order to ensure that the United Kingdom can compete internationally;

the fourth, raising the educational attainment of children from poorer backgrounds. On the surface, none appear controversial. In practice they have inspired fierce political debate not only between rival parties but often within the same government. Some factions want to concentrate on reducing the educational achievement gap between socio-economic classes and increasing the success rate of children from poor backgrounds (usually defined as those eligible for free school meals). Others believe it more important to develop the brightest children so they can compete in a global knowledge-based economy. Another group believes parental choice of schools is more important. Over the years reforms have aimed to do all of these, in order for the United Kingdom to compete in a global economy, improve educational attainment among poorer children and provide diversity of school type through more academies and free schools.

Yet there is a strand of education reform running from Thatcher through New Labour to the Coalition, each refining and adapting what has gone before, from City Technology Colleges, grant-maintained schools and local management of schools to foundation schools, academies and 'free schools' under the Coalition. Ofsted faced fierce opposition when it was launched, yet survived successive governments. Endless experiments have been attempted into breaking down the socio-economic obstacles that condemn children from deprived or troubled family backgrounds to low achievement at secondary schools. Supporters of the few grammar schools still in existence argue that they allow bright, working-class children to escape from their environment in a way that the comprehensive system, with its focus on catchment area, cannot. Opponents say it condemns those who failed 11-plus to a second-class education. Either way governments struggle with ways of improving achievement among children from deprived areas. As David Cameron said in November 2011:

> For a long time in our country there has been a scandalous acceptance of under-performing schools. It's the attitude that says some schools – and let's be frank, people normally say this about schools in the poorest areas – will always be bad. I think this is so wrong. It meekly accepts educational failure as a fact of life, and I think that is patronising nonsense.[5]

Not all initiatives survive changes of government. Mrs Thatcher considered introducing education vouchers which in her view 'would give parents a fixed, perhaps even means-tested, sum so that they could shop around in the public and private sectors of education for the school which was best for their children'.[6] Later when the Education Reform Act 1988 introduced per capita funding for schools which in her words 'meant that state money followed the child to whatever school he attended', she also knew that 'in effect we had gone as far as we could towards a "public sector voucher" '.[7]

Reform case study (1): Devolving powers to schools

Since the 1980s many politicians, Conservative, Labour and Coalition, have taken the view that schools function best when headteachers and governing bodies are independent of their local authorities which have traditionally been responsible for providing education. Supporters of more independent state schools claim that local authorities impede the ability of schools to decide their own policies and are influenced by party political considerations depending on their political control. They believe that local councils should focus on their strategic role, with responsibility for allocating places, planning supply and ensuring special needs provision. In practice, government funding for schools in England through formula grant and the dedicated schools grant has for some years been 'passported' through local authorities to schools with councils having little access to the money.

The history of education reform in the past three decades is littered with government initiatives to separate schools from local authority control, with periodic resistance not just from local authorities but often from government departments. Under the Thatcher government 1979–1990 moves towards more independent state schools had begun with the local management of schools programme and the creation of City Technology Colleges. But the first major initiative under Thatcher, grant-maintained schools, was introduced in England and Wales in the 1988 Education Reform Act. Governors of grant-maintained (GM) schools allowed to opt out of local authority control following a ballot of parents, were allowed to manage budgets, appoint staff and head-teachers, and agree admissions policy while funding came direct from the Department of Education and Science (DES) rather than through local authorities often enabling GM schools to access better financial support as a result. Thatcher thought that 'the very fact of having all the important decisions taken at the level closest to parents and teachers, not by a distant and insensitive bureaucracy, would make for better education'.[8] The new concept faced opposition not just from local government but even in the DES. Thatcher herself recalled that the DES 'hated' the phrases 'direct grant' or 'independent state schools' and kept trying to remove them from her speeches, preferring the 'bureaucratically-flavoured grant-maintained schools'.[9] And she added: 'The vested interests working against the success of GM schools were strong. The DES, reluctant to endorse a reform that did not extend central control, would have liked to impose all manner of checks and controls on their operation'.[10]

Thatcher herself, even though she was the daughter of a councillor, envisaged a slimmed-down local authority role in education 'leaving them with a monitoring and advisory role – perhaps in the long term not even that. It would been a way to ease the state still further out of education'.[11] Thirty years later the Coalition was on the way to achieving this through the hugely expanded academies programme.

Thatcher's successor, John Major, expanded the grant maintained schools programme. He called it 'a strikingly simple concept, devolving power from the centre to the schools, enabling them to make their own decisions on how to use resources and improve their performance, motivating heads and staff and giving them freedom from sometimes hostile LEAs' [Local Education Authorities]'.[12] He said there had been 'only of handful' of GM schools in 1990 when he became prime minister and he 'took huge satisfaction in seeing them grow in number – usually in the teeth of opposition from local Labour, Liberal and sometimes, even, deplorably Conservative councils' estimating that by 1997, 1,100 schools had opted for GM status.[13]

New Labour abolished GM schools in the Schools Standards and Frameworks Act 1998 although some GM schools acquired foundation status. Blair himself was not entirely convinced that it was the right decision later wondering whether he should instead have adapted 'these concepts of local self-governance to spread decentralised management across the state health and education systems but without the inequity inherent in the underfunded Tory reforms we inherited' and adding that 'in the NHS and schools... there were elements of [Tory] changes they had made that we needed to examine and learn from, not dismiss'.[14]

By 2000 the concept of academy schools was taking shape, drawing on past initiatives under the Conservatives. Blair himself recognised that they were 'based in part on the old Tory policy of independent technical colleges. However it aligned neatly with our thinking elsewhere; to give schools independence, to set them free from the local authority system of hands-on control; and to let them innovate, including in how they employed staff'.[15]

The original concept was to convert failing secondary schools with a history of under-performance, often in deprived areas, into academies managed by charitable companies with the support of private sector sponsors and directly accountable to the education department, not the local authority. In 2002/3, three academies opened, nine the year later and five in 2004/5 but the largest period of expansion under Labour occurred under Gordon Brown with 156 opening between 2007 and 2010. By August 2010 there were 203 academies, representing just over 6% of the 3,333 state-funded secondary schools in England and Wales. The proportion of pupils in academies from poor backgrounds, as recorded by the percentage of pupils eligible for free school meals, was about twice the national average.

In 2010 the NAO said that academies had a better record than schools with equivalent intakes in pupil attendance and a better rate of educational improvement. Of the 76 academies that had full Ofsted inspections by March 2010, 41 were judged as outstanding or good for overall effectiveness. Rates of exclusion were initially higher than in other schools though later fell faster. In particular the rate of ex-academy pupils entering work rose. Between 2006 and 2009 academies reduced by half the number of their pupils not going into employment, education or training. In 2008/9 nearly 43% of academy pupils went onto the sixth form in the same academy, up from 32% in 2006/7.[16] Department for Education figures issued in January 2012 showed that in 2011 for the 166 academies with results in both 2010 and 2011, the percentage of pupils achieving five or more good GCSEs including English and Maths rose from 40.6% to 46.3%, an increase of 5.7% or twice the level seen across all state schools. The average rate across all state secondary schools was 58.9%.[17]

Of the 75 academies inspected in 2010/11 by Ofsted, 40 were judged to be good or outstanding and five inadequate for overall effectiveness. The proportion of academies judged good or outstanding was similar to that of all secondary schools but the proportion of those outstanding was higher at 16 out of 75, over 20%, compared to 14% for all secondary schools.[18]

In 2011 the Public Accounts Committee also judged the programme 'a substantial success' with educational achievement (5 A*–C pass grades at GCSE) improving at a faster rate than schools with a similar intake.[19] The committee heard evidence from sponsors that the prime reasons for improvement were high-quality leadership with a strong ethos and high expectations from staff and pupils, a relentless focus on standards, a curriculum reflecting the needs and aspiration of pupils and creativity and innovation. Many pupils arrived from primary schools into academies at 11 with a reading age of nine requiring extra work in the first two years to enable them to catch up.

The Coalition government in 2010 announced plans to extend the academies programme to all schools, initially from those judged outstanding by Ofsted who were known as 'converters'. This was a major departure from Blair's original concept of academies as a means of improving poor-performing schools in deprived areas and was more akin to the Thatcher model of creating grant-maintained schools. By January 2011 there were 407 academies of which 271 were sponsored and 136 'converters'. By September 2012 there were 2,309 academies in total.

As the numbers escalate, measuring the success of the academies programme will be more challenging. Even before the programme expanded the NAO warned in 2010 that some academies faced financial problems, were owed money from sponsors and posed governance and accountability issues. It warned:

> It cannot be assumed, however, that academies' performance to date is an accurate predictor of how the model will perform when generalised over many more schools. Existing academies have been focused on improving underperformance in deprived areas, whereas the future academy population is likely to include schools with a much wider range of attainment, and operating in very different community settings.[20]

An initiative unique to the Coalition was the introduction of so-called free schools based on models developed in Sweden and the United States (where they are called Charter schools). The first 24 opened in September 2011 and a further 55 in September 2012. Although state-funded, non-profit-making, non-selective and subject to Ofsted inspection, free schools operate outside local authority control and can be set up by private groups including parents and charities to fill a local need such as lack of school places or absence of choice. There has to be local demand and a strong business case and the go-ahead has to be granted by the secretary of state.

The longer-term impact of the growth of academies and free schools will take time to evaluate. But one concern, as flagged up by the NAO, is the level required to monitor the schools' performance and governance, a concern also noted by Ofsted's Head Sir Michael Wilshaw. He told the education select committee in February 2012:

If there are going to be more academies and more independent, autonomous schools both in the primary and secondary sector...we need to think about how we are going to manage underperformance. Who is going to do it? Is it going to be the secretary of state and his officials at the centre or is it going to be another form of intermediary organisation? It seems to me that, if we do not think about this one carefully, we could have a situation where Whitehall is controlling an increasing number of independent and autonomous schools, and finding it very difficult to do so.[21]

He argued that local authorities still had an important role in monitoring academies and announced in spring 2013 a tougher Ofsted regime for checking that they did so despite complaints from councils that their role had been neutered by the opted-out academies programme.

Reform case study (2): Reducing the deprivation gap

In its annual report for 2010/11, Ofsted noted: 'There remains a strong relationship between deprivation and weaker provision and the gap in the quality of schools between socially deprived areas and more advantaged areas is a continuing concern'.

Ofsted found that the proportion of schools judged good or outstanding declines steeply as the proportion of deprived pupils at the school increases. A school serving the most deprived pupils in the country is four times more likely to be inadequate than one serving the least deprived. Of schools requiring special measures 6% were serving the least deprived areas whereas 29% were serving the most deprived.[22]

In January 2012 Department for Education data covering English state schools found that 33.9% of pupils from disadvantaged backgrounds, those on free school meals or in local authority care for at least six months, achieved five A*–C passes at GCSE including English and Maths compared to the national average of 58.2%. In 339 schools, with ten or more disadvantaged pupils, fewer than 20% of those pupils achieved five A*–C GCSE grades including English and Maths.[23]

Under-achievement by children in deprived areas is sadly not a new phenomenon and nor are efforts to address it. In its 1993 report *Access and Achievement in Urban Education*, Ofsted drew attention to the fact that while school standards were rising, the gap between the average performance and that of pupils in deprived backgrounds was growing wider. It was clear, added Ofsted, that the latter were not benefiting from education reforms. The issue was addressed in the 1997

White Paper *Excellence in Schools* which led to the creation of Education Action Zones and the Excellence in Cities programme, both supported by extra funding to focus on school improvement. The EAZs were partnerships between schools, businesses and local agencies to tackle under-achievement and actively encourage disaffected pupils to re-engage in education. The Excellence in Cities initiative (EiCs) aimed at improving poor attendance, poor behaviour and high exclusion rates among the most disaffected pupils. Ofsted found that EAZ programmes had only 'partial and mixed success' and concluded that both programmes worked best when there was already existing strong school leadership and dedicated staff and had very little effect where these attributes were missing.[24]

But the problems they were created to address refused to disappear. In May 2012, Education Secretary Michael Gove, in a speech that might have been written by a left-wing Labour politician, declared: 'More than almost any developed nation ours is a country in which your parentage dictates your progress. Those who are born poor are more likely to stay poor and those who inherit privilege are more likely to pass on privilege in England than in any comparable county'. Only 24% of disadvantaged children in the United Kingdom perform better than expected compared with 76% in Shanghai, 72% in Hong Kong and 46% in Finland and an average 31% in the OECD countries.

However, outlining his own reform agenda, the minister said that blaming socio-economic factors for low achievement by poor children was too simplistic. Good schools, he added, could make a difference pointing out there were 440 secondary schools across England where the average GCSE points score was higher for disadvantaged pupils than for all of them. The common elements for success were a focus on standards, an innovative curriculum and a 'burning sense of mission'. He added: 'Our reform programme is intended to ensure the virtues which characterise those schools are embedded across the school system. And we start with a relentless focus on overcoming disadvantarge'.[25]

Ofsted's own analysis for 2010/11 tends to support this claim; 71% of schools serving the least deprived pupils were good or outstanding, compared to only 48% of schools serving the most deprived. However, of schools serving the most deprived 7% were judged to be outstanding and most were in urban areas, showing, according to Ofsted, 'that it is possible to buck this trend'. Its own conclusion is that 'inspection and survey evidence has consistently shown that sustained and committed ambition on the part of school leaders and governors, with high levels of expectation for pupils irrespective of low prior attainment and a determination to deliver good teaching for all, are critical factors in breaking down barriers to achievement'.[26]

A new 'floor' was introduced for primary schools, defined as those having less than 60% of pupils achieving the 'basics' standard in English and Maths and fewer than the average making necessary progress between Key Stage 1 and Key Stage 2 tests. At that time there were 1,310 primaries below this floor, mostly in poorer areas with 200 converting to academy status with sponsors by autumn 2012. For secondary schools the floor in 2010/11 was 35% of pupils receiving five or more A* to C passes at GCSE including English and Maths rising to 50% in 2015. Ofsted envisages this to be a challenge as 38% of a sample of secondary schools inspected in 2010/11 were found to be below the 2015 floor standard.[27]

From April 2011 the 'pupil premium' was introduced as extra funding for pupils eligible for free school meals. A further trend in education policy has been 'federations' of schools, usually involving a high-performing school linking to one or more weaker schools. Ofsted has found behaviour and performance improving as a result in the weaker schools without any negative impact on the high-performing school.[28]

International comparisons also show the United Kingdom's social divide on education. The Commons education select committee noted that the OECD's PISA (Programme for International Student Assessment) study for 2009 showed that differences in the socio-economic background of schools in the United Kingdom accounted for 70% of performance variance between schools compared to say Finland's percentage of 30%.[29]

Supporters of the new free schools claim that they will benefit pupils from deprived areas as they have done in the United States while critics argue the opposite, that they will become the preserve of middle-class parents. The Department for Education claimed that of the first wave of free schools over a third (nine) were based in England's 20% most deprived areas and half in England's 30% most deprived areas, However, its own analysts admit these figures depend on how the areas are selected and conclude obscurely:

> This analysis suggests that, when areas of a size appropriate to school intakes are considered, there is no basis for the claim that more than half of Free Schools are in the country's least deprived areas. Only 3 of 24 schools are located in the 30 per cent least deprived Lower Super Output Areas. It is more reasonable to claim some concentration in the most deprived areas since 12 of the 24 schools are in the 30 per

cent of areas which are most deprived. Caution should be exercised, however, when arguments are based on larger areas such as Local Authority Districts, since many of these contain mixed pockets of deprivation and affluence.[30]

Separate analysis of free schools in Sweden shows that the majority were set up in urban, affluent or gentrifying areas and therefore the beneficial impact has been greater on more affluent and educated families while the impact on low educated families and immigrants 'is close to zero'. However, this analysis admits comparisons are difficult to make between the two countries because of various other factors.[31]

One cross-sector innovation which has been regarded as a success is the Sure Start Children's Centres programme first launched in 1998 as Sure Start but rolled out comprehensively as centres from 2004 under local authority management. They were described as 'intended to break the intergenerational transmission of poverty, school failure and social exclusion by enhancing the life chances for children less than four years of age growing up in disadvantaged neighbourhoods. More importantly, they were intended to do so in a manner rather different from almost any other intervention undertaken in the western world'.[32]

The centres, of which there were over 3,600 costing in 2010/11 £1 billion, provide integrated childcare and learning for children under five and their families at convenient community locations as well as family health services and are aimed particularly at poorer families who may be reluctant to engage with authorities. The programme was described by the Commons education committee in 2010 as 'an entirely new form of public services, and a new way of configuring provision for very young children and their families [which] has been brought into being and made available to all in just twelve years'. The committee called it 'one of the most ambitious Government initiatives of recent decades and its aims and principles have commanded widespread support'.[33] Council funding cuts however have raised questions over the viability of the programme in its current form.

The educational divide continues to be a concern for all public sector professionals, politicians and policy commentators. Low educational attainment features prominently in welfare, criminal justice and troubled family programmes. Schools in deprived areas are frequently acting as surrogate parents for children whose real parents have relinquished responsibility for their offspring's welfare. Looked-after children in council care consistently have below average achievement rates and are over-represented in the prison population. Many of the problems of crime, drug and alcohol abuse, family breakdown, poverty and gang violence originate from low achievement at school, lack of qualifications and low self-esteem. In an ideal public sector world resources would be entirely focused on school years, leading to long-term savings downstream. But such a strategy with its implications for upfront funding and cross-departmental sharing of budgets is too complex for public sector institutions to develop in any substantial form.

Reform case study (3): The creation of Ofsted

One of the longest-surviving inspectorates has been Ofsted, the Office for Standards in Education, which was launched under a Conservative government in 1992, expanded under New Labour and survived the move to the Coalition. Ofsted, since 2007 the Office for Standards in Education, Children's Services and Skills, first emerged under the government of Prime Minister John Major who in his memoirs recalled of its predecessor body: 'The old inspectorate lacked rigour. It was an arm of the Department of Education whereas logically a standard-setter and a standard-checker should be separate. The Audit Commission had shown in 1989 that many LEAs were failing to fulfil their obligation to monitor school performance'.[34]

Major, like Thatcher before him, had little regard for the Department of Education calling it complacent and bureaucratic and recalled:

> From the outset I wished to set up a regular and fully independent inspection of schools. The idea had few friends in the education establishment but [education secretary] Ken Clarke carried it into legislation in 1992. Under its early chief inspectors Ofsted was quite fearless in condemning low standards and opening up information long hidden from parents.[35]

Although – or perhaps because of – many in the Labour Party as well as teachers' unions were opposed to Ofsted, the inspectorate thrived in the decade under Blair from 1997 and by 2010 was overseeing childminders, children's care, children's centres, adoption and fostering agencies and even adult skills and prison learning. The public too took to the idea of being able to examine the academic performance of their local schools and to compare it against others with a similar catchment area.

Teachers' unions however complained of the bureaucracy of inspection and at the way Ofsted forced schools to focus on meeting targets and passing tests. A simplified remit for inspection of schools was outlined by the Coalition in 2010 including a drop in routine inspection of outstanding schools but it rejected calls by the education select committee to split Ofsted into two.[36] On the surface school performance has improved in the past decade. Since 1997 the percentage of pupils achieving five A*–C passes at GCSE (the figures exclude Scotland) has consistently risen, at 69.8% in 2011 up by 0.8% on 2010 and the 23rd consecutive increase. In 2008 the figure was 65.7%, in 2005 it was 55.7% and was 46.3% in 1998. However, there were increasing complaints that GCSEs had become 'too easy'.

In Ofsted's annual report for 2011/12 its head, Sir Michael Wilshaw, appointed in 2012, looked back on Ofsted's creation 20 years before. The ex-headteacher recalled:

> Ofsted replaced a system of irregular and infrequent inspections that sampled the state of the nation but did little to hold individual schools and colleges to account...Ofsted set out the first national benchmarks for standards in schools, initial teacher education and further education colleges. The first framework and inspection handbook began a culture of setting clear criteria for evaluating performance, making rigorous, evidence-based judgements and reporting without fear or favour.

In 1992, the report added, only 38% of 16-year-olds achieved five or more GCSE passes at grades A to C. In 2012, the provisional figure was over 80%, with 59% of pupils attaining grades A* to C in five subjects, including English and Mathematics.[37]

The fact that Ofsted has survived changes of government and expanded its remit while adapting to demands for less bureaucratic inspection shows its value to ministers of all political shades in driving up standards. Its challenge will be to ensure they are also met in the new academies and free schools.

Conclusion

Successive governments have attempted to create new models of school governance with more managerial and financial powers handed to schools and headteachers on the basis that they know better than local or central government. The latest incarnation are free schools along with an expanded academies programme. It is too early to say what impact these will have on educational standards. At the same time a rigorous inspection regime through Ofsted continues to monitor performance. School exam results have improved but have aroused concern that real standards have actually remained static, leading to plans to replace GCSEs altogether.

The educational deprivation divide remains a continuing concern, causing costs to other parts of the public sector such as welfare, criminal justice and family care. Despite a decade of increased funding in education and family programmes such as Surestart, lower educational attainment in deprived areas continues to be a concern.

Part IV

The Role of Performance Regimes in Public Sector Reform

14
Measuring Performance

If a performance cannot be measured it cannot be managed. A National Audit Office report states: 'Measuring Government performance is vitally important. It also enables the government itself to assess whether it is achieving its key objectives and to learn how to achieve them more effectively and at lower cost'. The NAO notes that research in the private sector showed that 'effective use of measurement frameworks can result in 10–20% better performance against investment'.[1]

For governments a prime aim of reforming public services is not only to improve their output and performance but also to ensure that the public sees and appreciates the results. Informing citizens how their services perform, whether they have improved or deteriorated, needs to be supported by robust, objective data. The public's own personal experiences may still suggest that reform has made little impact. Conversely the public may believe their local services are satisfactory when in comparison to other parts of the country they are under-performing. Users who have traditionally received low levels of service will have lower expectations than those in areas where services have been at a high level. Objective indicators of improved performance help show the public how their services are improving and how they compare and how much of the government's aims in improved outcomes are being fulfilled. Supporters of benchmarking argue this prevents 'the postcode lottery' where services vary from one part of the country to the other. But against this is the Coalition's drive for 'localism' in which logically performance may vary from area to area depending on local priorities.

A system of inspection regimes, performance indicators, benchmarking and opinion polling has therefore grown up over the past 30 years of reform to monitor performance and encourage improvement. Most of these have been government-inspired through the creation of regulatory bodies such as Ofsted in education, the Audit Commission in local government and health, HM Inspectorate of Constabulary for police and various social care bodies from the Social Services Inspectorate and Commission for Social Care Inspectorate to the Care Quality Commission. Some have been private, such as the information company Dr Foster which analyses hospital data or the opinion pollster Ipsos MORI which examines public attitudes to their services. In turn the public sector monitoring regimes have been scrutinised by the NAO and parliamentary select committees to evaluate their success in measuring performance.

The performance monitoring regime can be broken into

- targets, which are promised minimum levels of performance backed by indicators;
- league tables, which are comparisons of performance between different service providers;
- standards, usually an expected level of service which the user can expect and the provider must meet;
- benchmarking, which is an analysis of comparative performance between different providers.

Four key factors as determined by the Treasury, Cabinet Office and National Audit Office in the 2010 NAO report are regarded as vital for effective accountability and performance management namely:

- clear objectives that lay out the government's desired outcomes (their beneficial impact on society);
- measurement of how much these outcomes are down to government policy or other influences;
- information which highlights the cost of performance monitoring;
- easy to understand information on progress.

How can productivity be measured? Using the health service as an example the NAO says:

NHS productivity is measured as the ratio between the volume of resources going into the NHS (inputs) and the quantity of healthcare provided by the NHS (outputs). If inputs rise faster than outputs, then productivity goes down. Productivity is focused on the measurement of inputs and outputs that are directly in the control of the organisation that produces them, rather than the outcomes that are not wholly within their control. For instance, a hospital can control the time a patient waits for an operation, but cannot fully control their long-term health.[2]

Labour productivity is defined by the ratio of outputs to number of staff to give an idea of average output per member of staff.

A detailed study from Bristol University described measuring productivity as 'relating a volume measure of the output of an organisation or sector of the economy (goods produced and services provided) to a volume measure of the inputs used to deliver them (employees, equipment and intermediate goods and services)'. The study added: 'Much of the discussion around the measurement of productivity in public services focuses on the accurate measurement of output'.[3]

But clearly measuring public sector productivity is more complex than measuring it in the private sector. Outcomes are more important than output and users may prefer quality at the expense of productivity. Similarly whereas a private sector company wants to sell more of its products thereby increasing productivity, a public sector organisation ideally wants to reduce its take-up, for example in better preventative treatment in health to avoid hospital visits or early intervention with troubled families. Paradoxically this helps outcomes but reduces output. The Office for National Statistics also produces a productivity index in which inputs are measured so as to remove the impact of pay and price changes and focus on growth in the volume of inputs. But the NAO admits: 'Measuring productivity is difficult – in particular, adjusting for quality change is challenging – and there – has been only limited useful work in other countries. Efforts to compare productivity of NHS hospitals to other organisations are made difficult by a lack of data and directly comparable bodies'.[4]

In order to measure productivity governments collect data on the varying performance levels of public sector bodies to enable comparison. With such data they can establish a picture of high, low and average performance levels. The Treasury noted in 2009: 'Robust performance and management data can be hard to obtain across public bodies. Such data is crucial in being able to compare the performance of various organizations within the public sector and with comparing the public sector to private sector experiences...Benchmarking can enable increased innovation'.[5]

Benchmarking is an efficiency tool which can be used to make an objective assessment of capability and expose poor performance, identify where other similar providers show higher performance whose model can then be applied to average and low performers and monitor whether improvements are working. For public service users benchmarking is in the form of league table comparators, most notably the annual school examination results which enable parents to compare results school by school. Until 2010 local government was measured by a league table, the Comprehensive Performance Assessment (later the Comprehensive Area Assessment) which ranked councils as 'excellent, good, fair, weak, poor' and later by a star system.

Governments use benchmarking data to assess their own departmental capabilities. In the 2009 Budget the Operational Efficiency Programme Final Report estimated that the government could save £15 billion a year on operational spend, of which £4 billion could come from reducing back office costs. Recognising the need to have some form of comparative data on spending the OEP recommended the collection of data on back office operations – finance, human resources, IT, procurement and property – for all government departments and agencies employing more than 250 staff.

In written evidence to the Commons Communities and Local Government Select Committee in November 2011, the NAO said: 'Learning from others whether through formal benchmarking or more informal networking, can help improve performance and efficiency'. It cited the example of how the former East of England Development Agency had used the performance data of other regional agencies to achieve a 5% saving in its own back office function.[6]

Gathering and publicising information is key to the monitoring process. Treasury-led guidance on performance information noted in 2001:

> Performance information is a cornerstone of our commitment to modernise government. It provides some of the tools needed to bolster improvements in public sector performance including improving accountability, performance management, risk management and business planning. Good quality information also enables people to participate in government and exert pressure for continuous improvement. In addition to empowering citizens, this information equips managers and staff within the public service to drive improvement. Performance information is thus a catalyst for innovation, enterprise and adaptation.[7]

Performance information helps identify where policies and processes work and why and is a key part of business planning, One approach to measuring performance, outlined in the Treasury report above, is to look at the relationships between inputs, outputs and outcomes, or economy, efficiency and effectiveness. An economy measure looks at the cost of acquiring the inputs such as hospital drugs, an efficiency measure examines whether we are receiving maximum outputs for the inputs such as number of hospital patients treated and an effectiveness measure looks at whether the outputs lead to the desired outcomes such as reduced waiting lists. The 'balanced scorecard approach' originally developed in the private sector monitors both short- and long-term goals, measuring the business, financial, learning and customer perspectives.

The Number 10 Strategy Unit once noted that top-down performance management, now out of fashion,

> exerts pressure for improvement on providers of public services through measures imposed from above (usually central government). These measures typically include: the setting of challenging performance targets for service providers; regular monitoring of performance data and indicators; regulation of activities; performance inspection; and external interventions to tackle failing or underperforming providers. The pressure is intended to motivate management and staff delivering front-line services and, in some respects, to replicate the internal management structures and processes found in well-managed private sector companies.[8]

An established form of performance monitoring and benchmarking presented in a form the public can understand is the 'league tables' system, a comparison of performance between different service providers. The Department for Education also publishes annually information on the performance of pupils in schools, including Key Stage 2 for primary schools, GCSEs for state and independent schools and AS and A-levels for schools and sixth form colleges. These are used by parents to ascertain the performance of local schools and have proved popular among the public.

But the performance monitoring regime has not been without its critics. When the Conservative-led Coalition took power in May 2010 there was a concerted drive to scale back the level of inspection, abolishing the Audit Commission which had been first created by the Conservatives in 1983, the Public Service Agreements launched in 1998, Local Area Agreements and performance indicators. The Coalition instead argued that by making more government information available to the public this would enable them to be their own 'armchair auditors', able to track financial information and make comparisons between public agencies. It therefore ordered local authorities to upload onto their websites all items of spending over £500 from January 2011 and Whitehall departments to publish their own spending.

The weakness of this system is that without accompanying explanation or context the data is difficult to interpret. A Treasury report noted: 'The cost of producing performance information should be balanced against the use of the information and how it will improve performance. The costs and benefits of the performance information system should be regularly reviewed'. Frequently different parts of the public sector still collect overlapping data but are either unable or unwilling to share it, despite the Treasury report recommending a common system as far ago as 2001.[9]

Reform case study (1): Measuring productivity

According to the Office for National Statistics during the period 1997–2007 public sector productivity fell by 3.4% or an average of 0.3% a year. This seems a modest figure. Yet the Institute of Fiscal Studies said that had productivity levels kept pace with those of 1997, the government could have delivered the services it did in 2007 for £42.5 billion less, or alternatively could have increased the quality and quantity of public services by a further 16% for the same cost.[10]

But what is productivity and how is it measured? One analysis concluded: 'Productivity is broadly defined as output per unit of input and is an important indicator of the efficiency with which resources are being used. So it is natural for people to want to compare different areas of the economy to see how efficiency compares. There is particular interest in comparisons between the private sector and the public sector'.[11]

The Office for National Statistics explains:

'There is (usually) no market for public services in which well-defined units of output are bought and sold for well-defined prices. So it is difficult to provide a measure of how much the quantity of service changes over time, or what "price" should be used to value the quantity, to combine with other sectors of the economy in an overall output total. There is, however, information on the inputs (of labour, goods and services and capital) used to provide the services. The output of public services in the National Accounts, therefore, used to be measured by assuming that output growth was simply equal to the growth in inputs. However since 1998, some parts of public service output have been measured using direct measures of activity such as pupil attendance or health procedures performed as the units of output; and unit cost weights have been used instead of market prices to add the different measures of activity together'.[12]

It cannot therefore be assumed that output automatically equals the input because this fails to take into account the quality of services. For example in explaining an apparent fall in productivity in children's care, an ONS report said: 'Total children's social care output, is measured directly. Within this category the relatively cheap (hence low cost weight) adoption, fostering and similar categories have expanded at the expense of higher cost residential care homes. This has been the deliberate focus of policy because adoption and similar placements have been shown to give better outcomes for the child. But the output measure is not adjusted for quality, so the net effect is to depress output growth'.[13]

These issues were first addressed in 2003 when the ONS, which had begun measuring government output directly in 1998, commissioned Nuffield College's Sir Tony Atkinson to review the measurement of government output and productivity. His final report in 2005 recommended a framework and set of principles for measuring key areas like health and education. His report concluded: 'How we measure government non-marketed output can make a considerable difference to the recorded growth rate of the economy. Yet the absence of market transactions means that it is hard to place a value on the services provided'.

The Atkinson report argued that input did not automatically equal output when it added:

> There is an intrinsic case based on public accountability for seeking to measure what is achieved by spending on public services. We cannot simply assume that outputs equal inputs in such a major part of the economy. To fail to measure the output would be to miss the essential complementarity between public services and private economic growth ... Direct measures of output should be continuously monitored to ensure that they are capturing changes in quality. ONS has to steer a careful course with regard to changes in government policy, guaranteeing the independence of the approach to measuring government output while ensuring that its implementation reflects the realities and circumstances of public spending.[14]

As a result of the review the UK Centre for the Measurement of Government Activity was set up within the ONS to improve measures of public service output (later abolished by the Coalition government).

ONS studies in 2009 and 2010 into total public sector productivity 1997–2007 and 1997–2008 warned of the difficulties of measuring this against the private sector. Nonetheless key points were that:

- over the period 1997–2008 total public services productivity fell by 3.4%, an average of 0.3% a year;
- productivity fell most in 2002 and 2003 by 1.4% in each year and by 0.9% in 2008;
- within these figures over 1997–2008, education productivity fell by 4.3%, adult social care by 15.3%, healthcare by 2.3% while children's social care rose by 1.9%.

The 2010 report concluded that while services had improved along with productivity they lagged behind the extra investment:

> Over the whole period 1997 to 2008 total public service output has increased substantially. This largely reflects the increase in the volume of inputs, where growth was particularly high between 2002 and 2004. But the growth in inputs exceeded the growth in output, so over the whole period productivity has not recovered to its 1997 level. After rising in 2006 and 2007 total public service productivity is estimated to have fallen in 2008. This was not because of a fall in output growth. Output growth in fact rose in 2008 compared to 2007. But input growth increased more.[15]

In its paper *Payment for Success*, KPMG argued that any reduction in output, that is cuts in frontline services, would make the public sector even less efficient unless it reduced its back office costs by a similar, or even greater level. KPMG suggested that raising the level of productivity in the public sector for average performers to the top quartile would be equal to savings of 20% to 30%. It claimed that if the average NHS hospital were as efficient in its treatments as the top quartile the NHS could provide 27% more treatments which would otherwise cost £12 billion to provide.[16]

A damning NAO report in December 2010 was highly critical of NHS productivity during the previous decade of high investment. Its head, Amyas Morse, commented: 'Over the last ten years there has been significant real growth in the resources going into the NHS, most of it funding higher staff pay and increases in headcount. The evidence shows that productivity in the same period has gone down, particularly in hospitals'.[17]

Its report pointed out: 'In 2000 the Department of Health published the NHS Plan, a ten year vision for reforming the NHS. The expectation was that a significant increase in NHS budgets would drive systemic change leading to improvements in the quality of care and increased productivity'. But quoting ONS figures, the report said that since 2000 total NHS productivity had declined by an average of 0.2% a year while hospital productivity fell by around 1.4% a year – inputs were up by 4.9% annually during this period but outputs grew by 4.7%. It concluded: 'The Department [of Health's] design and the NHS's implementation of national initiatives were predominantly focused on increasing capacity, quality and outcomes of healthcare whilst maintaining financial balance, rather than on realising improvements in productivity'.[18]

Reform case study (2): Public Service Agreements

Productivity fell during the decade of increased public spending at a time when top-down performance monitoring was at its peak, suggesting that such zealous control was not entirely successful.

However, among the most ambitious performance monitoring tools in recent years were Public Service Agreements (PSAs) Although abolished in 2010, the lessons of the PSAs continue to inform lighter-touch performance monitoring. Launched in 1998, a year after the Blair government took office, these aimed to set key objectives for public services and measure performance against them. Departments with the Treasury agreed PSAs as part of the spending review process. In return for funding the departments agreed to meet government targets in areas like reducing child poverty and youth unemployment, improving community safety and health care and tackling climate change and the PSAs were measured through a number of indicators. The NAO, which began monitoring PSAs from 2003, later commented: 'This was a step-change in the systematic formulation and measurement of government's objectives and performance'. Through PSAs, the government aimed to 'prioritise its interventions and secure the greatest possible efficiency for every pound of taxpayers' money it spends'.[19]

PSAs became a central feature of the Blair government's expanding performance monitoring regime. Initially there were some 600 performance targets for 30 areas of government activity, later reduced in 2000 to 160 and revised downwards from then on to 30. In 2007 Departmental Strategic Objectives, designed to focus on departmental objectives, were added to the PSA framework.

The PSA programme dominated the government's approach to monitoring public sector performance for 12 years and played a key role in evaluating the progress of public sector reform. But it was criticised for being over-centralist and bureaucratic despite being refined and simplified over the years while some targets proved counter-productive. For example, one target set up in 2000 pledged that all GP patients should be able to see their doctor within 48 hours with the unforeseen consequence that some surgeries were reluctant to make advance appointments for non-urgent cases and asked them to phone on the day leading to telephone queues at opening time. One study of performance noted:

> The GP waiting time target was designed to improve services for one group of patients (those seeking urgent appointments). Unwittingly it created a 'perverse incentive' to limit choice for other users who did not fit into that group. Targets and measures like this are not designed to cause problems. They are set in good faith, in the belief that they will help the services in question. However if they are set without adequate understanding of the impacts they can create inappropriate incentives.[20]

So were PSAs successful as a means of performance monitoring and do they hold lessons for a lighter-touch system? In 2003 the Public Administration Select Committee published a report into the government's performance targets regime for public services, in particular league tables and the PSAs. Its comprehensive analysis remains a valuable and objective account of the role of targets in performance monitoring. It concluded:

> The report recognises that every organisation needs to have a means for measuring its own performance internally and in comparison with others, if it is to learn, develop and motivate its staff. None of our witnesses seriously advocated that performance measurement should be swept away, and we recognise that much has been achieved by means of it. The increase in accountability and transparency which targets have brought with them has been valuable. Taxpayers and users of public services have a right to know how well their services are being delivered and who is accountable for them. We also acknowledge that where necessary the system has been adapted to changing circumstances.

But the PASC report added:

What we found is that these very laudable aims are in many cases not being fulfilled nor widely recognised as such by those on the front line whose job it is to deliver them. This is not least because of the lack of proper integration between the building of an organisation's capacity through what we call 'the performance culture' and tracking quantitative achievement in the public services through the 'measurement culture'. The result has been tension between those charged with centralised responsibility and those who are responsible for dispersed delivery of public services.[21]

It recommended greater local autonomy 'to construct more meaningful and relevant targets' and fewer of them, widening the targets consultation process to include professionals and service users, and a reform of the way in which targets were set to a less 'hit and miss' approach. This, the report added, would need to be underpinned by common reporting standards on PSA targets, independent assessment by the NAO and annual reporting on performance.

The report criticised targets for becoming an end in themselves and for being centrally imposed with little understanding of local conditions. The MPs on the select committee noted many of their witnesses were hostile to the performance regime believing it led to 'cheating, perverse consequences and distortions'.

The report asked whether targets actually delivered results and concluded that while the government was meeting the majority of the PSA targets which it had set itself, 'targets and results were different things' and there was a danger 'measurement ceases to be a means to an end and becomes an end in itself'. It warned that providers were directing their energies to meeting targets rather than improving the service and added:

Public services need to be seen as learning organisations, with learning aimed at improvement. This puts the apparatus of measurement, including targets and league tables into its proper context. A target may be missed, but if learning takes place in the process then that is a gain. While this seems to be understood by the best private sector organisations, in the public sector a missed target is likely to be the object of political and media attack. This is both foolish and damaging, and prevents target-setting playing its proper role in helping public sector organisations learn how to improve. Asking the right questions is, indeed, the key point about the proper use of targets and performance measurement generally.[22]

The targets and league tables have been accused of being over-centralist, bureaucratic and plain misleading. Tony Blair's Number 10 Chief of Staff Jonathan Powell later admitted: 'We didn't make it easy for ourselves by piling new bureaucratic requirements on staff, with endless form-filling, but equally it is difficult to justify pumping masses of public money into reformed services without some form of accountability and some way of measuring results'.[23]

In 2010 the NAO, having monitored PSAs since 2003, delivered its final verdict on their progress under the Blair and Brown governments, concluding that the 'PSA framework provided a clear focus on the objectives that mattered for the then government and had gradually improved over the years'. It did however find a mismatch between PSA indicators and financial information, a particular concern with looming spending cuts.

Learning the lessons from the PSAs for any future measurement systems, the NAO report identified four clear guidelines namely that: objectives, indicators and success criteria must be 'clearly and unambiguously expressed'; a 'business model' as a basis for measurement and reporting must be published linking inputs (the resources used) through outputs (goods and services delivered) to outcomes. The report argued this would 'help interpret performance and promote lesson learning'; a firm integration of performance measurement into public bodies' management systems such as budgeting, resource planning and performance review processes; and departmental information strategies that enable clearer published performance information.[24]

The Coalition government elected in May 2010 declared its hostility to the performance regime set up by Labour, arguing that it was centralist and bureaucratic, and in June abolished PSAs altogether. That year a report from consultants KPMG, one of whose authors Paul Kirby was later to move to Number 10, concluded:

> Instead of challenging public service providers to do more for less through tougher prices and more freedom to respond we have tried (and failed) to solve the efficiency problem from Whitehall...performance management has significantly improved across public service providers but it has focused on eliminating the worst performers, rather than liberating the best to thrive and grow.

Echoing the NAO report into PSAs the same year the KPMG study added: 'Performance management has in most cases been undermined by its disconnect from financial management which remains poor in many parts of the public sector'.[25]

It is accepted that the huge increase in public spending for the decade from 2000 was not matched by commensurate increases in productivity. But as the above studies have shown, measuring public sector productivity is difficult. Frequently it fails to take into account issues like quality of life that do not perform part of a performance regime. An over-reliance on meeting inflexible outputs leads to bureaucratic burdens that increase, rather than reduce, costs. The focus now is on *outcomes*, not *outputs*. These take into account quality of service issues rather than inflexible measurements and are behind many of the payment by results regimes that form part of ongoing public sector reforms.

A core issue as performance monitoring regimes are reduced is whether or not service users are prepared to tolerate varying levels of performance across the country in what is sometimes dubbed 'the post-code lottery'. The release of more benchmarking data in theory is aimed at helping users act as their own 'armchair auditors' enabling them to pressurise local public service providers to raise their performance to the level of the best. But under the 'localism' agenda local providers are encouraged to decide their own priorities which might mean one service, say adult care, receiving more attention at the expense of another, say leisure.

Conclusion

Measuring public sector productivity is a challenge but is important as a guide to whether the taxpayer is receiving value for money. Despite a decade of top-down performance measurement during the decade from 2000, public sector productivity actually went down as increases in output were matched by bigger increases in input.

The Labour government scaled down its target-driven performance measurement regime, recognising that it was becoming counter-productive by encouraging a bureaucratic tick-boxing culture. The Coalition further reduced its monitoring regime. The culture now is to achieve outcomes rather than simply output and these need to be determined with the frontline.

The Coalition believed making more information available to the public would act as its own performance regime, enabling users to measure

their local service against another and turning them into 'armchair auditors'. But information also needs interpretation in order to be of value
and this area is still developing.

The Coalition's policy of 'localism' may clash with national standards of performance creating the so-called 'postcode lottery' in which
services differ from area to area.

15
Monitoring Performance

Inspection and regulation is an integral part of the public sector performance monitoring regime. Public sector bodies are subject to many of the rules that cover private businesses but are also judged by government departments or by specialist inspectorates. Although inspection of public services has existed since Victorian times, it expanded in depth and scope from 1980 to 2010, as pressure to improve public sector performance became a government priority. The Coalition downplayed the role of inspection, believing that greater transparency through the free availability of comparative performance data by public sector bodies can act as a spur to improvement but it still remains an essential part of performance monitoring.

Inspection is not necessarily a party political issue. In opposition before 1997, Labour pledged to replace the Audit Commission with a Quality Commission; once in office it not only retained the Audit Commission but expanded its remit. In opposition before 2010 the Conservatives envisaged a changed role for the Audit Commission in monitoring the local government grant system; once in office it abolished the commission altogether.

The view from the central government spending watchdog, the NAO, which itself monitors central government auditing on behalf of Parliament, is as follows:

> Regulation – including guidance, inspection and reporting – is central to the delivery of effective public services and provides accountability for public funds and essential protection for citizens. Regulation also plays an important role in delivering improvements to services. For example, inspections and reporting can have a critical role to play in highlighting examples of good and bad performance and variations in public service.[1]

For services where there is an expected uniform level of provision such as in health or education benchmarks have to set standards. It is difficult to know how a particular school, hospital, care home, police force or council is performing without some objective analysis based on a set of pre-determined criteria benchmarked against similar organisations. Publishing the analysis enables the public to see how their own local public services are working compared to other localities over and above their own personal experiences. Such publicised comparative data give the public an informed perspective about the real performance of their local services. It puts pressure on the public service providers to ensure they operate at the highest level of their capabilities or risk being exposed and pilloried. The inspectorates cover all the main local public services in England (with similar bodies for the devolved governments of Wales, Scotland and Northern Ireland), in particular children's services and schools (Ofsted), police (HM Inspectorate of Constabulary), health and adult social care (Care Quality Commission) and local government (Audit Commission functions transferred to National Audit Office) and are a major part of the reform process.

In his memoirs John Major, under whose government Ofsted was founded, remarked that as chief secretary to the Treasury in 1989 he had concluded then that 'we needed to improve [the public sector's] use of resources, measure its performance more rigorously and make services act more responsively towards their users'.[2]

But this was not at the time met with wholehearted support either by the service providers or government departments. He recalled:

> The principle of independent inspection became widely accepted although in what I now regard as a mistake I did not press more forcefully to introduce it to the field of social services ... We did strengthen the Social Services Inspectorate but it was not enough. Throughout my time in Number 10 the Department of Health strongly resisted the idea of imposing inspection on the schools, prisons or police model and in the White Paper we accepted the compromise principle of in-house 'arm's length' inspection units. But on reflection I should have pushed further. Full external inspection is needed.[3]

Although the Audit Commission had been created as early as 1983 it was firstly under Major and then especially under Blair that the inspection regime expanded. In 1991 Major launched his Citizen's Charter which used comparative performance data to inform the public how their local services compared with those in other areas. He recalled:

As part of the information revolution we decided that standards for every service should be published, both as a benchmark for improvement and to show the public what they could expect. So, too, in and in clear comprehensive detail, should results. I wanted to see reports on performance placed in public libraries and in newspapers. These would show on a range of key measurements how local services were doing . . . Relative weakness would be a point of pressure on failing management to upgrade standards.[4]

In a seminar with ministers and officials at the prime minister's country house Chequers in June 1991 the foundations of an expanded inspection regime were laid. Major recalled that it

strongly endorsed separating the function of checking on performance from that of service provision. Independent inspection, most notably perhaps in education, was to be one of the foremost features of the [Citizen's] Charter. I was also keen to ensure that a lay element should, wherever possible, be included. Often providers and scrutineers came from the same charmed circle and shared the same unthinking professional assumptions. It was all too cosy.[5]

Blair's own public service reform agenda was underpinned by a rigorous inspection regime for health (Healthcare Commission), local government (Audit Commission), social services (Commission for Social Care Inspection from 2004), police (HM Inspectorate of Constabulary), schools (Ofsted) and housing backed up by National Service Frameworks, Public Service Agreements and Local Area Agreements. In 2002 a new Comprehensive Performance Assessment for local government from the Audit Commission introduced for the first time performance league tables on a scale of 'excellent' to 'poor' (later zero to 4). During its lifetime the scores steadily improved. Supporters said it showed inspection worked. Critics argued it merely showed councils had learned to play the system. Under Blair objectives, targets and indicators set improvement goals, regulation defined minimum standards on the quality and quantity of service expected while government intervention remained the last resort for failing services.

In his memoirs he defended inspection saying that while 'some criticism was valid and targets can be too numerous . . . don't think for an instant that in any other walk of life you would spend these sums of money without demanding a measurable output'.[6]

But inspection and regulation has also been criticised for creating centralised targets with little bearing on frontline realities, for stifling innovation, for increasing back office staffing costs by creating an army of bureaucrats doing little but meeting the demands of inspectorates. In some cases inspections have delivered verdicts on a service that has then been confounded by an incidence of under – or indeed over – performance that has raised questions over the validity of the inspection itself. Journalist and historian Andrew Marr wrote in his history of post-war Britain: 'The centre of government ordered and cajoled, hassled and harangued, always high-minded, always speaking for "the people"'. The interference was always well-meant but it clogged up the arteries of free decision-making and frustrated responsible public life'.[7]

The NAO, in a December 2009 report on the bureaucratic costs of inspection, noted that a study had found 35 regulators, auditors, inspectorates and accreditation agencies with a healthcare remit, much of them requesting the same data from health providers. One indicator on accessible information involved nine regulatory bodies. Inspection of the health and adult care sector was also subject to regular changes of agencies under the Labour governments of 1997–2010, a weakness recognised in a 2011 NAO report which said it had led to disruption and confusion.

Even Blair's own Strategy Unit recognised the limits of inspection when it said in 2006, after seven years of 'top down' performance management that there was 'now recognition that top down targets, regulation and performance assessment can only be one part of a 'self improving' system'.[8] In 2007 the government accordingly set out a strategy, *Cutting bureaucracy for our public services*, with the aim of reducing the number of data requests made by central government to the frontline by 30% by 2010 as part of better regulation.

There is also a cost attached to inspection and regulation. The NAO said in 2009 that government departments estimated savings of £1.5 billion 'might be' made in the public sector by 2010 through 'burden reduction', a figure never audited. It reported that common complaints from frontline staff were lack of co-ordination and data-sharing between departments, duplicate information requests, long-winded process and poor use of IT. However, the NAO also pointed out that 'to date there has been no systematic quantification of the costs that complying with regulation imposes on frontline workers'.[9] Cutting inspection costs was a prime reason cited by Coalition ministers when they announced plans to abolish the Audit Commission in 2010 but savings have not been quantified.

Have the inspectorates led to improved performance? One difficulty in evaluating this is that during the decade to 2010 spending on public services increased each year and improvement in standards owes much therefore to higher investment. The question is whether improvement continues in the next decade despite spending cuts and despite the Coalition's reduction in inspections.

Certainly, school exam results have improved during the lifetime of Ofsted though there remain significant weaknesses for children from deprived backgrounds and the ONS maintained that productivity in education fell during the pre-2010 decade of investment. While health indicators have shown improved outcomes for patients, productivity also lagged behind investment according to the ONS (see previous chapter). The police inspectorate in 2010, just as the shutters were coming down on a decade of spending increases, reported there was still a billion pounds of efficiency savings to be found in police forces and that real transformation had yet to occur. In none of these core public service areas of health, education and police has there been clear evidence that inspection alone led to performance improvements.

One of the most damning indictments of inspection targets came with the results of an official public inquiry by Robert Francis QC into healthcare at Mid Staffordshire NHS Foundation Trust Hospital published in February 2013. It concluded that the 'appalling suffering of many patients' between 2005 and 2008 was in part a result of 'allowing a focus on reaching national access targets' despite a 'plethora' of scrutiny bodies.

Reform case study (1): transparency

The flipside of the Coalition's commitment to reducing inspection was its belief that if more information could be released by public service providers about their performance then users would become their own 'armchair auditors' replacing the bureaucracies of inspectorates by demanding higher standards and greater efficiencies. The policy was known as 'transparency' and described by the PAC as 'aligned with the government's wider public service reforms'.[10]

Its aims were to strengthen public accountability and help improvement by generating more comparative data. Cabinet Office Minister Francis Maude whose department was in charge of the programme said that 'transparency is at the heart of our agenda for government. We believe that opening up will empower citizens, foster innovation and reform public services...opening up public data is underpinning our public service reforms by offering people informed choices that simply haven't existed before, exposing what is inadequate and driving improvement'.[11]

As part of the Coalition's mantra on scaling back inspection in favour of making more data available to the public so they in turn can become their own 'armchair auditors', the Treasury business plan outlined how publishing departmental information would help inform the public about performance. This would enable 'users of public services to choose between providers and taxpayers to assess the efficiency and productivity of public services, holding them more effectively to account'. It added: 'By publishing a wide range of indicators, we will enable the public to make up their own minds about how departments are performing. We will use transparency to facilitate the choice and democratic accountability which will replace top-down targets and micromanagement'.[12]

The NAO in turn promised it would 'continue to apply the lessons from our work validating the PSA data systems when looking at Government's performance data in future'.[13] Data duly poured forth with the number of datasets on the government's *data.gov.uk* portal increasing from 2,400 in January 2010 to 7,865 in December 2011, making it one of the world's largest government data resources in the world according to the NAO.[14]

Such data ranged from civil service salaries and departmental organisational charts of managers to items of local government spending over £500. Much of it was incomprehensible to the ordinary member of the public. The PAC said that 'simply dumping data without appropriate interpretation can be of limited use and frustrating. Four out of five people who visit the Government website leave it immediately without accessing links to data'.[15]

A PAC report, while supporting the view that greater transparency would lead to 'better, more accountable government', also warned: 'While transparency is necessary it is not sufficient. We look to the Government to explain how the public in general, and the "user community" of statistics in particular will be empowered to use newly published information. "Data dumping" does not on its own constitute transparency and good governance. We recommend that the UK Statistics Authority should take a proactive role in ensuring that data released is intelligible, objectively interpreted and in a readily accessible format'.[16]

Conclusion

A degree of independent inspection is vital to ensure public services reach agreed levels of performance but over-zealous inspection is counter-productive, inhibits innovation and creates unnecessary bureaucratic costs.

It is difficult to quantify the impact of inspectorates on improving performance, some of which during 2000–2010 was due to higher public spending on services. In contrast it will be useful to see if standards continue to rise in the next five years despite spending cuts.

It will also be useful to monitor the impact of reduced inspection such as the abolition of the Audit Commission on service standards. The transparency agenda, which aims to create greater accountability to users and taxpayers by more release of data by public sector bodies, hopes to create 'armchair auditors' among the public which can replace much of the 'top down' inspection regimes.

16
The International Context

Despite the historic difficulties of reforming the United Kingdom's public sector its performance in comparison to the public sectors of other countries is relatively good. The decade of public spending investment from 2000 improved the quality of health, education, police and local government in the United Kingdom, bringing it up to and in some cases beyond the average of these sectors in developed countries. Among OECD countries the United Kingdom is average in terms of the percentage of its GDP taken up by public spending, below France, Sweden and Germany but above the United States, Canada and New Zealand. In most of the OECD countries, welfare, health and education are the top three spending sectors and the United Kingdom is in a similar position. League table comparisons put the United Kingdom's education system in the top ten of global performers. The United Kingdom's health system, as well as being free at the point of use, also comes out well for its spending levels per head although it has less doctors per head of population than west European countries. While the NHS may be outperformed on a technological level by many US hospitals, its overall standard of service remains high. The quality of Whitehall's administrative service, despite ministerial criticism, is well respected around the world.

It is more difficult to compare local government as responsibilities, structures and funding arrangements differ across countries but overall UK local government, particularly in its focus on customer-centric services and the use of external competition, has been a pioneer for other local government entities to follow. Many local authorities are experiencing similar budgetary reductions due to the global fiscal downturn and seeking similar solutions, especially in partnering and shared services and new revenue-generating models. As a result of their experience

in managing tight budgets and developing partnering and shared services, UK local authority chief executives are often poached by other
countries to run their councils, especially in English-speaking nations.

But the era of austerity in public finances for the next decade puts
huge pressures on public sector managers in Europe and the United
States to maintain performance with fewer resources. The NHS, for
example, faces annual rising demand of 4% a year with budget increases
of 0.1%. Yet a McKinsey survey of efficiencies made in hospitals in other
countries for the Department of Health found that none had achieved
annual savings of more than 5% year-on-year.[1] European countries are
all experiencing falls in health spending. Similarly the restructuring of
Whitehall occurs just when its budgets are being cut, a combination
which even Sweden, much admired by many UK ministers for the way
it solved its own budget deficit in the 1990s, avoided.

Data to make international comparisons is difficult to gather but
the following examples may provide some idea of the United Kingdom's relative performance compared to other countries, especially
those with similar levels of development like Europe, the United States
and Australia.

Case study (1): Health

Pressures on UK health spending are increasingly the norm across other
countries' health services. Health spending fell across 35 European states
including the 27 members of the European Union in 2010, as governments curbed spending to help reduce budgetary deficits according
to data from the OECD and the European Commission. This drop in
spending per person and as a percentage of GDP reversed increases
in the decade before the recession, when health spending per person grew two or three times faster than incomes in many countries.
From an annual average growth rate of 4.6% between 2000 and 2009,
health spending per capita fell to –0.6% in 2010. This is the first time
health spending has fallen in Europe since 1975. The data also shows
that health spending as a percentage of GDP was 9.6% in 2010 in the
United Kingdom compared to an EU weighted average of 10.3% (that
is, the total health spend divided by total GDP across the EU). European
countries which devoted more of their GDP to health spend than the
United Kingdom in 2010 included Austria, Belgium, Denmark, France,
Germany, Greece, the Netherlands, Portugal and Serbia. However, the
number of doctors increased between 2000 and 2010 especially in the
United Kingdom while it had the lowest rates of private health insurance

among European countries. The survey also contains detailed comparative data on public health, mortality and illnesses across European countries.[2]

Global health spending statistics are collected by the World Health Organisation. The 2012 survey showed that in 2009 total health spending per head from all sources was 3,440 US dollars. The United Kingdom was 16th in the list of European and ex-USSR countries, below the United States at $7,960 and Canada, France ($4,840), Germany ($4,723) but above the southern European countries. The highest per capita health spend was Luxembourg at $8,262.

The survey said that as a percentage of GDP health spending in the United Kingdom was 7% in 2000 and 9.8% in 2009. The United States was 13.4% in 2000 and 17.6% in 2009. But general government spending on health in the United Kingdom as a percentage of total health spend was 79.2% in 2000 and 84.1% in 2009. In the United States, which does not have a nationalised health service, it was 43.2% in 2000 and 47.7% in 2009. Sweden's government funding in 2009 was 81.5% while France's was 77.9%, down from 79.4% in 2000.[3]

A separate survey of the United Kingdom's public services industry (PSI) – the amount spent by the public sector on commissioning goods and services from the private sector – found it was 6.2% of GDP, the same as Sweden and Australia, and much the same as the United States where public spending was lower. In France and Spain, PSI was lower as a share of GDP at 3%, in the case of France due to a higher share of services being operated directly by the public sector.

In the health sector, the US health sector accounted for 14% of consumer spending compared to 4% elsewhere mainly because the US government spends far less on health itself. The United Kingdom in 2008 had the lowest combined private and public healthcare spend as share of GDP. Europe has a higher number of doctors per population than the United Kingdom.[4]

Case study (2): The civil service

A survey of central government administration looked at eight OECD countries generally regarded as having the most advanced government systems in the world namely the United States, Canada, Australia, New Zealand, Germany, France, Sweden and Finland. The researchers used indicators broken into values, outcomes, and enablers. Values included being responsive, transparent, accountable, equitable, and with a public service ethos. Outcomes were defined as high-quality services, public confidence and trust, well-informed policy advice, value for money, and stability and continuity. Enablers were seen as having a good performance management regime, skilled public administration, good leadership and capacity for change.

The United Kingdom compared well with the above, its administration having good performance management systems in place, strong leadership and capacity for change and a culture of value for money although it was not so good on delivering customer-centric services. There was also a discrepancy between how well the civil service performed and how it was perceived by the users. The report, which came out as the financial crisis ending the longest run of public investment since the 1940s was breaking, added:

> The UK performs less well than the chosen countries when it comes to providing high quality services with the public largely dissatisfied with service provision and pessimistic about them becoming better. But the British public have a lesser level of confidence, trust and satisfaction with the performance level of their public services. The public in the UK feel particularly pessimistic about how public services will progress in the coming years. They also feel as if they have no influence over how public services are delivered.[5]

Case study (3): Local government

Research by PricewaterhouseCoopers based on replies from the leaders of 64 global cities including five in the United Kingdom during 2011 found many similarities between the problems faced by their administrations especially in light of the downturn in public finances. Of the replies two-thirds cited financial constraints as a barrier to implementing their strategies while 40% said deciding how to prioritise spending as a result was the next barrier.

While 87% of city leaders backed partnering with the private sector and 77% with the voluntary, only 18% 'strongly agreed' that outsourcing was necessary. While three-quarters were using public/private or public/public partnerships and 50% public/voluntary sector partnerships just under half (44%) were already outsourcing shared services although 26% expected to do so. Commissioning or buying external service provision was seen as important or very important for well over half of respondents when it came to: transportation and infrastructure (85% cited it as important), economic development and investment (73%), tourism and cultural promotion (73%), sanitation and waste management (72%), security and safety (65%), e-government services (61%), housing (60%) and social care (60%).

Almost 40% believed payment by results, an increasingly popular means of charging providers in the United Kingdom, was 'extremely effective' but the report authors warned:

> Payment by results and outcomes is, in our view, the direction of travel where services are delivered by outside providers. But local governments will only really know if they have delivered value for money if they have the systems in place to measure outcomes and measure progress towards key milestones. This is one of the key challenges facing service delivery in local government in the next few years, especially as budgets continue to be tight.

The study concluded:

> Good intentions are being expressed but local governments are falling short on execution. Local government leaders know that financing is important as are new ways of delivering services but they do not appear to know how to achieve either. This is despite the financial challenges facing many in local government... In our view, the root cause can be traced back to the lack of finance capacity and capability in many local governments. Without a finance function with sufficient capability and business insight expertise, it is difficult for local governments to source the new forms of finance needed to help invest in new services and ways of doing things.

The report concluded that rather than a sign of failure this was 'a wake-up call to the need to upskill and resource effectively local government finance functions'.[6]

Case study (4): Education

International comparisons of education performance have become increasingly prevalent as educational skills become a major contributor to a country's competitive edge in a global economy. Education professionals across the world are also keen to learn from other successful education systems such as through the Organisation for Economic Cooperation and Development's Programme for International Student Assessment (PISA) surveys which began in 2001. There have been other international studies into global school performance. One, from consultants McKinsey and Company in 2007, *How the world's best performing schools systems come out on top*, found that school systems across the world shared similar challenges in stagnant performance despite high levels of spending. Its authors, one of whom was Tony Blair's ex-adviser Michael Barber, concluded that South Korea and Singapore – and indeed England – proved that low-performing education systems could become high-performing with decades. Essential ingredients are dedicated, well-paid and trained teachers and strong leadership in both schools and the system wholly focused on delivering high-quality teaching to every child. High-performing countries like Finland and Singapore also ensure that pupils who are lagging behind, especially those from deprived backgrounds, receive extra support.[7] This was followed in 2010 by McKinsey's *How the world's most improved school systems keep getting better* which analysed 20 education systems, including England's, around the world.[8]

Sir Michael Barber was also involved in a later global league table survey in 2012 conducted by Pearson, where he was now chief education adviser. This put the United Kingdom's education system at sixth in the developed world. It used 60 indicators based on inputs such as spending, pupil teacher ratio and salaries, outputs such as measured cognitive skills, graduation rates, employment levels for school leavers plus socio-economic data covering the period 2006–2010. The global league table published by Pearson put Finland at the head of the top ten followed by South Korea, Hong Kong, Japan, Singapore, the United Kingdom, Netherlands, New Zealand, Switzerland and Canada. The survey concluded that while the level of education spend was important, so too was the attention paid to it, that choice was not the most vital factor, Finland and South Korea having the lowest levels of school choice, and that while having motivated well-paid teachers was important there was no link between pay and performance.[9]

Ofsted's annual report for 2011/12 cited the PISA survey of the reading, mathematics and science skills of 15-year-olds in 2009 among OECD countries which found England doing 'relatively well' in science but about average for reading and maths. The survey found that the literacy of 15-year-olds in England was about the same as that of Denmark, France, Germany and the United States but behind other English-speaking countries like New Zealand, Australia and Canada and especially behind China and Singapore. In the annual report Ofsted Chief Sir Michael Wilshaw said that England's score of having 70% of schools good or better was 'not good enough' for an 'aspiring leading nation in a global economy'.[10]

Conclusion

The United Kingdom's public sector generally compares well internationally, and certainly compared to countries with similar developed economies like Europe, the United States, Australia, Canada, Japan and New Zealand. Levels of performance and public spending are similar except for the United States where public spending is lower especially on health, while school performance in the United Kingdom comes out towards the upper end of the league tables. All developed countries are struggling with the impact of the fiscal downturn on their public spending along with rising demand from increasingly elderly populations. The UK government's efforts to reduce its deficit and change the public sector are being closely observed by other nations with similar challenges.

Conclusion: The Next Steps for Reform

It would be tempting to conclude this book with a list of the pantomime heroes and villains of public sector reform. On the side of the heroes might sit the selfless workers as represented by the unions, the doctors, the police and the nurses while on the side of the villains are the grasping private sector shareholders eager to drive up profits by privatising services and forcing down workers' pay. Or is it the other way round? Are the heroes the private sector offering an efficient, technologically based, managerially led means of delivering efficient public services while staff producer interests are blocking change? And what of the politicians? Are they the problem or the solution or both?

Either way the debate is sterile. There are no heroes or villains. Private, public, voluntary sector, unions, shareholders, staff, managers, civil servants and politicians of all parties are united, in theory at least, in wanting to provide the best public services for the people who fund them through their taxes. But that is the easy bit. The problem is that the funding is under pressure, the services have to adapt to the new long-term austere fiscal environment and, as this book has showed, change in the public sector is complex.

There have been numerous failures in efforts to reform public services in the United Kingdom but there have also been successes. Educational standards are higher than a decade ago, hospital care has improved after a decade of above-inflation funding even though there is still much room for improvement, the administration of local and central government is more professional. New funding ideas are being tried such as social impact bonds while payment by results seeks to link remuneration to outcomes. But change is ongoing and service structures still have yet to be fully reconfigured to cope with the era of austerity in the public finances. For as Ofsted Chief Sir Michael Wilshaw said in his 2012 annual report, seven out of ten is not good enough. There is much more to be done.

Ten key lessons from reform

Let us be clear about the reality of what efficiency and transformation implies for public service directors or more importantly, their employees; as staff are about the biggest cost of an organisation it means doing more with less of them particularly as sharing services becomes more widespread. But this is not a case of arbitrarily reducing headcount, cutting wages or freezing salaries even though these initiatives have all contributed to previous efficiency savings. Poorly paid and demotivated staff and managers will not deliver high-quality services. *Firstly* therefore public service employers in the future will need to reduce staffing, especially middle management, as they have done since 2010 but remaining employees need to be properly remunerated, well-trained and well-led. Pay freezes are a short-term tactic, not a long-term strategy.

Secondly, driving down procurement costs and making efficiency savings means cutting margins for private sector suppliers. In the first two years of the Coalition there was much media speculation about how the public spending squeeze would mean a bonanza for the private sector as cash-strapped public service managers sought private sector help and investment. In fact, in many cases the opposite occurred. Public sector commissioners who had become complacent about the prices they were paying to suppliers now forced down prices, renegotiated contracts and demanded savings. As we have seen in this book, there is a substantial private sector market based round public services, and recent efficiency savings have cut margins or even forced some providers out of business. The government drive to push down suppliers' prices also hits small businesses which do not have the economies of scale of large companies. Public sector procurement skills are still questionable, especially when it comes to handling large projects; as they improve, which they must, there will be further downward pressure on the prices paid by private sector providers.

Thirdly, politicians and ministers are as much the problem as the solution to reforming public services. They are notoriously short-term while transformation is a long-term process. Ministers with a shelf-life of a couple of years in their department are prone to want to make their mark quickly and move on. They also tend to take a departmental, silo-based approach when evidence shows that real efficiency savings can be made by taking a cross-cutting approach and sharing budgets.

Public spending cuts have only worsened Whitehall departmentalism. Politicians also need to avoid political point-scoring when it comes to addressing longer-term challenges about public sector change such as police numbers or the closure of small hospitals.

Fourthly, reform has been dogged by the twin syndromes of 'not invented here' and 'reinventing the wheel'. In the case of the former, ideas or initiatives are discarded because they were proposed by a previous government, or a previous minister, or even another department. A classic example is the cross-cutting, transformational Total Place programme, invented under Labour in 2009, scrapped by the Coalition in 2010, then re-launched as 'community budgeting' in 2011 thereby wasting at least 18 months. The 'not invented here' syndrome leads to 'reinventing the wheel' syndrome when incoming ministers and governments come up with ideas they believe are new but which have already been tried, tested and in many cases rejected. Watching reruns of the 1980s comedy *Yes Minister* will show how so many apparently brand new initiatives have in fact been doing the Whitehall rounds for decades. There is insufficient attention paid to institutional memory with the results that the same mistakes keep getting repeated.

Fifthly, the one common theme from all the select committee, Institute for Government and National Audit Office reports on public sector reform is the importance of leadership. It is already accepted that the calibre of the headteacher is the most important ingredient in producing a high-performing school. The same applies to the Whitehall permanent secretary, the council chief executive, the hospital manager and the police chief. This means ministers paying serious attention to managerial training, not cutting it to save a few pounds or castigating managers for 'awaydays', and if necessary paying over the odds to attract outstanding leaders from the private sector, not arbitrarily benchmarking top public sector salaries to what the prime minister earns. Local government has many successful examples of ex-private sector managers becoming council chief executives. Organisational change in particular requires strong leadership and a defined strategy which is imparted to staff who need to be clearly aware of what is required from them as well as to users, the public. These leaders need to be supported, especially during periods of transition when the forces against change are attempting to block it.

Sixthly, public sector managers must avoid the temptation to go for the easy savings without a strategic rationale, or which make no impact on budgets or are likely to lead to further costs down the line. Local authorities, for example, when faced with major spending cuts from

2010, put the squeeze on voluntary sector providers, the very organisations whose long-term help they will need. In turn ministers castigating public sector managers for attending training events or networking at conferences makes good politics but having untrained, ill-informed managers during the worst crisis in public finances in half a century makes little strategic sense. In addition while the focus of cost-cutting since 2010 has been on back-office services it is now recognised reducing these alone can no longer plug the funding gap.

Seventhly, public sector organisations have to get over their obsession with corporate identity and territories. The public are not interested in what agency provides which service. Too many sensible efforts to share services, either across local government, or between public sector agencies, have foundered because of cultural or territorial jealousy by producer interests whether workforces or leaders with large egos.

Eighthly, reducing costs to the taxpayer associated with socio-economic issues like welfare dependency, family breakdown, drug and alcohol abuse, crime or low educational attainment is long-term, expensive and requires a highly targeted approach. One advocate of the Coalition's troubled families initiative said if necessary a social worker should come into the household of failing parents and make a proper breakfast for the children if that was what was needed to get them to school and ensure a proper diet. It means a 'tough love' approach but the alternative which has already been tried, of endless multi-agency interventions which provide little help to the troubled family or value for money for the taxpayer, has proved so far to lead to poor outcomes.

Ninthly, the public have to 'get real' about what long-term austerity in public finances means to their expectations. If public sector transformational reform is successful it will ensure that resources are focused on the frontline not lost within the organisation. But even with this it will be difficult, even impossible, to provide the same level of services that existed pre-recession when there was above-inflation investment in the public sector for a decade. Demographic changes with people living longer, often with chronic illnesses that require expensive care, places a major burden on already strapped public finances. The public and the media must also be prepared for more risk-taking by the public sector if innovation is to become standard. Public sector managers are rightly castigated for poor performance and incompetence but if the public and media are not prepared for the tiniest margin of error then public sector managers will always avoid trying new initiatives for fear of failure and reprimand. In the private sector risk-taking is part of innovation.

Tenthly, much greater attention must be paid by governments, central and local, to breaking down public sector institutional silos. Public spending must be seen as one pot delivering outcomes to users. This involves accountability issues and indeed new accounting arrangements as well as workforces on similar terms and conditions so that merging different parts of the public sector is no longer problematic for staff. The Treasury already itemises UK government spending by cross-departmental subject, under such headings as social protection, public order and safety and economic affairs in its annual Total Managed Expenditure figures. This should be applied locally.

Taking a 'whole place' approach

There are still millions of pounds locked up within public sector organisations that could be released to the frontline. Most of this spend is trapped because of institutional weaknesses such as overmanned middle managements resistant to change because they will be the losers, a reliance on process, silo-based budgeting focused on outputs not outcomes, duplication of functions by overlapping agencies and aversion to risk-taking. This statement that millions can still be released is not plucked from the air. Local authorities, for example, are constantly producing new initiatives, often not even especially innovative, that produce savings without adversely affecting frontline services. While some senior public service managers have had to grapple with huge downturns in their budgets, others admit privately that spending cuts announced in the 2010 Spending Review gave them the 'burning platform' excuse to make organisational changes, save millions of pounds and yet still have no negative impact on services (although the next Spending Review is more of a challenge for them). Identified savings from the 'community budget' pilots already run into hundreds of millions of pounds and yet such transformational change in merging service budgets has scarcely begun.

One of the biggest challenges the public sector faces is managing the rising costs of elderly care which impact primarily on the NHS and local government. Dire warnings from the Local Government Association in June 2012 that adult care would swallow up most councils' budgets within eight years have been followed by other pessimistic analyses of the pressures on the NHS, outlined in earlier chapters. Health and local government services are increasingly working together but with the NHS having to deliver efficiency savings and councils cutting their own budgets the need for a transformational change in delivery is even more pressing. The question is whether the move towards more personalised home-based care, personal budgets and greater use of technology to enable the elderly to be supported in their own homes will be sufficient.

For the culture of the public sector and indeed of many past reform efforts is too often reactive, dealing with symptoms rather than causes. One analogy is that of a householder whose leaking water tank in the attic causes the ceiling to collapse. The public sector fixes the ceiling but leaves the leaking water tank untouched so the ceiling collapses again. Welfare reforms address the symptoms, the rising cost of paying benefits but not the causes, whether unemployment, better training or lack of social housing for the low paid. The number of children taken into care has risen despite both the cost of care and the fact that looked-after children perform worse in schools and tend to be disproportionately represented in the prison population. Yet tackling family breakdown at a granular level remains a challenge for public sector agencies many of which deal with the results rather than the causes.

Unlike private firms which need to increase the number of customers and boost demand, the public sector seeks to reduce them. To repeat the water tank analogy, the leak needs to be fixed in order to prevent the ceiling collapsing again. There is recognition of this through the creation of the behaviour change unit in the Cabinet Office which seeks to manage down demand through changing lifestyles by persuasion and peer pressure. The Troubled Families Unit at the DCLG was set up in recognition that a minority of families had ingrained problems that cost the welfare and criminal justice systems millions but were being poorly addressed by existing agencies. In transferring public health from the NHS to local authorities the Coalition appreciated that the latter was better placed to deal with the causes of poor health because of its remit in housing, planning, education, economic development and social services.

But the biggest obstacle to dealing with these difficult socio-economic challenges is the structure of the public sector itself. The community budget 'whole place' pilots outlined in Chapter 10 identified that early, targeted intervention across different agencies to tackle, say, the number of elderly people needlessly in hospital or to reduce repeat youth offending or prevent children entering care will reduce costs in the long term. But the public sector operates in separately funded silos like police, local government, health, schools, further education, welfare, each jealously guarding their budgets, each with their own workforce structures and terms and conditions. Early results from the Total Place pilots in 2009 showed that a particular disincentive to joint working was that one arm of the local public sector, such as the council, was incurring the costs of an initiative only to see the benefits in terms of savings pass to another arm, say the police or local NHS. Reducing the number of elderly people kept in hospital requires an adult care support service able to ensure that they can be looked after in their own homes or in residential care, thereby involving two budgets, those of the NHS and local government. Many government initiatives have involved trying to get round this problem with financial incentives or financial penalties to encourage more cross-sector working.

The final word perhaps should lie with Sir David Varney who laid out a vision of what the ideal public sector of the future might look like in 2020. He envisaged all services, central and local, being accessed through a single portal based around the needs of the user which would have the added benefit of reducing duplication, a major and unnecessary cost for the public sector. His report concluded that this ought to be 'the public service aspiration for government'. It remains an aspiration because as he recognised, it requires 'a fundamental shift of models of current service delivery'.

His observations were made in 2006 before the recession and the consequent crisis in public finances made implementing his vision not less but even more relevant for the millions of people who rely on the public sector and its managers to deliver their vital services.[1]

Notes

The Politics of Public Sector Reform: From Thatcher to the Coalition

Introduction

1. Dr Campbell Christie, foreword (June 2011). *Commission on the future delivery of public services.* APS Group Scotland.
2. Oral evidence. Public Administration Select Committee (January 2010). *Public administration and the fiscal squeeze.*
3. HM Treasury (July 2012). *Public spending statistics.*
4. HMIC/Welsh Audit Office/Audit Commission (July 2010). *Sustaining value for money in the police service.*
5. No 10 Strategy Unit (June 2006). *The UK government's approach to public service reform.* Cabinet Office.
6. ibid.
7. Dr DeAnne Julius (July 2008). *Understanding the public services industry: how big, how good, where next?* Public Services Industry Review. Department for Business, Enterprise and Regulatory Reform.
8. Institute of Fiscal Studies (May 2010). *Election briefing note.*
9. Greg Clark (December 2012). *Decentralisation: an assessment of progress.* DCLG.
10. National Audit Office (Sept 2011). *A summary of the National Audit Office's work on the Department for Education 2010–11.*
11. Roger Latham and Malcolm Prowle (2012). *Public services and financial austerity. Getting out of the hole?* (Basingstoke, Palgrave Macmillan, p. 108).
12. Alistair Darling (2011). *Back from the brink* (Atlantic Books, London, p. 267).
13. Public Accounts Committee (October 2011). *The Efficiency and Reform Group's role in improving public sector value for money.*
14. Adam Roberts, Louise Marshall and Anita Charlesworth (December 2012). *A decade of austerity? The funding pressures facing the NHS from 2010/11 to 2021/22.* Nuffield Trust.
15. No 10 Strategy Unit (June 2006). *The UK government's approach to public service reform.* Cabinet Office.
16. Lord (Michael) Bichard (15 November 2012). Quoted in *The MJ (Municipal Journal).*
17. Public Administration Select Committee (September 2011). *Change in government. The agenda for leadership.*
18. Charles Levy (May 2011). *Making the most of public services. A systems approach to public innovation.* The Work Foundation.
19. Roger Latham and Malcolm Prowle (2012). *Public services and financial austerity. Getting out of the hole?* (Basingstoke, UK, Palgrave Macmillan, p. 108).

1 Reform Under the Conservatives 1979–1997

1. Margaret Thatcher (1993) *The Downing Street Years* (London. Harper Collins, p. 6–7).
2. ibid., p. 6.
3. ibid., p. 6, 13.
4. ibid., p. 32.
5. ibid., p. 606.
6. ibid., p. 607.
7. ibid., p. 607.
8. David Marsland (2005) *Margaret Thatcher's Revolution*, Edited Subroto Roy and John Clarke (Continuum, p. 167).
9. Roger Latham and Malcolm Prowle (2012) *Public services and financial austerity. Getting out of the hole?* (Basingstoke, Palgrave Macmillan, p. 101).
10. David Marsland (2005) *Margaret Thatcher's Revolution*, Edited Subroto Roy and John Clarke (Continuum, p.168).
11. John Major (1999) *The Autobiography* (London, HarperCollins, p. 203).
12. ibid., p. 248.
13. ibid., p. 248.
14. ibid., p. 246–247.
15. ibid., p. 246.
16. ibid., p. 245, 249.
17. ibid., p. 203.
18. ibid., p. 248.
19. Sarah Hogg and Jonathan Hill (1995) *Too Close to Call Power and politics – John Major in No 10* (Little, Brown and Company, p. 15). Sarah Hogg was head of Major's policy unit 1990–95 and Jonathan Hill was Major's political secretary and head of his Political Office 1992–94.
20. John Major (1999) *The Autobiography* (London, HarperCollins, p. 249).
21. ibid., p. 250.
22. Public Administration Select Committee (July 2008) *Public services: putting people first.*
23. Sarah Hogg and Jonathan Hill (1995) *Too Close to Call Power and politics – John Major in No 10* (Little, Brown and Company, p. 104).
24. ibid., p. 93.
25. John Major (1999) *The Autobiography* (London, HarperCollins, p. 261).
26. ibid., p. 262.
27. Sarah Hogg and Jonathan Hill (1995) *Too Close to Call Power and politics – John Major in No 10* (Little, Brown and Company, p. 97, 104).
28. Public Administration Select Committee (July 2008) *Public services: putting people first.*
29. Ofsted (November 2012) *Annual Report* 2011/12.
30. John Major (1999) *The Autobiography* (London, Harper Collins, p. 387).

2 Reform Under Labour 1997–2010

1. Jonathan Powell (2011). *The New Machiavelli: How to Wield Power in the Modern World* (London, Vintage Books, p. 180).

2. Alastair Campbell (2007). *The Blair Years: Extracts from the Alastair Campbell Diaries* (London, Hutchinson, p. xll).
3. Tony Blair (2010). *A Journey* (London, Hutchinson, p. 214).
4. ibid., p. 214.
5. ibid., p. 212.
6. ibid., p. 262.
7. ibid., p. 685.
8. Duncan Campbell-Smith (2008). *Follow the Money: A History of the Audit Commission* (Allen Lane, p. 413).
9. Tony Blair (2010). *A Journey* (London, Hutchinson, p. 124).
10. ibid., p. 206–207.
11. Jonathan Powell (2011). *The New Machiavelli: How to Wield Power in the Modern World* (London, Vintage Books, p. 26–27).
12. Tony Blair (2010). *A Journey* (London, Hutchinson, p. 254).
13. Anthony Seldon (2004). *Blair* (London, The Free Press, p. 423).
14. Tony Blair (2010). *A Journey* (London, Hutchinson, p. 255).
15. ibid., p. 271.
16. ibid., p. 288.
17. ibid., p. 267.
18. ibid., p. 272.
19. ibid., p. 273.
20. ibid., p. 283–284.
21. ibid., p. 284.
22. ibid., p. 270–271).
23. ibid., p. 481.
24. Anthony Seldon with Peter Snowdon and Daniel Collings (2007). *Blair Unbound* (London, Simon and Shuster, p. 114).
25. Tony Blair (2010). *A Journey* (London, Hutchinson, p. 499).
26. No 10 Strategy Unit (June 2006). *The UK Government's Approach to Public Service Reform* (Cabinet Office).
27. Anthony Seldon and Guy Lodge (2010). *Brown at 10* (London, Biteback Publishing, p. 82).
28. Tony Blair (2010). *A Journey* (London, Hutchinson, p. 481).
29. Alistair Darling (2011). *Back from the Brink* (London, Atlantic Books, p. 11).
30. Tony Blair (2010). *A Journey* (London, Hutchinson, p. 286).
31. ibid., p. 480.
32. Jonathan Powell (2011). *The New Machiavelli. How to Wield Power in the Modern World* (London, Vintage Books, p. 132).
33. Anthony Seldon and Guy Lodge (2010). *Brown at 10* (London, Biteback Publishing, p. 19).
34. ibid., p. xix–xx.
35. Peter Snowden (2010). *Back from the Brink: The Extraordinary Fall and Rise of the Conservative Party* (London, Harper Press, p. 289).
36. Anthony Seldon and Guy Lodge (2010). *Brown at* 10 (London, Biteback Publishing, p. 82).
37. Cabinet Office (2009). *Working Together: Public Services on Your Side.*
38. Anthony Seldon and Guy Lodge (2010). *Brown at* 10 (London, Biteback Publishing, p. 81).
39. ibid., p. 420.

40. ibid., p. 421.
41. ibid., p. 82.
42. ibid., p. 83.
43. ibid., p. 291.
44. The Stationery Office (June 2009). *Building Britain's Future.*

3   Reform Under the Coalition 2010–2015

1. Peter Snowden (2010). *Back from the Brink* (London, HarperPress, p. 289).
2. Oliver Letwin, BBC News online (18 Sept 2009). Quoted in *Back from the Brink.*
3. Spending Review. HM Treasury (Oct 2010).
4. ibid.
5. Letter from the chair of the UK Statistics Authority to Secretary of State for Health disputing ministers' claims of a real-term increase in health spending (4 December 2012). See also the Treasury's Public Spending Statistics (July 2012) which show that health spending fell by £20 million in 2011/12 or –0.2%.
6. Spending Review. HM Treasury (October 2010).
7. 11th Report. Public Administration Select Committee (July 2008).
8. ibid.
9. ibid.
10. The Big Society. Public Administration Select Committee (December 2011).
11. The Big Society Audit 2012. Civil Exchange (May 2012).
12. David Lewis in The Big Society Debate (2012) Edited Armine Ishkanian and Simon Szreter (Edward Elgar).
13. National Audit Office (November 2012) Managing the expansion of the academies programme.
14. Iain Duncan Smith. Speech at Arlington Centre (11 September 2010).
15. Universal credit: welfare that works (November 2010). White Paper. Department of Works and Pensions.
16. *The Guardian* (10 February 2012).
17. Open Public Services (July 2011) White Paper. Cabinet Office.
18. ibid.
19. Open Public Services 2012 (March 2012). Cabinet Office.
20. Dr Campbell Christie, foreword. Commission on the Future Delivery of Public Services (June 2011) APS Group Scotland.
21. ibid.
22. Department of Communities and Local Government (November 2012) 50 Ways to Save.

4   Number 10 and the Cabinet Office

1. Jonathan Powell (2011). *The New Machiavelli: How to Wield Power in the Modern World* (London, Vintage Books, p. 29). A useful study of No 10 and the Cabinet Office up to 2005 can also be found in Paul Fawcett and Oonagh Gay, Parliament and Constitution Centre, House of Commons

Library (December 2005). The Centre of Government – No 10, *The Cabinet Office and H M Treasury*. Research Paper 05/92.

2. Peter Thomas (July 2012). *Civil Service Reform: Our Verdict on the New Reform Plan* (Institute for Government).
3. Jonathan Powell (2011). *The New Machiavelli: How to Wield Power in the Modern World* (London, Vintage Books, p. 18).
4. ibid., p. 17.
5. ibid., p. 29.
6. ibid., p. 43, 45.
7. ibid., p. 29.
8. Margaret Thatcher (1993). *The Downing Street Years* (London. Harper Collins, p. 31).
9. Jonathan Powell (2011). *The New Machiavelli: How to Wield Power in the Modern World* (London, Vintage Books, p. 180).
10. Tony Blair (2010). *A Journey* (London, Hutchinson, p. 338).
11. Public Administration Committee (Feb 1997). *Governing for the Future.*
12. Margaret Thatcher (1993). *The Downing Street Years* (London. Harper Collins, p. 277).
13. John Major (1999). *The Autobiography* (London. HarperCollins, p. 248).
14. ibid., p. 252.
15. Jill Rutter (Nov 2010). Institute for Government Blog. http://www.instituteforgovernment.org.uk/blog/1096/strategy-unit-rip/
16. Andrew Blick and George Jones (June 2010). *The Power of the Prime Minister* (History and Policy, http://www.historyandpolicy.org/papers/policy-paper-102.html).
17. Tony Blair (2010). *A Journey* (London, Hutchinson, p. 338–339).
18. ibid., p. 339.
19. Public Administration Committee (July 2002). *The New Centre.*
20. ibid.
21. Public Administration Select Committee (March 2007). *Governing the Future.*
22. Tony Blair (2010). *A Journey* (London, Hutchinson, p. 339).
23. ibid., p. 339.
24. Prime Minister's Strategy Unit (June 2006). *The UK Government's Approach to Public Service Reform.* Cabinet Office.
25. ibid.
26. Public Administration Select Committee (March 2007). *Governing the Future.*
27. Andrew Blick and George Jones (June 2010). *The Power of the Prime Minister.* (History and Policy, http://www.historyandpolicy.org/papers/policy-paper-102.html).
28. Jonathan Powell (2011). *The New Machiavelli: How to Wield Power in the Modern World* (London, Vintage Books, p. 81).
29. Institute for Government (Jan 2010). *Shaping up – a Whitehall for the Future.*
30. Alistair Darling (2011). *Back from the Brink* (London, Atlantic Books, p. 169).
31. *The Coalition: Our Programme for Government* (May 2010). Cabinet Office.
32. Cabinet Office (November 2010).*Business Plan* 2011–2015.
33. Public Administration Select Committee (September 2011). *Change in Government. The Agenda for Leadership.*
34. Peter Thomas (July 2012). *Civil Service Reform: Our Verdict On the New Reform Plan.* Institute for Government.

5 The Treasury

1. HM Treasury (March 2008). *The Budget.*
2. Paul Fawcett and R.A.W Rhodes (2007) in *Blair's Britain: 1997–2007.* Edited by Anthony Seldon. Cambridge University Press, p. 95–98).
3. City of London/PwC (December 2010). *The Total Tax Contribution of UK Financial Services.*
4. Jonathan Powell (2011). *The New Machiavelli: How to Wield Power in the Modern World* (London, Vintage Books, p. 113).
5. Alistair Darling (2011). *Back from the Brink* (London, Atlantic Books, p. 7, 9).
6. HM Treasury (March 2008). *The Budget*, p. 77.
7. Alistair Darling (2011). *Back from the Brink* (London, Atlantic Books, p. 39, 41).
8. ibid., p. 100.
9. ibid., p. 218.
10. ibid., p. 178.
11. ibid., p. 270.
12. HM Treasury (2009). *Pre Budget Report*, p. 98.
13. Gershon Efficiency Review (2004). *Releasing Resources to the Frontline. Independent Review of Public Sector Efficiency.* HM Treasury.
14. ibid.
15. ibid.
16. Commons Treasury committee (July 2009). *Evaluating the Efficiency Programme.*
17. National Audit Office (July 2010). *Progress with VFM Savings and Lessons for Cost Reduction Programmes.*
18. Public Accounts Committee (October 2010) *Progress with VFM Cost Savings and Lessons for Cost Reduction Programmes.*
19. Sir Philip Green (October 2010). *Efficiency Review by Sir Philip Green – Key Findings and Recommendations* (Cabinet Office).
20. Her Majesty's Inspectorate of Constabulary (2010). *Police Governance in Austerity.*
21. Alistair Darling (2011). *Back from the Brink* (London, Atlantic Books, p. 312).
22. Cabinet Office Website (Sept 2012). http://www.cabinetoffice.gov.uk/news/chief-operating-officer-government-appointed.
23. Grahame Allen (December 2001). *The Private Finance Initiative (PFI). Research Paper* 01/117 (Economic Policy and Statistics Section. House of Commons Library).
24. HM Treasury (March 2011). *UK PFI projects. Summary Data.*
25. Public Accounts Committee (August 2011). *The Private Finance Initiative.*
26. Treasury Notice (15 November 2011).
27. HM Treasury and Cabinet Office (April 2011) *Major Project and Assurance Guidance.*

6 The Role of Parliament

1. Meg Russell and Meghan Benton (June 2011). *Selective Influence: The Policy Impact of House of Commons Select Committees* (Constitution Unit. University College, London).

2. ibid.
3. Public Accounts Committee (August 2011). *The Private Finance Initiative.*
4. House of Commons Liaison Committee (March 2012). *Select Committees and their Effectiveness. Written evidence.*
5. ibid.
6. Public Administration Select Committee (December 2011). *Big Society.*
7. Public Administration Select Committee (July 2008). *Public Services and the Third Sector: Rhetoric and Reality.*
8. Public Administration Select Committee (September 2011). *Change in Government. The Agenda for Leadership.*
9. Public Administration Select Committee (August 2007). *Skills for Government.*
10. Public Administration Select Committee (July 2008). *From Citizen's Charter to Public Service Guarantees: Entitlement to Public Services.*
11. Public Administration Select Committee (May 2008). *User Involvement in Public Services.*
12. Public Administration Select Committee (March 2010). *Too Many Ministers?*
13. Public Accounts Committee (October 2011). *The Efficiency and Reform Group's Role in Improving Public Sector Value for Money.*
14. Margaret Hodge Speech to Policy Exchange (16 March 2012). Press Association.
15. Michael Gove. Speech to Politeia (23 October 2012).

7 The Role of the Consumer and Competition

1. Sir Ronnie Flanagan (February 2008). *The Review of Policing. Final Report.* Home Office, p. 13.
2. John Clarke, Janet Newman, and Louise Westmarland (2007). Creating Citizen-Consumers? Public Service Reform and (Un)willing Selves. In Sabine Maasen and Barbara Sutter, eds. *On Willing Selves: Neoliberal Politics and the Challenge of Neuroscience* (Basingstoke: Palgrave Macmillan, p. 125–145).
3. Alan Milburn (April 2005). quoted in *Real Choice in the Health Service.* Royal College of Nursing.
4. No 10 Strategy Unit (2006). *The UK Government's Approach to Public Service Reform.* Cabinet Office.
5. Bernard Herdan (June 2006). *The Customer Voice in Transforming Public Services.* Cabinet Office.
6. 2020 Public Services Trust (May 2010). *Citizen Engagement: Testing Policy Ideas for Public Service Reform.*
7. Public Administration Select Committee (2008). *Public Services: Putting People First.*
8. ibid.
9. Public Service Committee (1997). *The Citizen's Charter.*
10. Public Administration Select Committee (2008). *Public Services: Putting People First.*
11. Bernard Herdan (June 2006). *The Customer Voice in Transforming Public Services.* Cabinet Office.

12. No 10 Strategy Unit (2006). *The UK Government's Approach to Public Service Reform.* Cabinet Office.
13. ibid.
14. Tim Curry. RCN South East Regional Office (April 2005). in *Real Choice in the Health Service.* Royal College of Nursing.
15. Liam Byrne (2009). Government response *to From Citizen's Charter to Public Service Guarantees: Entitlements to Public Services.* Public Administration Select Committee.
16. Cabinet Office (July 2011). *Open Public Services White Paper.*
17. National Audit Office (June 2012). *Delivering Public Services Through Markets: Principles for Achieving Value for Money.*
18. ibid.
19. National Audit Office (December 2011). *Digital Britain One: Shared Infrastructure and Services for Government Online.*
20. Sir David Varney (December 2006). *Service Transformation: A Better Service for Citizens and Businesses, A Better Deal for the Taxpayer* (HM Treasury).
21. Tom Gash and Theo Roos (August 2012). *Choice and Competition in Public Services: Learning from History.* Institute for Government. This report was based on four public Learning from History events the IfG held in spring 2012 on how choice and competition in public services has worked.
22. Dr DeAnne Julius (July 2008). *Public Services Industry Review. Understanding the Public Services Industry: How Big, How Good, Where Next?* (Department for Business, Enterprise and Regulatory Reform).
23. ibid.
24. ibid.
25. National Audit Office (June 2012). *Delivering Public Services Through Markets: Principles for Achieving Value for Money.*
26. ibid.
27. ibid.
28. Public Administration Select Committee (July 2008). *Public Services and the Third Sector: Rhetoric and Reality.*
29. ibid.
30. ibid.
31. ibid.
32. Public Administration Select Committee (December 2011). *The Big Society.*
33. Civil Exchange (May 2012). *The Big Society Audit.*
34. David Lewis (2012) in *The Big Society Debate.* Edited Armine Ishkanian and Simon Szreter (Cheltenham, Edward Elgar).
35. Public Administration Select Committee (July 2008). *Public Services: Putting People First.*
36. ibid.
37. Institute of Fiscal Studies (February 2012). *Green Budget.*
38. 2020 Public Services Trust (2009). *Drivers for Change: Citizen Demand in 2020.*
39. 2020 Public Services Trust (May 2010) *Citizen Engagement: Testing Policy Ideas for Public Service Reform.*
40. The Coalition. Our programme for government (May 2010).
41. *Annual Update* 2010/11. Cabinet Office.
42. Behavioural Insights Unit (December 2010). *Applying Behavioural Insight to Health.* Cabinet Office.

8 Whitehall

1. Institute for Government (February 2012). *An Open Letter: Two Challenges and an Opportunity.*
2. Public Administration Select Committee (September 2011). *Change in Government: The Agenda for Leadership.*
3. ibid.
4. James Page, Jonathan Pearson, Briana Jurgeit, Marc Kidson (November 2012). *Transforming Whitehall: Leading Major Change in Whitehall Departments.* Institute for Government.
5. ibid.
6. Public Administration Select Committee (September 2011). *Change in Government: The Agenda for Leadership.*
7. *National Audit Office/Accenture* (October 2008). An international comparison of the UK's public administration.
8. Tony Blair (2010). *A Journey* (London, Hutchinson, p. 19).
9. John Major (1999). *The Autobiography* (London. HarperCollins, p. 255).
10. Margaret Thatcher (1993) *The Downing Street Years* (London. Harper Collins, p. 47).
11. ibid., p. 31.
12. ibid., p. 45.
13. Peter Hennessy (1990). *Whitehall* (Fontana Press 1990, p. 632).
14. Margaret Thatcher (1993). *The Downing Street Years* (London. Harper Collins, p. 48).
15. Tony Blair (2010). *A Journey* (London, Hutchinson, p. 205).
16. ibid., p. 206.
17. ibid., p. 206.
18. Jonathan Powell (2011). *The New Machiavelli. How to Wield Power in the Modern World* (London, Vintage Books, p. 73–74).
19. Public Administration Select Committee (September 2011). *Change in Government: The Agenda for Leadership.*
20. Francis Maude (5 July 2010). *Speech to Civil Service Live.*
21. ibid.
22. *Open Public Services White Paper* (July 2011). Cabinet Office.
23. James Page, Jonathan Pearson, Briana Jurgeit, Marc Kidson (November 2012). *Transforming Whitehall: Leading Major Change in Whitehall Departments.* Institute for Government.
24. Public Administration Select Committee (September 2011). *Change in Government: The Agenda for Leadership.*
25. James Page, Jonathan Pearson, Briana Jurgeit, Marc Kidson (November 2012). *Transforming Whitehall: Leading Major Change in Whitehall Departments.* Institute for Government.
26. Sir Philip Green (October 2010). *Efficiency Review by Sir Philip Green: Key Findings and Recommendations* (Cabinet Office).
27. *The Civil Service Reform Plan* (June 2012). Cabinet Office.
28. ibid.
29. ibid.
30. National Audit Office (November 2009). *Commercial Skills for Complex Government Projects.*

31. Public Accounts Committee (July 2011). *Government and IT – a Recipe for Rip-Offs.*
32. Conservative Spring Forum (March 2011). *Cardiff.*
33. National Audit Office and Audit Commission (May 2010). *A Review of Collaborative Procurement Across the Public Sector.*
34. National Audit Office (March 2010). *Reorganising Central Government.*
35. ibid.
36. Public Administration Select Committee (September 2011). *Change in Government: The Agenda for Leadership.*
37. Matthew Flinders and Chris Skelcher (September 2012). *Shrinking the Quango State: Five Challenges in Reforming Quangos.* Public Money and Management. CIPFA).
38. ibid.
39. Public Accounts Committee (April 2012). *Reorganising Central Government Bodies.*
40. National Audit Office (November 2007). *Improving Corporate Functions Using Shared Services.*
41. National Audit Office (March 2012). *Efficiency and Reform in Government Corporate Functions Through Shared Service Centres.*
42. Cabinet Office (July 2011). *Government Shared Services: A Strategic Vision.*
43. National Audit Office (March 2012). *Efficiency and Reform in Government Corporate Functions Through Shared Service Centres.*
44. Public Accounts Committee (July 2012). *Efficiency and Reform in Government Corporate Functions Through Shared Service Centres.*
45. Justine Stephen, Robin Martin and David Atkinson (November 2011). *See-through Whitehall. Departmental Business Plans One Year On.* Institute for Government.
46. National Audit Office (February 2009). *Assessment of the Capability Review Programme.*
47. Cabinet Office (December 2009). *Capability Reviews. An Overview of Progress and Next Steps.*
48. National Audit Office (February 2009). *Assessment of the Capability Review Programme.*
49. Public Accounts Committee (July 2012). *Managing Early Departures in Central Government.*
50. Sir David Varney (December 2006). *Service Transformation: A Better Service for Citizens and Businesses, a Better Deal for the Taxpayer* (HM Treasury).
51. National Audit Office (December 2011). *Digital Britain One: Shared Infrastructure and Services for Government Online.*
52. Sir David Varney (December 2006). *Service Transformation: A Better Service for Citizens and Businesses, a Better Deal for the Taxpayer* (HM Treasury).
53. Lord Heseltine (October 2012). *No Stone Unturned in Pursuit of Growth.* Department for Business, Innovation and Skills.

9 The National Health Service

1. Adam Roberts, Louise Marshall and Anita Charlesworth (December 2012). *A decade of austerity? The funding pressures facing the NHS from 2010/11 to 2021/22.* Nuffield Trust, December 2012.

2. NHS Jobs Website (April 2012).
3. HM Treasury (July 2012). Public Spending Statistics and NAO (December 2012). *Progress in Making NHS Efficiency Savings.*
4. House of Commons Health Committee (May 2012). *Education, Training and Workforce Planning.*
5. Nicholas Timmins (July 2012). *Never Again? The Story of the Health and Social Care Act 2012. A Study in Coalition Government and Policy Making.* Institute for Government and the King's Fund.
6. See details of Qipp in *Briefing for the House of Commons Health Committee: Delivering Efficiency Savings in the NHS.* National Audit Office (September 2011).
7. NAO (December 2012). *Progress in Making NHS Efficiency Savings.*
8. Nicholas Mays and Anna Dixon (2011). In *Understanding New Labour's Market Reforms of the English NHS.* Nicholas Mays, Anna Dixon and Lorelei Jones (The King's Fund, p. 160).
9. Adam Roberts, Louise Marshall and Anita Charlesworth (December 2012). *A decade of austerity? The funding pressures facing the NHS from 2010/11 to 2021/22.* Nuffield Trust. December 2012.
10. Nicholas Timmins (July 2012). *Never Again? The Story of the Health and Social Care Act 2012. A Study in Coalition Government and Policy Making.* Institute for Government and the King's Fund.
11. John Major (1999). *The Autobiography* (London. HarperCollins, p. 391).
12. Margaret Thatcher (1993) *The Downing Street Years* (London. Harper Collins, p. 606).
13. ibid., p. 609.
14. ibid., p. 607.
15. ibid., p. 607
16. ibid., p. 607.
17. ibid., p. 607.
18. ibid., p. 609.
19. ibid., p. 615.
20. David Marsland (2005) *Margaret Thatcher's Revolution,* Edited Subroto Roy and John Clarke. (Continuum, p. 170).
21. John Major (1999). *The Autobiography* (London, HarperCollins, p. 390).
22. ibid., p. 391.
23. Tony Blair (2010). *A Journey.* (London, Hutchinson, p. 215).
24. ibid., p. 284.
25. National Audit Office (December 2010). *Management of NHS Hospital Productivity.*
26. Nicholas Mays, Anna Dixon and Lorelei Jones (2011). *Understanding New Labour's Market Reforms of the English NHS.* (The King's Fund, p. 1).
27. Tony Blair (2010). *A Journey* (London, Hutchinson, p. 283).
28. Nicholas Mays, Anna Dixon and Lorelei Jones (2011). *Understanding New Labour's Market Reforms of the English NHS* (The King's Fund).
29. Tony Blair (2010). *A Journey* (London, Hutchinson, p. 283).
30. Public Accounts Committee (December 2011). *Achievement of Foundation Trust Status by NHS Hospital Trusts.*
31. National Audit Office (June 2010). *A Short Guide: The NAO's Work on the Department of Health.*

32. National Audit Office (December 2010). *Management of NHS Hospital Productivity.*
33. Office of National Statistics (May 2011). *Expenditure on Healthcare in the UK.* ONS.
34. National Audit Office (December 2010). *Management of NHS Hospital Productivity.*
35. Anthony Seldon and Guy Lodge (2010). *Brown at 10* (London, Biteback Publishing, p. 19).
36. Nicholas Mays, Anna Dixon and Lorelei Jones (2011). *Understanding New Labour's Market Reforms of the English NHS.* (The King's Fund, p. 131).
37. Nicholas Timmins (July 2012). *Never Again? The Story of the Health and Social Care Act 2012. A Study in Coalition Government and Policy Making.* Institute for Government and the King's Fund.
38. Nicholas Mays, Anna Dixon and Lorelei Jones (2011). *Understanding New Labour's Market Reforms of the English NHS* (The King's Fund, p. 148).
39. Nicholas Timmins (July 2012). *Never Again? The Story of the Health and Social Care Act 2012. A Study in Coalition Government and Policy Making.* Institute for Government and the King's Fund.
40. ibid.
41. World Health Organisation (2012). *World Health Statistics.*
42. National Audit Office (December 2010). *Management of NHS Hospital Productivity.*
43. Office for National Statistics (March 2011). *Public Service Outputs, Inputs and Productivity: Healthcare.* This gives a detailed breakdown of inputs and outputs.
44. Commons Health Committee (December 2006). *NHS Deficits.*
45. Nick Bosanquet (2007). In *Blair's Britain 1997–2007.* Edited Anthony Seldon (Cambridge University Press, p. 389).
46. Public Accounts Committee (June 2008). Forty first report.
47. Nicholas Mays, Anna Dixon and Lorelei Jones (2011). *Understanding New Labour's Market Reforms of the English NHS* (The King's Fund, p. 133).
48. National Audit Office (December 2010). *Management of NHS Hospital Productivity.*
49. Department of Health (May 2010). *Achieving World-Class Productivity in the NHS. 2009/10 to 2013/14: Detailing the Size of the Opportunity.*
50. Public Accounts Committee (January 2011). *PFI in Housing and Hospitals.*
51. National Audit Office (June 2010). *The Performance and Management of Hospital PFI Contracts.*
52. Treasury Select Committee (August 2011). *The Private Finance Initiative.*
53. Public Accounts Committee (December 2011). *Achievement of Foundation Trust Status by NHS Hospital Trusts.*
54. Public Accounts Committee (September 2011). *Lessons from PFI and Other Projects.*
55. HM Treasury (December 2011). *Reform of the Private Finance Initiative.*
56. Treasury Select Committee (January 2012). *Private Finance Initiative.*
57. Public Accounts Committee (October 2012). *Securing the Future Financial Sustainability of the NHS.*
58. National Audit Office (February 2011). *The Procurement of Consumables by NHS Acute and Foundation Trusts.*

59. ibid.
60. ibid.
61. National Audit Office (June 2010). *A Short Guide: The NAO's Work on the Department of Health.*
62. Public Accounts Committee (August 2011). The National Programme for IT in the NHS. An update on the delivery of detailed care records systems. Also *National Audit Office* (May 2011). The National Programme for IT in the NHS. An update on the delivery of detailed care records systems.
63. Department of Health Announcement (22 September 2011).

10   Local Government

1. Author's Recollection, The MJ (Municipal Journal). December 2009.
2. National Council for Voluntary Organisations. 21 February 2006.
3. Local Government Association (June 2012). *Funding Outlook for Councils from 2010/11 to 2019/20: Preliminary Modelling.*
4. Sir Michael Lyons (2007) *Place-Shaping: A Shared Ambition for the Future of Local Government.* HM Treasury/DCLG.
5. Audit Commission (March 2009). *Final score: The Impact of the Comprehensive Performance Assessment on Local Government.*
6. Audit Commission (2002). First CPA Report.
7. Sue Charteris (2006). In *Double Devolution: The Renewal of Local Government.* Smith Institute.
8. Audit Commission (July 2006). CPA – *The Harder Test.*
9. Department of Communities and Local Government (2006/7). *Best Value User Satisfaction Surveys.*
10. Ministry of Justice (July 2007). *The Governance of Britain.* Green Paper.
11. Audit Commission (July 2008). *Tougher at the Top.*
12. Municipal Year Book (2013). London, Hemming Group.
13. Councillors Commission (December 2007). *Representing the Future.* Department of Communities and Local Government.
14. Audit Commission (November 2007). *Healthy Competition.*
15. Audit Commission (January 2008). *For Better, for Worse.*
16. Cabinet Office (June 2012). *Civil Service Plan.*
17. Sir Michael Lyons (2007). *Place-Shaping: A Shared Ambition for the Future of Local Government.* HM Treasury/DCLG.
18. *Birmingham Total Place Pilot: Final Report* (February 2010). Be Birmingham. www.bebirmingham.org.uk also Be Birmingham/Ekos (2009). *Public Expenditure and Investment Study* which provided data for the pilot.
19. DCLG (November 2012). 50 *Ways to Save.*
20. DCLG examples (November 2012).
21. Lord Heseltine (October 2012). *No Stone Unturned.* Department for Business, Innovation and Skills.

11   The Police

1. Home Office (July 2010). *Policing in the 21st Century: Reconnecting Police and the People.*

2. Lord Blair of Boughton (5 May 2012) 'Enough Cosy Inefficiency. Go for Liberation'. *The Times*.
3. R. I. Mawby (1999). *Policing Across the World*. Issues for the 21st Century (Routledge, p. 139).
4. Sir Ronnie Flanagan (2008). *The Review of Policing* (Home Office, p. 11).
5. HMIC (2010). *Policing in an Age of Austerity.*
6. Home Office (July 2010). *Policing in the 21st Century: Reconnecting Police and the People.*
7. Home Affairs Select Committee (October 2008).
8. Tom Winsor (March 2011). *Independent Review of Police Officer and Staff Remuneration and Conditions. Part 1 Report.* (Home Office).
9. R. I. Mawby (1999). *Policing Across the World. Issues for the 21st Century* (Routledge, p. 138).
10. John Major (1999). *The Autobiography (London, Harper Collins, p. 389)*.
11. R. I. Mawby (1999). *Policing Across the World. Issues for the 21st Century* (Routledge, p. 139).
12. Tony Blair (2010). *A Journey* (London, Hutchinson, p. 121).
13. John Major (1999). *The Autobiography* (London, Harper Collins, p. 389).
14. Tom Winsor (March 2011). *Independent Review of Police Officer and Staff Remuneration and Conditions. Part 1 Report.* (Home Office).
15. Tony Blair (2010). *A Journey* (London, Hutchinson, p. 262).
16. Sir Ronnie Flanagan (2008). *The Review of Policing* (Home Office, p. 6).
17. ibid., p. 13.
18. ibid., p. 7.
19. ibid., p. 5.
20. HMIC (July 2010). *Valuing the Police: Policing in an Age of Austerity.* See also HM Treasury (July 2012). Public Spending Statistics.
21. Tom Winsor (March 2011). *Independent Review of Police Officer and Staff Remuneration and Conditions. Part 1 Report* (Home Office).
22. Lord Blair of Boughton (5 May 2012). 'Enough Cosy Inefficiency. Go for Liberation'. *The Times*.
23. HMIC/Welsh Audit Office/Audit Commission (July 2010). *Sustaining Value for Money in the Police Service.*
24. Sir Ronnie Flanagan (2008). *The Review of Policing* (Home Office, p. 11).
25. Home Office Select Committee (February 2011). *Police Finances.*
26. Sir Ronnie Flanagan (2008). *The Review of Policing* (Home Office, p. 45).
27. ibid., p. 39, 45.
28. Quoted in Home Office Select Committee. *New Landcape of Policing.* September 2011.
29. Tom Winsor (March 2011). *Independent Review of Police Officer and Staff Remuneration and Conditions. Part 1 Report* (Home Office).
30. Tony Blair (2010). *A Journey* (London, Hutchinson, p. 278).
31. Sir Ronnie Flanagan (2008). *The Review of Policing* (Home Office, p. 7).
32. Home Affairs Select Committee. October 2008. Policing in the *21st Century*.
33. HMIC (July 2010). Valuing the Police: *Policing in an Age of Austerity.*
34. HMIC/Welsh Audit Office/Audit Commission (July 2010). *Sustaining Value for Money in the Police Service.*
35. HMIC (July 2010). *Valuing the Police: Policing in an Age of Austerity.*
36. Sir Ronnie Flanagan (2008). *The Review of Policing* (Home Office, p. 20).

37. Home Affairs Select Committee. October 2008. *Policing in the 21st Century.*
38. Sir Ronnie Flanagan (2008). *The Review of Policing* (Home Office, p. 31, 81).
39. Home Office Select Committee (September 2011). *New Landcape of Policing.*
40. Home Office (February 2010). *High Level Working Group Report on Police Value for Money* (Home Office, ACPO, APA, HMIC and NPIA).
41. ibid.
42. ibid.
43. Sir Ronnie Flanagan (2008). *The Review of Policing* (Home Office, p. 39).
44. Home Office Select Committee (September 2011). *New Landcape of Policing.*
45. Lord Blair of Boughton (5 May 2012). 'Enough Cosy Inefficiency. Go for Liberation'. *The Times.*
46. Home Affairs Committee (22 March 2012). *The Role of Private Sector Companies in Policing: Oral Evidence.*

12   Welfare

1. HM Treasury (2010). *Spending Review.*
2. Speech by David Cameron (25 June 2012). Bluewater, Kent.
3. National Audit Office (January 2012). *The Introduction of the Work Programme.*
4. National Audit Office (September 2011). *A Summary of the NAO's Work on the Department for Work and Pensions 2010–11.*
5. National Audit Office/Department for Work and Pensions (November 2005). *Dealing with the Complexities of the Benefits System.*
6. David Freud (2007). *Reducing Dependency, Increasing Opportunity: Options for the Future of Welfare to Work.* Department for Work and Pensions.
7. For a full list of changes, see Appendix 2. *The Evolution of the UK Social Security System in NAO/DWP: Dealing with the Complexities of the Benefits System* (November 2005).
8. Margaret Thatcher (1993) *The Downing Street Years* (London, Harper Collins, p. 629).
9. ibid., p. 629.
10. David Freud (2007). *Reducing Dependency, Increasing Opportunity: Options for the Future of Welfare to Work.* (Department for Work and Pensions).
11. Alistair Darling (2011). *Back from the Brink* (London, Atlantic Books, p. 312).
12. James Browne and Andrew Hood (November 2012).*A Survey of the UK Benefit System.* Briefing note, Institute of Fiscal Studies/ESRC.
13. Institute of Fiscal Studies (September 2009). Briefing note. *A Survey of Public Spending in the UK.*
14. National Audit Office/Department for Work and Pensions (November 2005). *Dealing with the Complexities of the Benefits System.*
15. HM Treasury (October 2010). *Spending Review.*
16. Department for Work and Pensions (1 November 2011). *Press Statement.*
17. National Audit Office (January 2012). *The Introduction of the Work Programme.*
18. ibid.
19. National Audit Office (December 2012) *A Commentary for the PAC on the Work Programme Outcome Statistics.*
20. Speech by David Cameron (25 June 2012). Bluewater, Kent.
21. Tony Blair (2010). *A Journey* (London, Hutchinson, p. 204).

22. Frank Field (December 2010). *The Foundation Years. Preventing Poor Children becoming Poor Adults. The Report of the Independent Review on Poverty and Life Chances* (Cabinet Office).
23. Households below average income 2008/9. DWP. Quoted in Frank Field's The Foundation Years. Preventing Poor Children Becoming Poor Adults (Cabinet Office, December 2010).
24. ibid. Frank Field.
25. Centre for Social Justice (May 2012). *Rethinking Child Poverty.*
26. Graham Allen and others (July 2011). *Early Intervention: Smart Investment, Massive Savings.* Second report. (Cabinet Office).
27. Department of Communities and Local Government (March 2012). *Financial Framework for the Troubled Families Programme's Payment by Results Scheme for Local Authorities.*
28. National Audit Office (November 2012). *Managing the Impact of Housing Benefit Reform.*

13   Education and Schools

1. Michael Gove (2012). *Speech at Brighton College.* 10 May 2012.
2. Ofsted (2011). *Annual Report* 2010/11.
3. OECD (2009). *Education Systems Compared.*
4. HM Treasury (February 2012). *Statistical Bulletin. Public Spending Statistics.*
5. David Cameron (September 2011). Speech at Free School, Norwich.
6. Margaret Thatcher (1993) *The Downing Street Years* (London, Harper Collins, p. 591).
7. ibid., p. 591.
8. ibid., p. 592.
9. ibid., p. 571.
10. ibid., p. 592.
11. ibid., p. 597.
12. John Major (1999). *The Autobiography* (London, HarperCollins, p. 398).
13. ibid., p. 399.
14. Tony Blair (2010). *A Journey* (London, Hutchinson, p. 212, 262).
15. ibid., p. 285.
16. National Audit Office (September 2010). *The Academies Programme.*
17. Department for Education. 26 January 2012.
18. Ofsted Annual Report 2010/11.
19. Public Accounts Committee (January 2011). *The Academies Programme.*
20. National Audit Office (September 2010). *The Academies Programme.*
21. Education Select Committee (February 2012). *Annual Report of Ofsted. Oral Evidence.* 29 February 2012.
22. Ofsted Annual Report. 2010/11.
23. Department for Education. 26 January 2012.
24. Ofsted (May 2003). *Excellence in Cities and Education Action Zones: Management and Impact.*
25. Michael Gove (2012). *Speech at Brighton College.* 10 May 2012.
26. Ofsted (November 2011). *Annual Report* 2010/11.
27. ibid.

28. ibid.
29. Education Select Committee (March 2011). *The Role and Performance of Ofsted.*
30. Department for Education (September 2011). *Deprivation Banding of Free Schools. Infrastructure, Funding and Longitudinal Analysis Division.*
31. Rebecca Allen (2010). *Replicating Swedish 'free school' Reforms in England* (Institute of Education. Research in Public Policy. Summer 2010).
32. J. Belsky, J. Barnes and E. Melhuish (eds) *The National Evolution of Sure Start.* Quoted in Education select committee. *Sure Start Children's Centres.* March 2010.
33. ibid.
34. John Major (1999). *The Autobiography* (London, Harper Collins, p. 395).
35. ibid., p. 397.
36. Education Select Committee (March 2011). *The Role and Performance of Ofsted.*
37. Ofsted (December 2012). *Annual Report 2011/12.*

14 Measuring Performance

1. National Audit Office (July 2010). *Taking the Measure of Government Performance.*
2. National Audit Office (December 2010). *Management of NHS Productivity.*
3. Helen Simpson (December 2006). *Productivity in Public Services* (Centre for Market and Public Organisation, Bristol Institute of Public Affairs, University of Bristol).
4. National Audit Office (December 2010). *Management of NHS Productivity.*
5. HM Treasury (2009). *Benchmarking the Back Office.*
6. NAO evidence to House of Commons DCLG Committee: 2011.
7. Treasury/Cabinet Office/NAO/Audit Commisssion/ONS (2001). A Framework *for Performance Information.*
8. Prime Minister's Strategy Unit (June 2006). *The UK Government's Approach to Public Service Reform* (Cabinet Office).
9. Treasury/Cabinet Office/NAO/Audit Commisssion/ONS (2001). *A Framework for Performance Information.*
10. Institute of Fiscal Studies (May 2010). Election Briefing Note.
11. Mike G. Phelps (2009). *Comparing the Different Estimates of Productivity Produced by the ONS* (UK Centre for the Measurement of Government Activity).
12. Office of National Statistics (2010). *Total Public Service Output, Inputs and Productivity.*
13. ibid.
14. Sir Tony Atkinson (2005). *Final report. Measurement of Government Output and Productivity for the National Accounts* (Office for National Statistics).
15. Office for National Statistics (2010). *Total Public Service Output, Inputs and Productivity.*
16. KPMG (June 2010). *Payment for Success – How to Shift Power from Whitehall to Public Service Customers.*
17. National Audit Office (December 2010). *Management of NHS Productivity.*
18. ibid.

19. National Audit Office (July 2010). *Taking the Measure of Government Performance.*
20. Briony Smith (2007). *What Gets Measured: Contracting for Delivery (Serco Institute).*
21. Public Administration Select Committee (July 2003). *On Target? Government by Measurement.*
22. ibid.
23. Jonathan Powell (2011). *The New Machiavelli. How to Wield Power in the Modern World* (London, Vintage Books, p. 181).
24. National Audit Office (July 2010). *Taking the Measure of Government Performance.*
25. KPMG (June 2010). *Payment for Success – How to Shift Power from Whitehall to Public Service Customers.*

15 Monitoring Performance

1. National Audit Office (December 2009). *Reducing Bureaucracy for Public Sector Frontline Staff.*
2. John Major (1999). *The Autobiography* (London, HarperCollins, p. 248).
3. ibid., p. 256.
4. ibid., p. 251.
5. ibid., p. 255.
6. Tony Blair (2010). *A Journey* (London, Hutchinson, p. 338).
7. Andrew Marr (2007). *A History of Modern Britain* (London, Macmillan, p. 543).
8. Prime Minister's Strategy Unit (2006). *The UK Government's Approach to Public Service Reform* (Cabinet Office).
9. National Audit Office (December 2009). *Reducing Bureaucracy for Public Sector Frontline Staff.*
10. Public Accounts Committee (August 2012). *Implementing the Transparency Agenda.*
11. Cabinet Office (June 2012).*Open Data White Paper: Unleashing the Potential.*
12. HM Treasury Business Plan 2011–2015.
13. National Audit Office (June 2010). *The NAO's work on HM Treasury. June 2010.*
14. National Audit Office (April 2012). *Implementing Transparency.*
15. Public Accounts Committee (August 2012). *Implementing the Transparency Agenda.*
16. Public Administration Select Committee (September 2011). *Change in Government. The Agenda for Leadership.*

16 The International Context

1. National Audit Office (December 2012). *Progress in Making Efficiency Savings.*
2. OECD (2012), *Health at a Glance: Europe 2012*, OECD Publishing, http://dx.doi.org/10.1787/9789264183896-en.
3. World Health Organisation (2012). *World Health Statistics.* 2012 Figures.
4. Oxford Economics for the Department for Business Enterprise and Regulatory Reform (July 2008). *The Market for Public Services: International Comparisons.*

5. National Audit Office/Accenture (October 2008). *An International Comparison of the UK's Public Administration.*
6. PricewaterhouseCoopers (2011). *Making It Happen. A Roadmap for Cities and Local Public Services to Achieve Outcomes.* (PwC Public Sector Research Centre).
7. Michael Barber, Mona Mourshed (September 2007). *How the World's Best Performing Schools Systems Come Out on Top.* (McKinsey and Co.).
8. Mona Mourshed, Chinezi Chijioke, and Michael Barber. *How the World's Most Improved School Systems Keep Getting Better.* (McKinsey and Co.).
9. *The Learning Curve. Lessons in Country Performance in Education. 2012 Report.* (2012). (Pearson/The Economist Intelligence Unit).
10. *Ofsted Annual Report* 2011/12. (November 2012).

Conclusion: The Next Steps for Reform

1. Sir David Varney (December 2006). *Service Transformation: A Better Service for Citizens and Businesses, A Better Deal for the Taxpayer* (HM Treasury).

Index

Printed and bound in Great Britain by
CPI Antony Rowe, Chippenham and Eastbourne